Life Adrift

Geopolitical Bodies, Material Worlds

This series publishes studies that originate in a range of different fields that are nonetheless linked through their common foundation: a belief that the macro-scale of geopolitics is composed of translocal relations between bodies and materials that are only understandable through empirical examination of those relations. It is the interaction of these elements that produces the forces that shape global politics, often with outcomes that differ from the predictions of macro-scaled theories. This world poses questions: how do materialities such as the built environment and the body reproduce global power structures, how are they caught up in violent transformations and how do they become sites of resistance? How do assemblages of human and non-human elements both fortify and transform political space? What possibilities for political change are latent within the present?

Series Editors

Jason Dittmer, Professor of Political Geography at University College London.
Ian Klinke, Associate Professor in Human Geography and Tutorial Fellow at St John's College, Oxford.

Titles in the Series

The Geopolitics of Real Estate: Reconfiguring Property, Capital and Rights, Dallas Rogers.
Choreographies of Resistance: Mobilities, Bodies and Politics, Tarja Väyrynen, Eeva Puumala, Samu Pehkonen, Tiina Vaittinen, Anitta Kynsilehto.
Life Adrift: Climate Change, Migration, Critique, Andrew Baldwin and Giovanni Bettini.

Forthcoming

Territory Beyond Terra, Kimberley Peters, Philip Steinberg, Elaine Stratford.
The Politics of Bodies at Risk: The Human in the Body, Maria Boikova Struble.

Life Adrift

Climate Change, Migration, Critique

Edited by
Andrew Baldwin and Giovanni Bettini

London • New York

Published by Rowman & Littlefield International, Ltd.
Unit A, Whitacre Mews, 26-34 Stannary Street, London SE11 4AB
www.rowmaninternational.com

Rowman & Littlefield International, Ltd. is an affiliate of Rowman & Littlefield
4501 Forbes Boulevard, Suite 200, Lanham, Maryland 20706, USA
With additional offices in Boulder, New York, Toronto (Canada), and Plymouth (UK)
www.rowman.com

British Library Cataloguing in Publication Data
A catalogue record for this book is available from the British Library

ISBN: HB 978-1-7866-0119-3
    PB 978-1-7866-0120-9

Library of Congress Cataloging-in-Publication Data Available

ISBN 978-1-78660-119-3 (cloth : alk. paper)
ISBN 978-1-78660-120-9 (pbk. : alk. paper)
ISBN 978-1-78660-121-6 (electronic)

∞™ The paper used in this publication meets the minimum requirements of American
National Standard for Information Sciences—Permanence of Paper for Printed Library
Materials, ANSI/NISO Z39.48-1992.

Printed in the United States of America

Contents

Chapter 1

Introduction

Life Adrift

Andrew Baldwin and Giovanni Bettini

Migration is life.

—Anonymous

Migration is one of the defining features of contemporary political life. Figured in opposition to the citizen, the nation and the sedentary, migrants are constitutive of some of today's most cherished political identifications. Celebrated or denigrated as a matter of political expedience, migrants bear the mark of the other. They are racialized, sexualized and dehumanized, even while represented as hardworking, desirable and prosperous. That migration has and will continue to shape the twenty-first-century global order is a truism evident in the ever-increasing number of migrants in the world today alongside a full-fledged political antipathy for immigration. But in addition to migration, global climate change looms over the present as another world-shaping phenomenon. Indeed it is now a commonplace in today's global political economy to argue that climate change is itself a migration crisis in the making.

As climate change becomes ever more apparent, many expect large areas of the planet to become uninhabitable, producing what some have referred to as 'dead zones' (see Goldberg and Colebrook, this volume). But what of the inhabitants of these dead zones? What fate awaits those who will bear the brunt of climate change while having contributed the least to its creation? One view is that the impacts of climate change, whether in the form of sea-level rise, extreme weather events or drought, will 'induce' a complex pattern of human mobilities, including migration, displacement and resettlement, on an unprecedented scale. Such mobilities, whether real or imagined, are mobilized for quite different political ends. Some characterize environmentally induced displacement as one of climate change's most severe injustices. The popular yet deeply fraught figure of the 'climate refugee' here becomes

1

a touchstone for planetary fate, humanity adjudicated on the ethical stance adopted in relation to it. For others, the anticipated mobilities induced by climate change are a potentially ungovernable, and therefore, dangerous, phenomenon. Here, climate change promises the radical redistribution of people around the world, with those expected to be set in motion, in turn, inscribed with the near-mythical power to disrupt entire economies, political institutions and identities. Climate change thus becomes dramatized not only as a problem of excessive greenhouse gas emissions, but also as one that demands new mechanisms for anticipating and controlling 'flows' of people who, many expect, will be unleashed by climate change. At a time of heightened political anxiety when the figures of the migrant and refugee are easily mobilized to undermine European integration, or when both feature centrally in hateful political speech (i.e. Trumpism), how we approach the relation between climate change and migration is of profound significance.

Life Adrift intervenes in the problem space opened up when climate change and human migration are made to intersect, when climate change is configured as a problem of migration. The contributors to this volume represent an eclectic mix of the humanities and interpretive social sciences – political and cultural theory, literary criticism, linguistics, migration studies, philosophy, geography and media studies. The essays gathered together in this volume thus offer a wide-ranging, and we hope fresh set of, insights for thinking anew the relation between climate change and human migration. Common across these essays is a shared conviction amongst the authors that climate change is a real, material circumstance with potentially dire consequences for much of the world's population, especially those already living on the fringes of capital. In compiling these essays, our intention is not to trivialize this. Like so many other forms of violence, including imperialism, colonialism, economic austerity, genocide and patriarchy, the violence of climate change will reverberate for generations to come. It may even threaten long-term human survival. Yet in this introduction we take a slightly counter-intuitive view; we argue that the *relation between climate change and human migration* must be understood foremost as a relation of power rather than as a hard fact awaiting to be discovered, or an empirically observable phenomenon. Climate change designates a real crisis of contemporary political economy, but its migration effects are mediated at every turn by all manner of other social, cultural, political and even geological, relations (on the geological see Clark, this volume). Consequently, we argue that the very act of thinking (or speaking or imagining) climate change as a problem of migration is explicitly political. By bending our view of the world, such thinking becomes a powerful means by which social attitudes are governed, which is what we mean when we say that climate change and human migration is a relation of power. In its more hegemonic expressions, it orients publics to climate change in a way that reinforces the exceptional status of the migrant or refugee. It demands that we view the migrant and refugee as the 'other', the constitutive outside or excess of what is otherwise imagined as the pairing of 'normal' even if fraught geopolitical and climatic conditions. It reinforces the belief, erroneous in our view, that life internal to the modern nation state is settled, sedentary and at some degree of remove from the transnational flows of labour, capital and technology, imagined to lie beyond state borders. And in a more abstract sense, it is a relation that often constructs movement and change as inimical to social order rather than as its founding and ongoing condition (Nail, 2015). (Later, however, we discuss how this relation of power might be used to reimagine the future.)

As a system of power, the discourse of 'climate change and human migration' – by which we mean a representational schema in which climate change is configured as a problem of migration, displacement and resettlement – achieves all of this by privileging climate change as the main 'agent', 'determinant' or 'trigger' of migration. One effect of this is that it obscures the always historical circumstances that lead people to migrate from or flee their homes. It is, in this sense, a form of power, or discursive regime, reliant upon what the climate scientist-cum-cultural theorist Michael Hulme (2011) calls 'climate reductionism'. Climate reductionism is 'a form of analysis and prediction in which climate is first extracted from the matrix of interdependencies which shape human life within the physical world ... then elevated to the role of dominant predictor variable' (p. 247). Simply put, this is the belief that one can anticipate the appearance of future social life simply by modelling climate change. For Hulme (2011), the inherent danger of such reasoning is that it forecloses the future as a site for creatively reimagining the world, as a site for democratic politics. Climate reductionism is also the central organizing logic in the discourse of climate refugees. When a climate justice activist, a military general or scientist declares that climate change will result in millions of people seeking refuge from their homelands, each mobilizes the ideology of climate reductionism. And yet what remains blurred by such claims are the countless other counter-histories, both macro (i.e. currency devaluations, structural inequality, civil war, land reform) and micro (i.e. the intimacies of daily life), that account for migration, whether understood as a voluntary or involuntary act. The discourse on climate change and human migration thus draws its power by superseding these counter-histories in favour of the perceived primacy of climate change, by reducing mobility to climate.

But if climate reductionism is a prevalent trope in discourses on climate change and human migration, then, paradoxically, so too is its refusal. Indeed, the refusal of climate reductive reasoning is now a commonplace in most mainstream accounts of climate and human migration, the basic premise being that migration is multicausal and therefore irreducible to climate change. Prominent examples of this refusal include the UK Foresight report (2011) on *Migration and Global Environmental Change*, the *Fifth Assessment Report of Intergovernmental Panel on Climate Change* (2014) and research published by the International Organization for Migration. But we could cite countless other studies similarly premised on its refusal. In one sense, the retreat from reductionism is a welcome development insofar as it offers a refreshing alternative to the reductive logic common in popular media and political rhetorics and in the casual, everyday use of concepts like 'climate refugee'. And yet it is also deeply equivocal. For even while much of the discourse on climate change and migration is predicated on the refusal of climate reductionism, the fixation on *climate* as the first among equal drivers of migration decisions nevertheless remains. If migration is truly irreducible to climate, then why not simply refer to 'migration'? Why isolate 'climate' or 'environment'? It would seem that even while the explanatory value of climate is routinely downplayed by those seeking to understand the interactions of climate and migration, the urge to speak about *climate* and migration as a singular phenomenon remains for many as strong as ever. The act of refusing climate reductive logic, while simultaneously reinforcing the explanatory value of climate, is a peculiar feature of the discourse on climate change and human migration. It is precisely through the inclusion of the social, the historical and the political, albeit in a position that is subordinate to climate, that the discourse is rendered self-evident and its power dissimulated.

So, even while we concur with Hulme's critique of climate reductionism, even while we adhere to the truism that human mobility is irreducible to climate change in reason of its complexity, we nevertheless remain sceptical about the critique of climate reductionism insofar as it has been misappropriated into the wider discourse on climate change and human migration and made to serve a set of ends different than those intended by Hulme. Our scepticism is bolstered by two additional observations. First, when researchers seek to explain specific instances of migration as the outcome of a mixture of climatic variation alongside cultural, economic and political variables, they assume that the knowledge they produce accurately reflects the phenomena it purports to represent, and, relatedly, they assume that such realist representations are value free (see, for example, McLeman, 2014). Such positivist assumptions, however, run counter to another basic truism in contemporary social science, which is that 'fact' and 'value' are not separate domains but are mutually imbricated elements of thought (Cf. Latour, 2004, Harvey, 1974). To assume otherwise merely papers over the normative component intrinsic in the act of inscribing an element in a discourse. The power effects of such empiricism begin to appear when we fully historicize this knowledge. The example of Hurricane Katrina is illustrative. When Katrina is constructed as an event in which *climate change* is said to bear directly on migration, such reasoning downplays the significance that nearly four centuries of structural racism in America *also* had on this displacement event. More specifically, a judgement is made concerning the relative value accorded to the hurricane as opposed to American racism in explaining this displacement. In other words, our scepticism lies in the way the undeniable eventfulness of the hurricane is oftentimes mobilized as a fact which is then used to sustain the belief that climate change is a problem of migration – when it would be equally justifiable to posit the displacement effects of Hurricane Katrina as nothing but a crisis of American racism. How we comprehend these phenomena matters greatly.

This leads us to our second observation, which is that the empiricist conceit running through the discourse on climate change and human migration leaves little room for conceiving of the intricacies of knowledge and power. We can begin tracing these intricacies by considering the way in which the relation between climate change and human migration is overly represented as a crisis that demands technical and expert solutions. We find this form of representation across all manner of policy domains, from international organizations like the International Organisation for Migration, the United Nations High Commission for Refugees and the Asian Development Bank, regional bodies like the European Commission and the African Union, and national institutions, such as UK Foresight. It is also embedded in the United Nations Framework Convention on Climate Change (UNFCCC). In 2010, for example, the Cancun Adaptation Framework (2010) called on national governments 'to enhance understanding, coordination and cooperation with regard to climate change induced displacement, migration and planned relocation'. More recently, negotiators at the Paris climate summit (2015) upped the ante by striking an expert task force to 'avert, minimize and address displacement related to the adverse effects of climate change'. One could scrutinize the unique power/knowledge formations specific to each. But together what these examples point towards is the coming into being of an epistemic community of experts and researchers, bound together through a shared set of assumptions about the nature of human mobility in the context of climate change. Foremost among these assumptions is that expert knowledge of this relation is required to ensure that the migration effects of climate are properly managed.

Noel Castree (2014) reminds us that 'epistemic communities gain their distinctiveness, and sense of self-identity, through a mixture of their value-set, ontological beliefs, questions of interest, objects/domains of concern, methods of inquiry, the criteria favoured for determining worthy ideas, knowledge or information, and their chosen genre of communication' (p. 42). Epistemic communities are significant for numerous reasons but arguably most importantly for the way they draw boundaries around what can and cannot be said about a specific area of knowledge, distinguishing, sometimes formally, sometimes tacitly, the parameters for legitimate speech. This significance can be appreciated in relation to the above-mentioned example about Hurricane Katrina. It matters significantly that this event can be mobilized to consolidate a set of truths about climate and migration, especially if doing so displaces the politics of race and racism. For example when commentators claim that climate change will result in more such extreme weather events and therefore greater levels of human displacement, they render the politics of American racism secondary to those of climate change. This is not inconsequential inasmuch as it purifies the discourse of climate change from any meaningful discussion about race and racism. And the epistemic community on climate and human mobility matters more generally too because insofar as it configures migration in the context of climate change as exceptional and thus in need of expert management, it negates the more fundamental notion that migration is *not* exceptional but central to the multiplicities of human existence. And this, we would suggest, has the effect of prohibiting more fundamental questions from being asked about, for example, what migration might come to mean in the context of climate change, how it relates to democratic and public life, and what it can tell us about humanness today.

All of this is hardly unprecedented. The mechanisms by which the discourse on climate and migration displaces these fundamental, political questions are a recurring feature of environmental discourse. Numerous critical interventions (for instance, Swyngedouw, 2010, Žižek, 2010, Harvey, 2011) have made the argument that doom-and-gloom scenarios, the invocation of 'facts' (in its more or less reductionist variants) and the delegation of action to techno-managerial communities are instrumental to depoliticization. A priority for critical scholarship is therefore to surface the political questions that mainstream discourses on climate and migration have otherwise left unaddressed.

Life Adrift should be read as an attempt to do just this, to expose the political subsurface of the discourse on climate change and migration. It offers a set of interventions that run counter to many of the epistemological and ontological assumptions that proliferate across the epistemic community of climate change and migration. Its purpose, however, is neither to repudiate nor to valorize the relation between climate change and migration, but to offer instead a fresh suite of concepts, approaches and questions that might be used to *politicise* migration and life in the overlapping and ever-shifting contexts of climate change, the Anthropocene, neoliberal rationality and shifting geopolitical dynamics. Developing such resources, we argue, is a necessary precursor for bringing into existence new and, we hope, progressive ways of living in common as a condition for inhabiting political and social lifeworlds that are by definition always in transition (Berlant, 2016). Resilience, however, is not the point. Its inherent conservatism plays no part in our aspiring lexicon (Reid and Evans, 2014). Instead, we find inspiration in the idea that 'since it is at least possible – if not indeed likely – that human creativity, imagination, and ingenuity will create radically different social, cultural, and political worlds in the future than exist today, greater effort should be made to represent these possibilities in any analysis about the significance of future climate change' (Hulme, 2011 p. 266).

Towards the Political Subsurface

In 1974 the geographer David Harvey wrote an essay entitled 'Population, Resources and the Ideology of Science', now a classic text in Marxist geography. In it Harvey developed a powerful methodological critique of the Neo-Malthusianism, which at the time was shaping popular environmental narratives about overpopulation and resource use. Arguing against the ethical neutrality of science, and specifically Malthus' logical empiricism, Harvey's fundamental claim was that method and result are 'integrally related' (p. 270). If one naturalizes scarcity, even while we know scarcity to be a social relation, then this will inevitably colour how one reads population: population can always be said to exceed scarce resources. But the significance of Harvey's argument lies equally in its political implications. Harvey reminds his reader, for example, that Malthus wrote his influential '*Essay on the Principle of Population* in 1798 as a political tract against the utopian socialist-anarchism of Godwin and Condorcet and as an antidote to the hopes for social progress aroused by the French Revolution' (p. 258). And later, he argues that overpopulation is easily mobilized by elites 'as part of an elaborate apologetic through which class, ethnic, or (neo-) colonial repression may be justified' (p. 274). And Harvey, of course, wrote *his* important essay amidst and *against* what he saw as a Malthusian revival occurring at a tumultuous time in the West when various societal transformations, including the civil rights movement, calls for indigenous self-determination, decolonization and student protests, all threatened elite rule. Within such a context, argued Harvey, claims about scarcity resurfaced as a means for blaming the poor for their condition while diverting attention from the real culprit, exploitative capitalism.

We foreground Harvey's important essay here because it remains as pertinent today as it was when it was first written over forty years ago. This is because much of the discourse on climate change and migration is Malthusian in tone if not in political intent. Indeed, we find in many accounts of the relation between climate change and migration elite anxieties about an ungovernable poor threatening elite power in the face of combined ecological and economic crises. Take for example the popular documentary film, *Climate Refugees*, noteworthy only for its unstated racism (Baldwin, 2013).

One prominent political actor in that film makes direct reference to Malthus, noting that the popular notion of climate wars derives from Malthus' original thesis about resources and overpopulation. Malthusian references are implied by numerous others in the film. A similar appeal to Malthus is conjured up by the extremely popular thesis put forward in Robert Kaplan's popular 1994 essay 'The Coming Anarchy', which orientalizes Africa through tropes of poverty, corruption and bloodshed. Uncritical embraces of Kaplan's thesis are still commonplace in the discourse on climate change and migration, in spite of the fact that the Malthusian basis of Kaplan's essay has since been the subject of numerous important criticisms (Dalby, 2002, 1996).

Harvey's analysis therefore still has much to offer. First, it reminds us that when Malthusianism 'seizes hold in a society dominated by an elite, then the non-elite invariably experience some form of political, economic, and social repression' (p. 273). Harvey's examples include 'Britain shortly after the Napoleonic Wars', 'the conservation movement in the United States at the turn of [the last] century', Hitler's Germany and the 'twilight years of the British Empire' (p. 273). These are not equivalent events. But in each, Malthusian notions of overpopulation are used to ground elite authority and justify social repression. Our contention is that the discourse on climate change and migration is similar in a few key respects. If an epistemic community is able to configure climate change as a problem of runaway migration, which by implication may threaten elite authority, then labelling huge portions of the world's population, notably the poor, as potential climate migrants or refugees offers elites a means to exercise their authority over those so labelled. Elsewhere Baldwin (2013, 2012) has argued that temporalizing the poor this way amounts to a specific form of racial violence by robbing them of their history. Second, Harvey reminds us that context matters. Thus, to comprehend the discourse of climate change and migration, one must account for the wider political, economic and cultural contexts from which its meaning derives. Important here is that, even while the discourse on climate change and migration has a lengthy genealogy (Saunders, 2000), its recent popularity coincides sharply with the 2008 financial crisis and the ensuing uncertainty in the global economy. Recall, for example, its first mention in the UNFCCC in 2010. One could also point to the mounting sense of geopolitical crisis throughout the West in the 2000s, given the pace of economic growth in China. And indeed climate change itself represents a formidable crisis that threatens to undermine elite authority. Within such a context, the promise of controlling flows of 'climate migrants' or 'climate refugees' offers elites a way of shoring up their own perceived waning authority. Romain Felli's (2013) argument that climate migration is a strategy of labour management and thus of capital accumulation under conditions of climate change is exemplary in this respect.

And finally, Harvey's analysis is helpful because, drawing from Marx, it situates dialectical materialism as an important counter method to the logical empiricism that characterizes Malthusianism. One aspect of this method, yet another truism in the interpretative social sciences, concerns the relational 'nature' of objects by which Marx 'means that a "thing" cannot be understood or even talked about independently of the relations it has with other things' (Harvey, 1974, p. 265). Thus, a body of knowledge, such as climate change and migration, owes its existence to those things by and from which it is composed (i.e. institutions, epistemic communities, power). In this sense, climate change and migration should be conceived as a relation; we stand to learn much about it if we interpret it as such. But perhaps more importantly, Harvey reminds us that as a method for social transformation, dialectical materialism begins with categories already in circulation and then goes about transforming them, and thus their social relations, from within. This is the hope we invest in *Life Adrift*.

The Political Subsurface: Labour, Borders and Race

In the remainder of this introductory chapter, we identify three analytical categories that we have found useful for accessing, and we hope transforming, the power relation of climate change and migration: labour, borders and race. We are under no illusions that each is cleaved from the other two; all three are interdependent. Nor do we pretend this is an exhaustive list. It could be easily expanded to include all manner of other categories including gender, sex, affect, assemblage, space, place, strata, materiality and dozens of other concepts. Not all essays in this volume engage with all three categories. We have chosen them, however, as we think they are among the themes that have proved the least reducible to the depoliticized terms of the mainstream discourses and as a consequence have been most fiercely pushed out of the frame.

Labour

Labour seldom figures within contemporary accounts of climate change and migration, the notable exception being Romain Felli's aforementioned contribution (2013). Instead, reductionism, empiricism and naturalism all conspire to purify the climate – migration relation of its connections to the (re)production, mobilization and disciplining of labour under planetary capitalism. We find this erasure of labour *striking* and *concerning* – striking because it represses one of the defining social relations under capitalism, and as Arun Saldanha reminds us in his chapter contribution, the planetary crisis of the Anthropocene is *also* a crisis of capitalism; and concerning because,

in the absence of an analytics of labour, the ways in which labour is rearticulated, mobilized and harnessed as a precondition for the expansion and
survival of capital amidst these planetary transformations become obscured.
To be sure, mobility is often woven into the plot of the global climate crisis
and even that of the Anthropocene. For many, population movements are
among the most topical and concerning symptoms of these planetary transformations. Most interventions on the Anthropocene feature some variation
of the figure of the climate refugee or environmentally displaced or ecologic
nomad, all of which dramatize the radical transformations and disruptions
at the horizon (Cf. Hamilton et al., 2015, Ghosh, 2016, Nail, 2015; see
also Clark, Colebrook, Dalby, this volume). But while the concept of the
Anthropocene reveals the ways in which human mobility and settlement
are changing, commentators seldom interrogate these as *labour* relations.
This is a significant omission and can be read against the tendency, shared
by mainstream articulations of the Anthropocene and of climate change, to
dehistoricize the planetary transformations they narrate and to overlook their
essential entanglement with capital(ism) (cfr. Malm and Hornborg, 2014,
Haraway, 2015, Moore, 2015). The Anthropocene and climate change reveal
the unprecedented scale and depth of the crises through which the planet is
living. Both make visible the planetarity of capital, its novel productions
of horizontal (i.e. territory) and vertical space (i.e. geologic depth), as well
as the new political domains opened up when capital relations extend ever
deeper into the strata of human and non-human life. The failure to include
the reconfigurations of labour and class relations in this story of planetary
transformation, which is also the story of capital, is a source of concern. Not
only is it symptomatic of the sanitization of current discourses on climate
change and migration, it gestures towards a rather bleak reconfiguration of
politics itself.

In the opening essay of *Life Adrift*, Wendy Brown argues that the crisis
of humanism brought about by climate change/the Anthropocene, neoliberal
rationality and the spread of slums and refugee camps is most immediate
in the contemporary supersession of democracy. Her argument resonates
strongly with what we take to be the 'repression' of labour as a term of art
in the discourse on climate change and migration. Brown reminds us that
democracy means 'rule by the people'. But in place of rule by the people, in
the climate–migration relation we find instead new forms of population management in which labour (i.e. people) is disciplined by neoliberal rationality.
This is nowhere more apparent than in the fashionable 'migration-as-adaptation' thesis (Foresight, 2011, Black et al., 2011, Warner and Afifi, 2014,
McLeman and Smit, 2006). Often praised for avoiding the reductive, Malthusian logics of 'climate refugees' and climate wars, and for foregrounding
migrant agency, the thesis holds that migration can be a desirable means of

adapting to climate change (rather than a failure to adapt). At first glance, the migration-as-adaptation thesis seems a welcome alternative to its Malthusian antecedent. It appeals to liberal ideals of unconstrained human mobility and laborious individuals engaged in securing and improving their living conditions. But, as several have now shown, the thesis recalls the neoliberal rationality present within the domain of climate change adaptation. It posits that vulnerable populations should manage (climate) risk by mobilizing their human capital and financing their adaptation by participating in migration and the global remittance economy. As such, the thesis merely repackages development policy that has been in circulation for decades within the so-called 'migration-development' nexus (Bettini and Gioli, 2016). With climate change, these 'old' discourses are simply rearticulated, for instance according to the logics and ontology of resilience (Baldwin, 2016, Bettini et al., 2016, Methmann and Oels, 2015), and inherit its peculiar subjectivities and mechanisms of government (Chandler and Reid, 2016, Evans and Reid, 2014, Reid, 2012). In particular, the thesis implies that surviving climate change is conditional on one's ability to mobilize one's own resources (i.e. one's labour) to withstand the impacts of climate change. The neoliberal character of the thesis is unmistakable. It interpolates surplus labour into remittance economies through a logic of self-entrepreneurship, a first step in extending 'insurance' to those otherwise deemed 'uninsurable' (Baldwin, 2016), offering little hope to those unable to mobilize their labour in this way.

The migration-as-adaptation thesis is not a model for free migration. It is, rather, another instance in the disciplining of labour and class control under capitalism. Autonomy and democracy play little or no part in the migration-as-adaptation thesis. Those for whom the thesis is designed – surplus labour, the rural and urban poor – are imagined not as political agents or citizens of democracy but as a docile labour force in the service of capital's endless requirements for expansion and adaptation to its ongoing crises. In this respect, the policies that would govern, discipline and curb the flows of mobilized 'climate labour' are reminiscent of those used in the Global South to manage 'dangerous' populations in the wake of decolonization (Duffield, 2007, 2001). So too, environmental stress and 'disasters' have long been involved in the mobilization of labour (primitive mode of accumulation) crucial to capital accumulation and linked by Marx to the emersion and role of surplus populations (Marx, 1983). Ranabir Samaddar's rereading of migration and famines in India under British imperial rule (this volume) provides an exemplary case in point. Understanding how labour and its mobility are rearticulated in the face of climate change (and the Anthropocene) is thus crucial, both analytically and for the political questions it raises.

The Border

It is almost impossible to think about migration in today's global political economy without – sooner or later – running up against the semantics of the border. The building of fences and walls against migration is a trademark rallying cry for all manner of contemporary right-wing populisms. But the 'enforcement' of borders enjoys political currency and ethical legitimacy in liberal circles as well, as does the violence that such enforcement often entails (Doty, 2011). Border enforcement is, for example, a standard component of European and North American migration policy. The recent decision to deploy NATO vessels to 'stem flows' in the Aegean is a vivid illustration of the open militarization of border controls and its overlap with humanitarian interventions (Pallister-Wilkins, 2015). Both Sweden's decision to re-establish border checks across the Oresund and the slightly surreal quarrel between France and the United Kingdom over who should be in charge of the walls and security devices protecting the entry into the Calais tunnel make evident how borders are a common part of the way states govern and bargain. Plenty are the interests that converge around the military, intelligence and industrial complexes tasked with securing terrestrial and maritime frontiers, justified through the irregularization and securitization of migration (Andersson, 2015, Jansen et al., 2015). Intense is the violence exercised and heavy are the casualties, while scant is the evidence that border militarization actually reduces migration (see the conclusions of the longitudinal study on the US – Mexico border by leading migration scholar Douglas Massey and colleagues, 2016). The border has also become a key signifier for struggles in support of migrants and against xenophobia, with 'no borders' representing one of the main banners – together with the fight against austerity and precariatization – for radical antagonistic movements (Mezzadra, 2015, Burridge, 2014).

The border thus imposes itself as a key object of investigation. It is important at several levels, but also in the context of climate change and migration where fences, barbwires and 'barbarians' are key visual signifiers in narratives on 'climate refugees'. Border fortification is often invoked by those in the affluent North concerned by the prospects of mass climate-induced displacement from the Global South (Schwartz and Randall, 2003). Katherine Russo's investigation of Australian media discourses (this volume) traces the transnational flows of people and affect that are harnessed through the figure of 'climate refugees' and the bordering impulse this figure more or less explicitly invokes. Not surprisingly, the border has been investigated in relation to climate change and mobility in a number of international relations and securitization studies (e.g. Boas, 2015, Rothe, 2015, Baldwin et al., 2014, Oels, 2013). Gregory White (2011), for example, focusing on the migration channels linking North Africa and Europe, has documented the impacts that climate change is having on border regimes across a spectrum of countries. For White, discourses on global warming have become part of the securitization of borders in Europe and North Africa but also in the renegotiation of sovereignty amongst those states. And Simon Dalby's contribution to this volume also poses important questions on the radical transformation that sovereignty (and borders) may undergo with regard to the scramble for territory and settlement that climate change is expected to bring about.

But alongside this important work, we highlight another approach: one inspired by Sandro Mezzadra and Brett Neilson (2013) which provides useful resources for a non-reductionist account that draws together the entwined themes of labour and the border. Mezzadra and Neilson's starting point is that borders are more than just 'things', mere lines that delimit territory. For them, borders are *relations*. Inasmuch as borders organize the intricate processes of selective exclusion and inclusion (triaging bodies on the basis of citizenship, the productivity of their labour, their race, etc.) borders become key sites by and through which power is reproduced and contested. Starting from such a conceptualization, Mezzadra and Neilson trace the deep interconnections between the proliferation of borders and of migration in contemporary globalized capitalism, and the (re)production and disciplining of labour. When we consider the environmental dimension, approaching the 'border as method' allows for connections to be drawn across a number of phenomena that otherwise appear disconnected in the discourse on climate change and migration. Territory, sovereignty and exclusion, the government of population and the role of mobile labour in capital accumulation all congeal 'at the border'. It is at the border that the reconfiguration of sovereignty in the face of globalized capital and planetary crises is negotiated (see Dalby, this volume). It is at and through the border that capital's attempts to secure a smooth mobilization of labour, as, for example, in the migration-as-adaptation thesis mentioned earlier, becomes visible. And it is through material and symbolic borders that transnational flows of racialized and colonial affects are channelled and amplified, surfacing in public discourse in the form of the anxieties and fears that characterize the present. Using the 'border as method' thus offers, among the other things, a promising analytic for countering the reductionism and empiricism prevalent in mainstream accounts of climate migration.

Race

If *Life Adrift* intervenes in the space opened up when climate change is said to be a problem of migration, then this must surely entail asking: For whom is migration in the context of climate change a problem? A simple perusal of the topic would suggest that it is predominantly European and

Western publics that adopt this view. This is certainly confirmed when we take account of the colonizing gaze through which low-lying islands states of the Pacific have been made available to Western audiences concerned with climate change (Farbotko, 2010a, 2010b, Farbotko and Lazrus, 2012). Colonial tropes, such as remoteness, smallness and victimhood, are partly the reason so many Pacific islanders refuse the label 'climate refugee' (McNamara and Gibson, 2009, Government of Tokelau, 2015). Not only does the label dehistoricize, it effaces the heterogeneity that characterizes political and cultural life in the expansive 'sea of islands' that comprise Oceania. So, when Europeans use the label 'climate refugee' to describe those they perceive to be at the greatest risk of climate change, even while the label is refused by those it purports to help (see Dalby, this volume), this merely confirms Epeli Hau'ofa's (1994) trenchant critique that 'academic and consultancy experts tend to overlook or misinterpret grassroots activities because these do not fit in with prevailing views about the nature of society and its development' (p. 148). There can be no doubt that when academics, activists and policymakers use the concept of 'climate refugees' they do so with the best of intentions. But as Sherene Razack (2011) writes, 'Colonizers always claim a commitment to the improvement of racialized peoples' (p. 269). Any account of the way climate change and migration function as a form of power that fails to account for this asymmetry in racial terms is simply missing the point.

It is entirely plausible to argue that the effects of climate change will be racialized, born disproportionately by people of colour. This claim is one of the pillars of climate justice. It is also correct to argue that climate change is a manifestation of racist political economy (think: oil extraction in the Niger delta). But to understand the relation between climate change and migration as a system of racial power means going beyond the reductive claim that a climatic injustice occurs when a person of colour relocates because of climate change. David Theo Goldberg's chapter offers a compelling way into the question of race through a focus on the sea: the sea as a cultural reference point, the sea as bearer of racial meaning and the sea as material force. As a form of natureculture, the sea mediates historically situated social relations. It is also a source of heterogeneity, where heterogeneity is a theme of racial threat that recurs throughout Goldberg's oeuvre (Goldberg, 1993, 2014). Oceans are also racially characterized, and the mode of the migrant's arrival is now racially indexed, superseding country of origin as a racial marker. Arrival by boat poses the threat of race, while arrival by plane is akin to fluidity, circulation and capital. Such racial indexing is thoroughly postracial (on postraciality, see Goldberg, 2015 and Baldwin, this volume). As climate change bears down the present, it carries implicitly the connotation of racial invasion.

And here we identify another related aspect of racial power: the way that enslaved and racially subjugated bodies always represent the possible dissolution of white supremacy. The abolition of slavery was a perilous prospect for both slave holder and abolitionist alike. For the slave holder, the slave always represented the possibility of rebellion, vengeful murder and rape. Abolition for the slave holder meant not only the loss of property and labour but the inevitable confrontation with the once-subjugated, now-equal freed slave (McWhorter, 2009). Better for slavery to continue than to risk unleashing race war. For the abolitionist, on the other hand, the newly freed slave stood for an excess of freedom. Mark Duffield (2007) locates this excess of freedom as the reason early liberals and missionaries sought to train newly freed slaves in self-government. To do otherwise, so went their reasoning, would risk imprudence and violence among those unversed in practices of freedom. This is why Thomas Jefferson, a slave holder *and* an abolitionist, advocated that freed slaves be deported from America (McWhorter, 2009). Doing so, he thought, was the only reliable method to avoid what he imagined was inevitable post-abolition race war.

The fear that the oppressed will one day seek revenge on the oppressor is a consistent theme in environmental narratives. The environmental historian William Cronon (1996) characterizes this fear as 'nature as demonic other, nature as avenging angel, nature as the return of the repressed' (p. 48). What this narrative expresses is the modernist worry that nature ultimately can never be fully subdued by man, that nature is forever the excess of the human. In racial terms, it is precisely this fear which is expressed by the slave holder; the naturalized other, the racial other, will return to destroy some cherished object, whether a family, a polity or civilization. King Kong taking over Manhattan and unstoppable zombies are pop cultural manifestations of this long and persistent trope (Giuliani, this volume). Narratives about climate change and migration express precisely this same concern. Unless contained or managed in some way, the figure of the climate change migrant in all its excessiveness represents the possibility of destroying civilization, a fear homologous with the midnight worries of the slave holder.

CLIMATE CHANGE AND MIGRATION: THE KINOPOLITICS OF STRATA

Our concern up until now has been to show how climate change and migration is foremost a relation of power. Labour discipline, bordering and racialization are all central (but by no means exclusive) features of this power. Together they instruct us to think about how, why and for whom managing human migration has become a central prerogative for climate change governance. If climate change represents for some a profound instability or the unruly movement of populations, then attending to these techniques can help us grasp how governing climate change is also partly about fixing certain relations in place, ensuring that population movements do not become excessive, and deciding upon the legitimate (and illegitimate) movement of bodies in the context of a changing earth system.

We wish to conclude, however, by outlining a very different if tentative ethics for rethinking human migration in the context of climate change, one that combines Nigel Clark's (forthcoming) *politics of strata* with Thomas Nail's (2016) theory of *kinopolitics*. Our starting point for this, however, is Claire Colebrook's chapter contribution in which she turns the climate–migration relation completely inside out. Whereas migration is conventionally understood in a changing climate as exceptional to an otherwise stable life, Colebrook argues that 'it is from movement and migration that relative stabilities are formed' (p. 117, this volume). Her point is that movement, flow and flux precede position and stability and, furthermore, that whatever anxiety we harbour about the migration effects of climate change is merely the effect of the stabilities that colonialism violently imposes on a world in motion. Her insight is significant for us because it redirects us to imagine human migration in relation to deep time, and not just decades and centuries but through millennia well before the advent of early hominids.

Enter Clark's politics of strata. Echoing a wider debate on the intercourse of geology and philosophy (Grosz, 2008, Yusoff et al., 2012, Deleuze and Guattari, 1987), Clark poses the question of geological strata to that of the political. 'Rather than simply affirming that the Anthropocene thesis has suddenly propelled geological strata into political significance', Clark suggests 'that interactions with the stratified composition of the earth's crust have long played a constitutive role in social and political formations' (forthcoming, p. 4). His point, however, is very far from a reaffirmation of determinist reasoning. Strata, for Clark, do no determine the worlds of political and social life. A focus on strata, for Clark, has a much more unsettling and creative potential, for strata are not to be understood as fixed layers of the earth – stratifications of rock and sediment – but as a geological archive reminding us of the earth's inherent volatility, its overfull potential for radical transformation. Strata are, in this sense, continuously forged and recomposed from below while at the same time are always extending outwards in their continuous reconfigurations. Although not immediately obvious, Clark's insights bear directly on the question of human mobility. We might, for example, imagine the existing distribution of matter and bodies across the surface of the earth as a particular stratum, one composed as much by the transatlantic slave trade and European colonialism as by the slow retreat of the Laurentide Ice Sheet over North America. In this sense, population is an irreducibly complex tangle of varying speeds of economic, ecological and historical change. But to arrest our analysis here would merely confirm the empiricist and depoliticizing lure inherent in the notion that migration is 'complex'. Clark's emphasis on strata reminds us then that like geological strata population strata are not spatially and temporally fixed but are always open to recombination and redistribution. Indeed, as many commentators now point out (Dillon, 2008, Dillon and Lobo-Guerrero, 2008; Cf. Colebrook, this volume), this ontogenetic capacity to combine and recombine according to no predetermined plan is precisely what defines life itself. In terms of climate change, a focus on the ontogenetic formations of strata means embracing the idea that the 'tectonic shifts' brought about by climate change promise to lead to the de- and reconfiguration of the forms of mobility (and accumulation, sovereignty, territory) that emerged in the modern period.

Such a position emerges in profound contrast with the assumption of stability and immobility (of territory, people, sovereignty and state) that inform mainstream discourses on migration and climate change. Thomas Nail's theory of *kinopolitics* offers an additional contribution in that direction. Not unlike Colebrook's claim that movement precedes position, kinopolitics is the idea that politics originates out of movement and flow rather than stasis and immobility as its default conditions. In this sense, power, sovereignty and border emerge as techniques designed to harness never-ending flows of flesh, rock, fluids and energy rather than as institutions designed to preserve a pre-existing, original, 'natural' state of stability (Nail, 2015). The flows – of energy, of materials, of territories, of people – that climate change and the Anthropocene are expected to put in train might then be seen as forces that impel us to renegotiate the very devices that attempt to harness those flows, rather than (only) as forces that threaten the disruption of pre-(and yet non-) existent stabilities. To put this in more practical terms: if we consider the function of containment that the stabilization of territory and the drawing of borders have had in modern history, the instability brought about by climate change and the Anthropocene might also represent an opening to the emergence of new ways to inhabit and to move across territory and indeed the emergence of new forms of political community and solidarity. What comes out of this condition of twilight, where we see the possible end of modern forms of inhabiting and dividing territory, can and should become a key political question for the present (see Colebrook, this volume). Life adrift is thus not some fatal condition. To be adrift is to be overfull with potential and with life.

REFERENCES

Andersson, R. 2015. Hardwiring the frontier? The politics of security technology in Europe's 'fight against illegal migration'. *Security Dialogue*, 47(1), 22–39.

Baldwin, A. 2012. Orientalising environmental citizenship: Climate change, migration and the potentiality of race. *Citizenship Studies*, 16.

———. 2013. Racialisation and the figure of the climate change migrant. *Environment and Planning A*, 45, 1474–1490.

———. 2016. Resilience and race, or climate change and the uninsurable migrant: Towards an anthroporacial reading of 'race'. *Resilience*, 1–15.

Baldwin, A., Methmann, C. & Rothe, D. 2014. Securitizing 'climate refugees': The futurology of climate-induced migration. *Critical Studies on Security*, 2, 121–130.

Berlant, L. 2016. The commons: Infrastructures for troubling times. *Environment and Planning D: Society and Space*, 34, 393–419.

Bettini, G. & Gioli, G. 2016. Waltz with development: Insights on the developmentalization of climate-induced migration. *Migration and Development*, 5, 171–189.

Bettini, G., Nash, S. & Gioli, G. 2016. One step forward, two steps back? The changing contours of (in)justice in competing discourses on climate migration. *The Geographical Journal*, doi:10.1111/geoj.12192.

Black, R., Bennett, S. R. G., Thomas, S. M. & Beddington, J. R. 2011. Climate change: Migration as adaptation. *Nature*, 478, 447–449.

Boas, I. 2015. *Climate Migration and Security: Securitisation as a Strategy in Climate Change Politics*. New York: Routledge.

Burridge, A. 2014. 'No Borders' as a critical politics of mobility and migration. *ACME*, 13, 463–470.

Castree, N. 2014. *Making Sense of Nature: Representation, Politics and Democracy*. Abingdon: Routledge.

Chandler, D. & Reid, J. 2016. *The Neoliberal Subject: Resilience, Adaptation and Vulnerability*. London: Rowman & Littlefield International.

Clark, N. forthcoming. Politics of strata. *Theory, Culture & Society*. Special Issue: Geosocial formations and the Anthropocene.

Cronon, W. 1996. 'Introduction: In search of nature'. In: Cronon, W. (ed.) *Uncommon Ground: Rethinking the Human Place in Nature*. New York: W.W. Norton and Company.

Dalby, S. 1996. The environment as geopolitical threat: Reading Robert Kaplan's 'coming anarchy'. *Ecumene*, 3, 471–496.

———. 2002. *Environmental Security*. Minneapolis: University of Minnesota Press.

Deleuze, G. & Guattari, F. 1987. *A Thousand Plateaus: Capitalism and Schizophrenia*. Minneapolis: University of Minnesota Press.

Dillon, M. 2008. Underwriting security. *Security Dialogue*, 39, 309–332.

Dillon, M. & Lobo-Guerrero, L. 2008. Biopolitics of security in the 21st century: An introduction. *Review of International Studies*, 34, 265–292.

Doty, R. L. 2011. Bare life: Border-crossing deaths and spaces of moral alibi. *Environment and Planning D: Society and Space*, 29, 599–612.

Duffield, M. 2007. *Development, Security and Unending War – Governing the World of Peoples*. Cambridge: Polity Press.

Duffield, M. R. 2001. *Global Governance and the New Wars: The Merging of Development and Security*. London: Zed Books.

Evans, B. & Reid, J. 2014. *Resilient Life: The Art of Living Dangerously*. Cambridge: Wiley.

Farbotko, C. 2010a. 'The global warming clock is ticking so see these places while you can': Voyeuristic tourism and model environmental citizens on Tuvalu's disappearing islands. *Singapore Journal of Tropical Geography*, 31, 224–238.

———. 2010b. Wishful sinking: Disappearing islands, climate refugees and cosmopolitan experimentation. *Asia Pacific Viewpoint*, 51, 47–60.

Farbotko, C. & Lazrus, H. 2012. The first climate refugees? Contesting global narratives of climate change in Tuvalu. *Global Environmental Change*, 22, 382–390.

Felli, R. 2013. Managing climate insecurity by ensuring continuous capital accumulation: 'Climate Refugees' and 'Climate Migrants'. *New Political Economy*, 18, 337–363.

Foresight. 2011. *Final Project Report – Foresight: Migration and Global Environmental Change*. London: The Government Office for Science.

Ghosh, A. 2016. *The Great Derangement: Climate Change and the Unthinkable*. Chicago: University of Chicago Press.

Goldberg, D. T. 1993. *Racist Culture: Philosophy and the Politics of Meaning*. Oxford: Blackwell Publishers.

———. 2014. *Sites of Race: Conversations with Susan Searls Giroux*. Cambridge: Polity Press.

———. 2015. *Are We All Postracial Yet?* Cambridge: Polity Press.

Government of Tokelau. 2015. 'Climate refugees' connotation rejected in Kiribati dialogue. Apia, Samoa: Office of the Council for the Ongoing Government of Tokelau, Apia, Samoa.

Grosz, E. 2008. *Chaos, Territory, Art: Deleuze and the Framing of the Earth*. Durham and London: Duke University Press.

Hamilton, C., Gemenne, F. & Bonneuil, C. (eds.). 2015. *The Anthropocene and the Global Environmental Crisis: Rethinking Modernity in a New Epoch*. New York: Routledge.

Haraway, D. 2015. Anthropocene, capitalocene, plantationocene, chthulucene: Making king. *Environmental Humanities*, 6, 159–165.

Harvey, D. 1974. Population, resources and the ideology of science. *Economic Geography*, 50, 256–277.

———. 2011. *The Enigma of Capital – and the Crises of Capitalism*. London: Profile.

Hau'ofa, E. 1994. Our sea of islands. *The Contemporary Pacific*, 6, 148–161.

Hulme, M. 2011. Reducing the future to climate: A story of climate determinism and reductionism. *Osiris*, 26, 245–266.

Ipcc 2014. Fifth Assessment Report, Working Group II: Impacts, Adaptation, and Vulnerability. Geneva: Intergovernmental Panel on Climate Change.

Jansen, Y., Celikates, R. & De Bloois, J. (eds.). 2015. *The Irregularization of Migration in Contemporary Europe: Detention, Deportation, Drowning*. London and New York: Rowman & Littlefield.

Latour, B. 2004. *Politics of Nature: How the Bring the Sciences into Democracy*. Cambridge: Harvard University Press.

Malm, A. & Hornborg, A. 2014. The geology of mankind? A critique of the Anthropocene narrative. *The Anthropocene Review*, 1, 62–69.

Marx, K. 1983. *Grundrisse*. London: Penguin Books.

Massey, D. S., Durand, J. & Pren, K. A. 2016. Why border enforcement backfired. *American Journal of Sociology*, 121, 1557–1600.

Mcleman, R. 2014. *Climate and Human Migration: Past Experiences, Future Challenges*. Cambridge: Cambridge University Press.

Mcleman, R. & Smit, B. 2006. Migration as an adaptation to climate change. *Climate Change*, 76, 31–53.

Mcnamara, K. E. & Gibson, C. 2009. 'We do not want to leave our land': Pacific ambassadors at the United Nations resist the category of 'climate refugees'. *Geoforum*, 40, 475–483.

Mcwhorter, L. 2009. *Racism and Sexual Oppression in America: A Genealogy*. Bloomington: Indiana University Press.

Methmann, C. & Oels, A. 2015. From 'fearing' to 'empowering' climate refugees: Governing climate-induced migration in the name of resilience. *Security Dialogue*, 46, 51–68.

Mezzadra, S. 2015. 'The proliferation of borders and the right to escape'. In: Jansen, Y., Celikates, R. & De Bloois, J. (eds.) *The Irregularization of Migration in Contemporary Europe: Detention, Deportation, Drowning*. 1st edition. London and New York: Rowman & Littlefield.

Mezzadra, S. & Neilson, B. 2013. *Border as Method, or, the Multiplication of Labor*. Durham: Duke University Press.

Moore, J. W. 2015. *Capitalism in the Web of Life: Ecology and the Accumulation of Capital*. London: Verso Books.

Nail, T. 2015. *The Figure of the Migrant*. Stanford: Stanford University Press.

Oels, A. 2013. Rendering climate change governable by risk: From probability to contingency. *Geoforum*, 45, 17–29.

Pallister-Wilkins, P. 2015. The humanitarian politics of European border policing: Frontex and Border Police in Evros. *International Political Sociology*, 9, 53–69.

Razack, S. 2011. 'Colonization: The good, the bad, and the ugly'. In: Baldwin, A., Cameron, L. & Kobayashi, A. (eds.) *Rethinking the Great White North: Race, Nature and the Historical Geographies of Whiteness in Canada*. Vancouver: University of British Columbia Press.

Reid, J. 2012. The disastrous and politically debased subject of resilience. *Development Dialogue*, 58, 67–80.

Reid, J. & Evans, B. 2014. *Resilience: The Art of Living Dangerously*. Cambridge: Cambridge University Press.

Rothe, D. 2015. *Securitizing Global Warming: A Climate of Complexity*. London: Taylor & Francis.

Saunders, P. 2000. 'Environmental refugees: The origins of a construct'. In: Stott, P. & Sullivan, S. (eds.) *Political Ecology: Science, Myth and Power*. London: Arnold Publishers.

Schwartz, P. & Randall, D. 2003. *An Abrupt Climate Change Scenario and its Implications for United States National Security*. Washington, DC: Environmental Media Services.

Swyngedouw, E. 2010. Apocalypse forever? Post-political populism and the spectre of climate change. *Theory, Culture & Society*, 27, 213–232.

UK Foresight. 2011. Foresight: Migration and Global Environmental Change (2011) Final Project Report. London: The Government Office for Science.

Warner, K. & Afifi, T. 2014. Where the rain falls: Evidence from 8 countries on how vulnerable households use migration to manage the risk of rainfall variability and food insecurity. *Climate and Development*, 6, 1–17.

White, G. 2011. *Climate Change and Migration: Security and Borders in a Warming World*. Oxford: Oxford University Press.

Yusoff, K., Grosz, E., Clark, N., Saldanha, A. & Nash, C. 2012. Geopower: A panel on Elizabeth Grosz's chaos, territory, art: Deleuze and the framing of the earth. *Environment and Planning D: Society and Space*, 30, 971–988.

Žižek, S. 2010. *Living in the End Times*. London: Verso Books.

Part I

POLITICS: TERRITORY, BORDERS AND SUBJECTIVITIES ON SHIFTING GROUNDS

Chapter 2

Climate Change, Democracy and Crises of Humanism

Wendy Brown

The worry that hovers over the explorations in this chapter is that *Demos-kratia*, rule by the people, has an incontrovertibly humanist heart, even as its practices and orientation may rightly undergo modification by posthumanist critique. Already challenged today by globalization and by the neoliberalization of political life, democracy cannot survive a total eclipse by posthumanist practices and commitments. Yet most serious climate change mitigation strategies, even those contoured by climate justice concerns, aim directly or indirectly at circumventing democracy. That is, from geoengineering to international agreements to carbon credits, these strategies do not rest on implementing the will of the people, even as present and future generations are presumed beneficiaries. This sidestepping – sometimes outright spurning – of democracy is no light matter, given democracy's more generally imperilled condition.

That we are living in the era of the posthuman is a commonplace, both in contemporary cultural and social theory and in quotidian existence punctuated by Siri's ubiquitous voice. What is meant by posthumanism varies, but for many scholars it converges in disturbing the centrism, and not only the distinctiveness, of the human as that which feels, thinks, deliberates and acts differently from other sentient life, on the one hand, and differently from inanimate things, including those of our making, on the other hand. Posthumanism emerges as well from a critique of the norms sedimented into historical humanisms – norms of gender, caste, race, culture, civilization and more. Thus posthumanism challenges ontologies and epistemologies of the human that would fix or stipulate human nature, render us unified and self-mastering and radically distinguish us from our productions, prosthetics and other sentient life. It also upsets the theology of God as a disembodied yet

25

anthropomorphized figure and of humans as God's miniatures, little sovereigns each.

There may be nothing that makes wrestling with posthumanism more urgent than climate change: it mandates a recognition that what was once quaintly called 'external nature' does not simply exist as our resource to plunder and that we must rapidly and dramatically accommodate our ways of life *and* problem-solving to this truth. And yet, in this call to do something historically unprecedented – to act collectively on behalf of the world's survival – is there not an intensification rather than supersession of humanism? Are we not required to mobilize distinctly human capacities of intellection, knowledge, will, institutions and acting in concert to bring us back from the cliff edge to which the species has run itself and the planet? Is such a hoped-for reckoning with and rectification of our global condition one that any other animate or inanimate entity can conceive, let alone perform? Perhaps we cannot either, but there is little question about the obligation to try. And there is a distinctly human imagination and drive behind every possible approach to climate change mitigation or adaptation, from cap and trade to global governance and policing, from micro-politics based on individual or local practices to global transformations of economy and polity, from dreamed of technological adaptations to continued high levels of fossil fuel burning and economic growth to a dreamed of U-turn's away from these practices. Even environmental economists who seek to alter energy utilization entirely through markets imagine a feat of unprecedented global human design. Each places a Herculean humanism at the heart of the solution they promulgate.

However, this humanism too is inflected by a certain undoing. It is shadowed by a fear that we may not be up to the task or by ironic recognition that humility and reckoning with limits, rather than hubris and visions of mastery, must hereafter frame the project of being human. It is also threatens to suspend or undermine political practices expressive of humanism. This chapter, then, is a modest exploration of the portion of the political topography of climate change where a flow of posthumanisms intersects a flow of humanisms.

*

The posthumanisms considered in this chapter, however, do not hail from theorists. Rather, my focus will be on what I take to be the historical unfolding of posthumanisms inherent in the arrival of the Anthropocene, in neoliberal rationality, in proliferating global slums and refugee camps and in disembowelled democracy.[1] I want to consider these material disruptions of the foundational humanist idea, cultivated in the European Renaissance, that humans make their own meanings, histories and worlds, that humans are a fundamental (though not necessarily exclusive) agency in their universe and that humans, rather than God, are the proper centre of their own political and cultural universe. This formulation precedes the high modern (Cartesian and then Kantian) inflection of humanism with unremitting rationalism, moral autonomy and the radical independence of nature – mind as its own steed. Yet there is already a strong notion of freedom hovering around early-modern humanism. Against a world view in which humans are presumed determined by the Divine, exist to know or comport with Divine truth or are condemned to naturalist orders (with their inherent hierarchies) or instinct (with their inherent drives), humanism's animating conceit is that we are unique in our capacities to act, give form to existence and are destined to struggle with meaning. Humanism is thus always at least modestly non-theistic and anthropocentric, as well as tethered to the human capacity for action based on deliberation and will, fashioning life together and making our own history. Most humanism posits these features of us as both ontological and good; some also reckon with their tragic dimensions – the uniquely human capability of wreaking horror, holocaust, protracted social and subjective misery and now, climate change.

This is what I take to be the rough concatenation of humanistic conceits animating Western modernity. Let us now turn to three fundamental ways in which they are materially challenged today.

THE ANTHROPOCENE

There is nothing inherent in the concept of the Anthropocene that disturbs humanist conceits; to the contrary, it can confirm them, which is one of several recent objections to this concept by certain left ecological scholars and activists.[2] The marking of ours as the age in which *Homo sapiens* became a significant geophysical force means that, more than simply special amidst a million varieties of life, we alone are capable of radically altering the planet and conditions of life for everything on it. If there was a God, we rival it now; and if there wasn't, we've become the God-myth's negative type. In contrast with Hobbes' infamous 'God makes and governs nature, man makes and governs the state', or with Machiavelli's cosmology in which manly *virtu* wrestles with the naturalized figure of *fortuna*, or with Marx's historiography of a long struggle with nature culminating in mastery through rational collective control of existence, the Anthropocene reflects us as bigger in our effects and destructive potential than any humanist imagined.

Here we come upon the first paradox of the Anthropocene for humanism. In no prior historical moment have human powers – economic, military, political, technological, representational and more – been so large, so complex or so thoroughly saturated the globe. Yet never have humans faced a challenge as daunting as climate change, one whose serious address requires global coordination and enforcement, and has implications for how the entire species lives, thinks, works and plays. If we of such unprecedented powers lack the crucial ability to harness rather than be buffeted by them, are they really powers after all, or only capacities? A neo-Marxist might render this as the familiar problem of powers humanly generated but not humanly controlled, only ramified across a greater spectrum of existence than Marx captured with his focus on production and class. No sooner are we taken into Marxist arms, however, than we are dropped by them. The Marxist solution to this condition depends upon the resolution of all ills – from alienation to resource depletion, sexism and racism to poverty – through communism, itself delivered by the magic of dialectics, historical progress, rationality, world civilization, the inexhaustible yearning for freedom and the human capacity to cooperate and plan absent centralized government. Stripped of these old tricks, the challenge of humanly generated powers that escaped their progenitors persists, while the resolution evaporates.

As Dipesh Chakrabarty has brilliantly illuminated, we are up against much more than broken promises here. Rather, the Anthropocene poses the problem of humanity in a novel way: as the unprecedented effect of *the species* qua species on the planet on the one hand, and the near impossibility of apprehending this effect at the level of individual consciousness on the other. For Chakrabarty, in the Anthropocene, the species that uniquely produces for its subsistence now produces more than its way of life and history; rather, it produces the history of the world as a whole. Yet it does so as a collective and non-human *force*. Here are the implications for humanism as Chakrabarty sees it:

> But what happens when we say humans are acting like a geophysical force? We then liken humans to some nonhuman nonliving agency. That is why I say the science of anthropogenic global warming has doubled the figure of the human – you have to think of the two figures of the human simultaneously: the human-human and the nonhuman-human. (Chakrabarty 2012, 11)[3]

Perhaps a third figure of the human is also emergent here: we might call it the *uberhuman*, sought for that which we have never before done, namely guided the endeavour, organized the existence and set the limits of the species, as a species. Through the *uberhuman*, the species would take itself in hand, as it were.[4]

This doubled or tripled figure of the human brings an end to the ontogeny/phylogeny homology, and the historical narrative based upon it, dominating much of Western historiography and history. In this homology, the organization, development or government of the species is imagined to be replicated in the organization, development or government of the individual. Far from being the exclusive preserve of discredited nineteenth-century evolutionary theory, the homology has many variations, including philosophical (Kant, Hegel, even Nietzsche), political (Plato, Hobbes, Bentham, Mill) and, of course, psychoanalytic (Freud). This indispensable yet intensely colonial trope for framing civilizational infancy and maturity, difference and not only development, has for millennia organized our understanding of the human and its possibilities. But when the project of preserving the species and the planet rests on a capacity that cannot be found within its individual members, when that project concerns what Chakrabarty terms the 'nonhuman human' and depends on what I am provisionally terming the *uberhuman*, ontogeny and phylogeny fall asunder: the former remains the site of the human/human and the latter migrates to the non-human/human and hoped-for *uberhuman*. This is a consequential development. For all that the ontogeny-recapitulates-phylogeny trope facilitated colonial discourse and social Darwinism, for all of its indefensible and error-ridden features, its disintegration has its own frightening implications. We are already missing it.

NEOLIBERALISM

The deep incompatibility of neoliberalism with prospects for serious climate change mitigation is obvious enough – there's little to add to the arguments of Naomi Klein (2014), Mike Davis (2006a), Adrian Parr (2012) and other similarly minded critics.[5] Unregulated markets allow near-term profit interests maximized through exploitation of cheap resources and immediate consumer desire to trump every other concern, especially those pertaining to the long term. Privatization means that public goods and public interests are concretely defunded and dismantled as well as ideologically demeaned. It also means that higher education as a site for cultivating thoughtful citizenship and of generating research in the public interest is divested of these purposes precisely when we require unqualifiedly public orientations to the unqualifiedly public predicament of climate change. And the neoliberal subordination of the state to the economy means that agglomerated financial interests dominate governments and postnational constellations, crowding out other kinds of political claims and constituencies.

These features of neoliberalism in relation to climate change are well known and often discussed. However, there are more subtle ones: populations are largely depoliticized through formal institutions of neoliberal subject production (even as some portion may be politicized by the conditions and problems neoliberalism generates), which makes mobilization for planetary-wide ends doubly difficult. Neoliberalism's new legitimations of inequality generate political insensitivity to climate justice and, among the well-off, a sense of entitlement to a large carbon footprint. Neoliberalism also equates freedom with self-interest and value with competitive positioning, thus taking an ethos of self-absorption and self-protection to new levels. Finally, precarity is increasingly universalized by financialization, neoliberalism's offspring. Almost no one is insulated from the vicissitudes of a financialized world whose root principle is speculation – inherent fluctuations along with episodic market blowouts and burst bubbles. This precarity, which adds a certain veracity to that otherwise strange class category, the 99%, understandably generates more self-absorption and less public mindedness even as it can occasionally generate political rebellion.

Much of this is familiar. But what humanist premises and practices does neoliberalism assault? What posthumanist predicament does it present? Notwithstanding its cold secularism, indeed its replacement of the divine and the hidden hand with the algorithm, the philosophy and practice of neoliberalism make five fundamental moves against persons as agentic, free and ends in themselves:

1. Neoliberalism reduces humans to *homo oeconomicus*, only and everywhere. Neoliberal subjects are market actors in all things and all domains. Conceptually, this compression of the value and meaning of the human is more total than any previous iteration of *homo oeconomicus*; it is exhaustive, meant to extend to every crevice of our being and activity. Practically, neoliberal orders are bringing this being and this world into existence; everything from learning to dating, preschools to human rights organizations and states to prisons are fashioned according to a figure of human capital enhanced by branding, self-investment aimed at attracting potential investors, and savvy marketing. The human rendered entirely as *homo oeconomicus* and *homo oeconomicus* rendered as a bit of capital together transform the meaning and definition of being human more radically than even secularism did. Neoliberalism today produces the human as a miniature firm – in its self-understanding, conduct, social relations and valuation.

2. This reduction of the human being to *homo oeconomicus* breaks radically with the formulation of human beings as uniquely capable of the intellectual and political freedom captured in Aristotle's notion of the 'good life' – life apart from concern with survival or wealth accumulation and oriented instead to the distinctly human practices of thinking and shared rule. *Homo oeconomicus* is by definition bound to 'mere life': across all of its activities, its calculations never exceed value enhancement, never move to practices of self-realization and freedom apart from this table of values.

3. Being *homo oeconomicus* and nothing but *homo oeconomicus* figures humans as fundamentally behavioural beings, shaped and stimulated by

environments that incentivize and otherwise conduct us. In neoliberal reason, we are not giving form to ourselves or the world, and we are not poets, democrats, philosophers, tillers of the soil or writers of the book. Rather, we are creatures whose conduct is shaped at the intersection of internal drives and external conditions and stimuli.[6] This is why, of course, the social science cottage industry exploring our 'hard wired' proclivities for everything, from alcoholism to gender identity, anxiety to infidelity, liberalism to conservatism, is complemented by another cottage industry: models and experiments that test environmental effects on political, social and economic behaviour. Each challenges the figure of the human as capable of giving creative form to itself and the world; the combination lays this creature in the grave.

4. Today's figure of *homo oeconomicus* (a protean being, varying just as economies themselves do) is that of human capital comprising a portfolio of credit-seeking assets (Feher 2017b). In a financialized neoliberal regime, we don't simply have but are human capital, for ourselves and for others. The human thus dissolves into the collection of skills, knowledge and assets that create their value (or lack of it) in any domain – whether as job or university applicant, as intern or founder of start-up, as participant on a dating, gaming or career networking website. More than simply monetizing or entrepreneurializing the human being, financialization renders persons as bits of self-investing capital seeking to attract investors. The consequences for humanism are evident simply by contrasting the figure of the worker with the figure of human capital: A worker alienates its labour to generate wages for survival while capital is a derivative and an abstraction, albeit an endlessly divisible, leverageable and transformable one. Marx's formulations of exploitation and alienation thus don't apply, but neither does a Kantian kingdom of ends.

5. The fifth assault on humanism contained in neoliberal rationality is contained in its principle that markets are both superior to humans in providing for human wants *and* properly beyond human control, a principle whose anti-humanist effects are compounded by the neoliberal dissemination of markets everywhere. More than simply marketizing everything, neoliberalism dreams of an order in which all value and activity is subordinated to markets – their imperatives, vicissitudes, anxieties and cast-offs. Markets organize the present and future of governments, universities, ecosystems, relations among nations, relations among peoples. Neoliberalism thus affirms as a norm the inversion Weber identifies as a tragic dimension of rationalization, wherein systems developed as instruments or means – his focus was capitalism and bureaucracy – become ends, dominating what they were intended to serve. Neoliberal reason sheds the Weberian analytics while affirming the principle of markets as

superordinate and ungovernable.[7] Certainly we may speculate in and about markets, attempt to corner, manipulate, stimulate or cajole them. But in its drive to economize everything, neoliberalism affirms the escape of everything from sovereignty – personal, political, theological.[8] If sovereignty was, according to Schmitt, a secularized theological concept, and if God was, according to Feuerbach, a theologized account of human powers, when neoliberal theory and practice dethrone sovereignty, they dethrone humanism in the same gesture.

6. On at least these five counts, then, the triumph of neoliberal rationality (*not* simply neoliberal economic policy) portends the death of Man.

GLOBAL SLUMS AND REFUGEES

More than a billion people (one in eight humans on the planet) now live in urban/suburban slums, mostly shantytowns, and that number is predicted to double in fifteen years. Over half the urban population of sub-Saharan Africa resides in slums, the favelas of Rio de Janeiro contain more than 11 million people, and the *ciudad perdida* outside Mexico City hosts around 5 million. Some slum dwellers are squatters, some are renters, most are lifers. Many are refugees, but another 20 million people live in refugee camps, increasingly inside the borders of the developed world, not only abutting war-torn or famine-plagued parts of Asia and Africa (Spiegel 2013). By 2015 UN estimates, more than 30,000 new refugees are produced daily, 14 million annually.[9]

Some slums and camps have electricity, water and sewage lines, access to public education for kids and public transportation to jobs, stores or health care. Many do not. Employment figures are impossible, given that most income comes through the so-called informal economy – ranging from off-the-books work as nannies and domestics, rickshaw drivers and day labourers, to selling drugs and other contraband, human organs and babies, and, of course, garbage. An ever-growing number of slum dwellers are in the garbage-picking business, sorting and selling their finds to recyclers for pennies; cast-off humans picking through human refuse.

Why treat slums and refugee camps as another scene for the crisis of humanism? How else would we depict this condition in the twenty-first century: a rapidly growing proportion of the species living without ordinary need-provision (protection from the elements, adequate food, potable water and sewage treatment) and without conditions for development (modest life stability and security, access to education, integration into culture, society and economy). Frequently perched on sites that are toxic, dangerous or both (abutting waste dumps or airports, situated on flood plains, crumbling cliffs or hollows), these are lives often deracinated several times over. Lack of civic or political belonging was imagined in the last century to be exceptional – the issue of catastrophe or war – and has become a structural feature of our time.

This is not to discount practices of social cooperation, government and economy present in many slums and camps. It is not to suggest that there is no humanity in them. Rather, it is to identify the crisis that this almost-unfathomable pile-up of *Homo Sapiens* generates for a humanism identified with civilization and its accoutrements (Davis 2006b). However one may appreciate strategies of survival, cohabitation and political organization in many camps and slums (and we would do well to remember that these are also features of concentration camps and prisons), objectively this is the warehousing and removal from civilization of steadily growing numbers of humans. Nor are there signs of it abating as steadily more are exiled from homelands by war, political persecution, gang rule or the effects of climate change – floods, draughts, rising seas, changing agricultural conditions (Scheffran et al. 2012).

Arendt famously characterized stateless refugees as 'outside the common world of humanity'. Absence of national belonging reduced them to political 'nakedness', not fully human because of living without recognized forms of belonging. Arendt reminds us that humanism secures personhood not through species membership but through removal from such membership to a normatively specified status of persons. This status, she argued, is politically conferred in modernity by nation state recognition and 'the right to have rights' (Arendt [1951]/1968; Hayden 2009). Arendt's formulation needs augmentation through appreciation of subnational and postnational forms of political recognition along with the shadowy place the undocumented occupy between belonging and statelessness. Above all, however, it needs updating with appreciation of how neoliberal valuation has transformed the very question of belonging. For this purpose, I want to draw on Michel Feher's (2017a) analysis of what he terms the problem of 'disposing of the discredited', an analysis that will help us link the two crises of humanism we have just considered: that pertinent to global slums and camps, and that entailed by neoliberal transformations.

Here, briefly, is Feher's argument: financialization radically transformed the nature of value in capitalism as it converts owners of capital (including human capital) from a focus on immediate profit to a focus on shareholder value – the latter an index of the capacity to attract investors. There is thus a global shift from concern with direct capital accumulation through pricing and sales in excess of costs, to concern with enhancing creditworthiness and credibility; from a concern with attracting buyers to a concern with attracting investors and hence on the rankings and ratings that attract them. This is why financialization changes the game for everything: from corporations that live and die by the stock market rather than quarterly earnings, to small businesses that live and die by Yelp ratings, to nation states that live

and die by bond, credit and currency ratings, to educational institutions that
compete for, manipulate and manage their rankings, to human beings whose
value oscillates according to their Facebook 'likes', and 'favorited' tweets.
Financialization, Feher argues, transformed the neoliberal dream of a 'world
where the mindset and behavior of corporations, governments and individuals – including wage earners and even the unemployed – would be modeled
on the reasoning and pursuits of the profit-seeking entrepreneur' to one in
which that mindset and behaviour was instead 'modeled on the reasoning and
pursuits of a credit-seeking asset manager' (Feher 2017a, 10). The new mandate is to do what will enhance one's credit and avoid what will depreciate it.
This is what it means to be human capital, and hence human, today. Through
branding, self-promotion and careful investments, not to mention cultivation
of inherited assets like whiteness, nationality, masculinity, money or beauty,
each of us fashions ourselves as credit-seeking portfolio managers across the
whole of our existence. So also does every institution, project, corporation,
programme, school, start-up or state fashion itself this way. And, of course,
the credit ratings of individuals in turn enhance those of the family, university, firm or nation state with which the individual is affiliated.

What has this to do with refugees, global slums and humanism? Feher
argues this way:

> While neoliberal governments make it their calling to support the creation and
> attend to the sustaining of capital markets, the social compact that they produce
> by means of protecting an ever-expanding range of assets is not one that pro-
> vides universal coverage. Quite to the contrary, the advent of a political regime
> devoted to the fashioning of credit seeking portfolio managers is bound to gen-
> erate an ever-growing number of discredited individuals whose very existence
> ends up being burdensome. Indeed, when reassuring bondholders and creating
> value for the shareholders are the respective priorities of public officials and cor-
> porate managers, people who lack valuable assets can neither be cared for nor
> simply left to fend for themselves. On the one hand, boosting their creditworthi-
> ness requires an expansive fiscal policy that investors are likely to find unap-
> pealing. Yet, on the other hand, allowing their sorry lot to appear in plain view
> will prove just as damaging to the attractiveness of the territory in which they
> reside. Therefore, no matter how unsavory, disposing of the discredited – either
> by rendering them invisible or by making them actually disappear – figures
> among the missions that real neoliberal institutions are expected to accomplish.
> (Feher 2017a, 12)

Feher then analyses various ways that the European Union (EU) has disavowed, disappeared or disposed of the discredited (most importantly,
but not only refugees) in the past decade. These include manipulation of
statistics about them, harassment, incentives to leave and most importantly,

for our purposes, curbing the 'inflow of people who are not presumed to be very bankable' (2017a, 28). Two statistics reveal the intensity of these latter efforts. First, Feher notes, in the past twenty years, approximately '25,000 people have died while trying to cross the Mediterranean, some from drowning, others because their boats were left to drift' (Feher's paper was written before 2015–2016 influx, so these numbers are several thousand short).[10] Second, he notes that until the 1990s, 85% of those seeking asylum in Europe obtained it, while, today, 85% is the rate of rejection (Feher 2017a, 28). The story in North America is similar: over the past two decades, border fortification between Mexico and the United States has dramatically increased the death rate from attempted crossing; more than 2,000 people have died in the attempt in the past decade. These difficulties deter return, and, combined with the near impossibility for illegal entrants to obtain citizenship, the result is that approximately 12 million US inhabitants labour in agriculture, construction, landscaping and domestic work, but lack civil belonging, political rights or access to state services, health care or police protection.

Feher's analysis helps us understand why the growing populations in global slums and refugee camps, rising migrant deaths and estimated 40 million 'sans papiers' around the world generate policy challenges for countries anxious about their creditworthiness but not the humanitarian crisis Arendt expected. He explains why the problem largely materializes as one of financial rather than moral–political valuation, notwithstanding occasional handwringing and encomiums to Kant. As the human is reduced to a bundle of credit-seeking assets – the contemporary iteration of human capital – those without such assets take shape as a problem organized and represented by financial coordinates (credit, debt, default, currency and bond ratings).[11] This was exquisitely expressed in a June 2015 *New York Times* op-ed authored by the eminent economist Peter Schuck. Schuck (2015) argued that the April 2015 migrant boat disaster in the Mediterranean called for a new EU approach to immigration and refugees. He proposed one that would oblige all EU states to offer protection to refugees but organize it through a market in which states could trade this obligation with one another. Implicitly likening refugees to carbon emissions, Schuck argued this way:

Just as cap-and-trade schemes enhance environmental protection, this market would maximize the number of refugees protected by exploiting differences in states' resources, politics, geography and attitudes toward newcomers. A more ethnically homogeneous or xenophobic state might eagerly pay a high price (in cash, credit, commodities, political support, development assistance or some other valuable) to more refugee-friendly states to assume its burden, rather than having to bring them in-country.

While noting the many potential problems with such a market – ranging from super-exploitation to refugees being sent places they are loathe to go – for Schuck, these negatives are preferable to doing nothing. And they may well be. For our purposes, what's clear is that this scheme borrowed from environmental policy renders refugees as the undesirable effluent of global 'civilization' – its toxic refuse, as it were. Which brings us to the real flaw in Schuck's analysis: if cap and trade for carbon emissions addresses use of fuels whose toxic emissions are ineliminable, the human refuse problem is more easily solved. As Feher suggests, it really can just be disappeared.

DEMOCRACY'S SUPERSESSION

The last scene I want to consider as a certain crisis of humanism pertains to democracy, or, more precisely, to democracy's supersession and undoing today. Its realization in large democratic nation states was always limited by liberalism and compromised by undemocratic forces (capitalism) and repositories of power. But the challenges posed by globalization and neoliberalism threaten to reduce it to a ghost. Globalization undermines the jurisdiction, definition and sovereignty of the nation state – still democracy's essential modern form – with flows of power, configurations of identity and postnational political challenges that together assault the meaning, attractiveness, quotidian practices and functionalism of rule by the demos. Even national elections, that bare icon of democracy, rarely serve as deliberation-based referenda on national problems and visions today. They are more often expressions of resentments and fears, or cathection to personalities, in response to challenges exceeding both popular comprehension and the locus of the nation state.

Neoliberalism also undercuts democratic practices, institutions and imaginaries. It does this in obvious ways by intensifying inequality, subordinating states to large capital interests and financialization, removing the welfare provisions that enfranchise at social and civic levels, tethering politicians and policy ever more tightly to corporate money and, more generally, privatizing public goods, purposes and spaces. But neoliberal reason has also transposed the meaning of democracy and its constituent elements. When human beings are wholly reduced to market actors, the very idea of a self-ruling people vanishes. On the one hand, the *demos* is literally disintegrated into bits of human capital, each preoccupied with enhancing its individual value and competitive positioning. So the idea of popular sovereignty becomes incoherent – there's no such thing in a market. On the other hand, democratic political life reduced to a marketplace loses its distinctive value, cadences and coordinates. It ceases to be a domain of deliberation about how we should live together, and of sharing and equalizing power to determine common values and ends. Instead, political life is figured as a domain of (appropriately deregulated) competing capitals. Here, liberty loses its political valence and becomes nothing more than the unrestricted capacity to enhance ones human capital portfolio. Equality, hardly a value in markets, becomes only the equal right to compete in this way. So, neoliberalism undoes the very idea of democracy as that which depends on distinctively political forms and meanings of freedom, equality, personhood and popular sovereignty. This undoing occurs concretely through neoliberal law and economic policy. It occurs at the level of the political imaginary through the dissemination of neoliberal reason to every quarter of life. Democracy and markets, always in high tension, are barely able to coexist when the essential elements of democracy are explicitly nourished and protected. But democracy cannot survive being reduced to market values, terms and practices. This reduction is at the heart of the neoliberal anti-democratic revolution today, a revolution of extraordinary dimensions and consequences.

But again, what has this to do with humanism? Democracy is *the* humanist form of rule (anarchism would be a candidate save for its fundamental, indeed etymological, opposition to rule). Democracy holds the promise that humans will rule themselves as a whole rather than be subject to a part or an outsider – kings, tyrants, despots or priests, the highborn or the wealthy, the propertied or the owning class, bureaucracies, technocrats, experts, truth (religious or secular), unaccountable government institutions or markets. Against all of these, democracy holds out the promise that the people set the principles and conditions of their own collective existence. The term 'democracy' does not say how this shall be done. It only insists on the unique legitimacy of this political form. To give up on it, or allow it to thin to the point of irrelevance, is to give up humanism in its political form, which is the aspiration to govern our existence together.

CONCLUSION

Let me draw these strands into a provisional conclusion. Philosophical, cultural, ecological, feminist, queer, disability and interspecies critiques of humanism are indispensable to critical political and intellectual work. The violences and exclusions of humanism's normative emergence and trajectory – and not only its wrongheaded positioning of the human in relation to other species of life – are indisputable. But like all intellectual developments of this kind, posthumanist thought and politics themselves emerge from material disruptions; Donna Haraway (2009) is astute on this point. The digital technological revolution and the manifest effects of the Anthropocene are most familiar in this regard. I have sought to bring into relief disruptions posed by the imbricated phenomena of neoliberal rationality, the effective exclusion from civilization of over 1 billion people, and disintegrating democratic institutions and imaginaries. I am also suggesting that the practical prospects for addressing each, and climate change itself, likely rest with (neo) humanist retorts to these posthumanist developments and orders of valuation. Here, we may need to remind ourselves of two things. First, that critique is not rejection but depends profoundly upon what it subjects to its force, and that it is often a profound affirmation of an un- or under-realized ideal. Second, that 'post' denotes a condition of being after but not over – the signal event or formation may be past but we remain claimed by it. Moreover, I have suggested that to seek to be finished with humanism now risks complicity with the deep nihilism – the assault on human worth and human capacity – already too available in the nearly overwhelming challenge of climate change, in neoliberal reason, global slums and abandonment of democracy. These are the dark posthumanisms through which humans are politically and socially devalued, devitalized or discounted, and that lie in wait for the creature critical theorists might hand it.

As many have argued, our historical conjuncture with regard to climate change is such that we need emergency political responses to an emergency predicament, where the emergency itself is unavailable to extant categories of thought, analysis and politics. (This is the foundational meaning of *krisis* from which our term, 'critique', emerges.) We cannot expect compelling accounts of this condition's scope or implications nor can we expect viable responses, from the notions of the human and its relationship to nature, or its practices of economics and politics, that have brought us to this pass. Nor can we rely on old tropes of progress, dialectics, contradiction, democracy's equation with the good, or market solutions to every problem – all of these now appear as so many variations on a theological theme. On the other hand, we must be wary of conceptual and political coinages that attempt to overleap or fly off from our histories and ourselves. One worry here is irrelevance, but the more serious one may be the risk of their unintended comportment with the forms of domination they mean to contest.

NOTES

1. Some, like James Lovelock (2010), suggest that suspension of democracy is now in order.

2. For a useful review of these objections, see Vansintjan (2015).

3. As Chakrabarty puts it later, 'But in becoming a geophysical force on the planet, we have also developed a form of collective existence that has no ontological

dimension. Our thinking about ourselves now stretches our capacity for interpretive understanding. We need non-ontological ways of thinking the human'.

4. This would be God and human finally reunited as world maker.

5. Economic policies that favour deregulation and facilitates the domination of policy by large financial interests could serve these interests *only* if one subscribes to the creed that markets can solve every problem, including one that much of the world's population is indifferent to and whose address is incompatible with the imperative of growth, the appetite for cheap goods and 250 years of unplanned development premised on burning fossil fuels. It is one thing to get 30,000 liberal upper-middle-class Los Angelicans to buy Priuses and install solar panels on their roofs; it is another to imagine reorganizing the greater metropolitan LA area, population approximately 18 million, as one in which fossil fuels are no longer fundamental to existence. This would be difficult to pull off under Leninist or democratic socialist state planning; it is inconceivable in a world dominated by unregulated free trade amongst financial giants.

6. This intersection isn't simple, but neither is it distinctively human.

7. The principle of (neo)liberal governmentality, according to Foucault, is that the economy and economic man are untouchable because unknowable – 'government may not touch because it cannot know'.

8. 'Economics is a discipline without God . . . without totality', writes Foucault, 'a discipline that . . . demonstrate[s] not only the pointlessness but also the impossibility of a sovereign point of view' (Foucault 2008, 282–3).

9. In June, *before* the massive exodus from Syria, the UN Refugee Report claimed that, 'Globally, one in every 122 humans is now either a refugee, internally displaced, or seeking asylum'. See the following: http://www.nytimes.com/interactive/2015/06/21/world/map-flow-desperate-migration-refugee-crisis.html

10. Feher details overt policies of neglect and abandonment of African immigrants seeking access to Europe, as well as the literal outsourcing of detention camps from Europe (where they are controversial) to Morocco and Libya where Europeans don't see them and need not be concerned with their conditions.

11. Of course there is no essential human thing here – that will always be a semiotic depiction, represented through particular vocabularies drawn from theology, philosophy, politics, etc.

REFERENCES

Arendt, Hannah. [1951] 1968. *The Origins of Totalitarianism*. New York: Harvest.
Chakrabarty, Dipesh. 2012. "Postcolonial Studies and the Challenge of Climate Change". *New Literary History*, 43(1): 1–18.
Davis, Mike. 2006a. *Planet of the Slums*. New York: Verso Books.
———. 2006b. "Humanity's Ground Zero A Tomdispatch Interview With Mike Davis". posted on May 9, 2006. http://www.tomdispatch.com/post/82655/tomdispatch_interview_mike_davis_turning_a_planet_into_a_slum
Feher, Michel. Manuscript, forthcoming in 2017a. "Disposing of the Discredited: A European Project". First presented at the 2015 Neoliberalism + Biopolitics Conference at UC Berkeley.

Feher, Michel. Manuscript, forthcoming in 2017b. *Rated Agencies: Political Engagements With Our Invested Selves*. Brooklyn: Zone Books.

Foucault, Michel. 2008. *The Birth of Biopolitics: Lectures at the Collège de France, 1978–1979*, ed. Michel Senellart, trans. Graham Burchell. New York: Picador.

Haraway, Donna. 1991. "A Cyborg Manifesto: Science, Technology, and Socialist-Feminism in the Late Twentieth Century" In *Simians, Cyborgs and Women: The Reinvention of Nature*. New York: Routledge.

Hayden, Patrick. 2009. "From Exclusion to Containment: Arendt, Sovereign Power, and Statelessness". *Societies Without Borders*, 3(2): 248–269.

Klein, Naomi. 2014. *This Changes Everything: Capitalism vs. The Climate*. New York: Simon & Schuster.

Lovelock, James. 2010. "Humans are too Stupid to Prevent Climate Change". posted to *The Guardian* on March 29, 2010. http://www.theguardian.com/science/2010/mar/29/james-lovelock-climate-change.

Papademetriou, Demetrios G. 2005. "The Global Struggle with Illegal Migration: No End in Sight". posted on September 1, 2015. http://www.migrationpolicy.org/article/global-struggle-illegal-migration-no-end-sight.

Parr, Adrian. 2012. *The Wrath of Capital: Neoliberalism and Climate Change Politics*. New York: Columbia University Press.

Scheffran, Jurgen, Michael Brzoska, Hans Gunter Brauch, P. Michael Link, and Janpeter Schilling. 2012. *Climate Change, Human Security and Violent Conflict: Challenges for Societal Stability*. Berlin: Springer.

Schuck, Peter. 2015. "Creating a Market for Refugees in Europe". *New York Times* (June 9, 2015).

Spiegel Online Staff. 2013. "Fortress Europe How the EU Turns Its Back on Refugee". posted on October 9, 2013. http://www.spiegel.de/international/europe/asylum-policy-and-treatment-of-refugees-in-the-european-union-a-926939.html.

Vansintjan, Aaron. 2015. "The Anthropocene Debate: Why is Such a Useful Concept Starting to Fall Apart"? posted on June 26, 2015. http://www.resilience.org/stories/2015-06-26/the-anthropocene-debate-why-is-such-a-useful-concept-starting-to-fall-apart.

Chapter 3

On 'Not Being Persecuted'

Territory, Security, Climate

Simon Dalby

New Zealand has deported a Kiribati man who lost a legal battle to
be the first person granted refugee status on the grounds of climate
change alone. Ioane Teitiota, 39, has argued that rising sea levels in his
homeland meant his family would not be safe there. . . . His deportation
on Wednesday night follows a failed appeal against a New Zealand
high court decision that he could not be a refugee as he was not being
persecuted.

BBC News (24 September 2015
http://www.bbc.com/news/world-asia-34344513)

If the relationship between political and scientific atomism has been
disrupted by the emergence of more recent science, it may be worth-
while considering whether such disruptions bear any implications for
the fundaments of not just the physical but also the political world.
If sovereignty is premised upon an atomistic conception of the state
of nature, then surely a more interconnected understanding of nature
raises the question whether the basic presumption of autonomy that
undergirds sovereignty should shift in favour of a politics of interde-
pendence.

Chantal Thomas (*Melbourne Jnl of Law* 2014, p. 57)

TERRITORY AND SECURITY

The geopolitical order of modernity is apparently one of states, of a fixed
territorial arrangement, and supposedly stable arrangements where state

sovereignty is tied to an agreed set of fixed boundaries. All else supposedly follows from this mode of governance; this system of states is sovereign, the overarching principle that orders humanity's affairs. It is an especially elegant resolution to the political difficulties of reconciling universal aspiration and political particularity (Walker 2010). We can all be modern within the boundaries of our state; citizenship understood in geographical terms as related to distinct, exclusive territorial states is the most basic political identity for people. From this elegant arrangement, the modern 'global covenant' in Bob Jackson's (2000) terms, all other questions of politics can supposedly be derived. Stable states may be threatened from abroad by military and other dangers, or internally by subversion, sedition and domestic protest, but the category of the permanent territorial state is unquestioned most of the time.

The territorial fixity norm underpins much of the United Nations system, and insofar as it has operated to reduce the frequency and severity of international warfare has, despite the protestations of the United Nations' frequent critics, been an important matter in the reduction of large-scale, if not persistent smaller-scale, violence. This key theme in contemporary geopolitics suggests both that state boundaries are stable and that minor demarcation readjustments are possible but major boundary changes or accretion by aggression are no longer acceptable parts of state practices.

In part this territorial state cartography is premised on arguments that states represent nations; culture is, following the Wilsonian principles of self-determination, a geographical matter. Ethnicity, in the form of a common identity, supposedly resides in places that can be at least approximately mapped into bounded territories.

> This confused imaginary [of pure ethnicity] was born with a territorial basis that was then spread materially throughout the world via Western imperialism. This territorial legacy of the Peace of Westphalia of 1648 renders it that much more difficult to think through, or outside of, this confused imaginary as distinct 'nations' become affixed to distinct 'states' in an elision which essentializes non-essences (nations) thereby according 'them' agency. (Archer 2007: 120)

Politics is thus now fundamentally a geographical matter; territory is key to this even if as a category it was slow to emerge as a key organizing principle in human affairs (Elden 2013). That said, the United Nations has been reluctant to link nations explicitly to territories in the neat Wilsonian cartography. Peoples, relating to residents of the territory rather than members of a specific ethnicity, are frequently the entity understood to be sovereign within specified borders.

Here and there are to be distinguished by drawing lines and demarcating spaces in which certain forms of jurisdiction are paramount and where certain cultures and ethnicities reside and are to be administered in terms of residential location. One's geographical address is key to one's identity; 'where do you come from?' is very much more than a conversation opener in many parts of the world. The United Nations arrangement in the 1940s codified the tentative League of Nations aspirations to non-intervention and fixed state boundaries in the 1933 Montevideo Convention on Rights and Duties of States. Decolonization and practices of boundary drawing, partition and population relocations were frequently violent in the aftermath of the Second World War as the violence of India and Pakistan as well as Israel and Palestine made clear, and the huge numbers of people in the category of displaced persons exemplified in Europe.

But at least in theory, once these disruptions were accommodated and people's papers put in order, permanently fixing boundaries removed a major cause of warfare (Zacher 2001). Irredentism and further territorial adjustment by violence were outlawed; military interventions were only allowed in matters deemed self-defence and supported by United Nations actions to protect the new territorial order. Honoured in the breach frequently, nonetheless this arrangement has become the geopolitical norm of modernity. The lines on the map will remain, and if adjustments must be made, they are done on the basis of antecedent administrative arrangements and fixed territorial jurisdictions. The fact, as has frequently been suggested in regard to the 1880s Berlin Congress where European colonial powers divided up Africa, that the cartographers who dreamt up some of these lines may have been inebriated, incompetent or both is an unfortunate reality in many cases. As this chapter shows, all this is now made more complicated by global environmental change.

After the Cold War this system of states, while specified as the given geopolitical arrangement, has been beset by frequent anxieties about globalization, economic sovereignty and cultural nationalism. While patriotism may indeed be, in Dr Johnston's famous phrasing, the last refuge of the scoundrel, nationalist anxieties have been a recurrent part of geopolitical discourse driven by globalization and its militarized version in the war on terror, and European and American concerns about jihadism and Islamic threats of various sorts. Distinctions between us and them, locals and foreigners, those worthy of moral solicitude and those beyond the ambit of responsibility rely on such categories to the degree that the territorial fixity assumption that underlies this is not usually questioned. In Oscar Wilde's dark rephrasing of Dr Johnston, patriotism is the virtue of the vicious. In these terms security is about the invocation of culture and territorial identity in ways that assert a sovereign right to exclude those specified as different, from somewhere else, regardless of the consequences for those so excluded.

NON-TRADITIONAL SECURITY

There is, however, much more to the questions of sovereignty and security than these ideal types and overarching view of the system of states suggests, however elegant and persuasive their categories are in establishing the terms of political discourse. In the aftermath of the Cold War, security has been challenged in terms of the dominance of the state-centric formulations. After all national security premised on the promise of mutually assured destruction in the Cold War provided a very dangerous form of political order. Nuclear issues continue to overshadow international politics and the potential for all-out warfare due to miscalculation continues to haunt the international system even if the dangers seem much less immediate than they were in the Cold War period.

The inability of states to protect their own populations and the vulnerabilities of people to various global disruptions generated a large discussion of matters in terms of global dangers and the possibilities of a human security agenda (Stiglitz and Kaldor 2013). These formulations have subsequently fed into discussions of a responsibility to protect and more general discussions of non-traditional security threats (Hameiri and Jones 2015). The term 'non-traditional security' is of course somewhat of a misnomer because security has never been only about narrowly defined national interests, but nonetheless the term encompasses a broader agenda than the earlier focus on military rivalries and the supposed dangers of domestic subversion. Crucially with the rise of international trade and the rivalries that go with it, economic matters have been discussed in terms of stability and security even if the largest threats are to domestic populations. In Europe recently, and earlier in the Asian crisis of the 1990s and the Argentinian debt crisis, international financial arrangements are obviously the greatest threat to the well being of particular national populations.

Beyond this focus on economic and political matters there is a growing realization of just how dramatically humanity is changing the material circumstances that provide the context for the state system. Global environmental change now challenges the principles of territorial stability, admittedly, so far, mostly at the margins, but with long-term implications for how geopolitics will play out (Dalby 2013). The rise of an earth system understanding of global biophysical processes is now making it clear that humanity is a geological scale actor in a period now sometimes called the Anthropocene (Vidas, Zalasiewicz and Williams 2015). This directly challenges assumptions of a given earth with a stable environmental context on which the human drama, and the processes of development, can play out (Dalby 2014). Climate concerns have become the predominant theme in this discussion. Sustainable development has been recently supplemented by discussions of resilience, adaptation and environmental security. Much of this has been a reworking of earlier themes of economic development as a necessary strategy to pre-empt peripheral insecurities and disruptions threatening metropolitan order. This is especially ironic given that environmental change is predominantly driven by metropolitan consumption rather than peripheral activities (Dauvergne 2008). But this isn't a new pattern; environmental security has long been about metropolitan fears of those dispossessed by the expansion of its political economy (Dalby 2002).

Nonetheless the implicit assumption that the metropoles do provide an order that has to be perpetuated is key to the formulations of security that currently purportedly address climate change (Boas 2015). Epitomized by the repeated focus on climate as a threat multiplier, where environmental disruptions will supposedly aggravate political instabilities, or in the worst cases cause states to degenerate into violent conflict over diminishing water and food supplies, and become 'failed states', the security agenda remains in danger of perpetuating a focus on symptoms of climate change rather than its causes (CNA 2014). It is metropolitan consumption that is changing the climate, but focusing on peripheral political symptoms rather than metropolitan root causes obscures the key causal relations while the victims are portrayed as a security threat to the perpetrators (Buxton and Hayes 2016).

Most glaringly the contradictions of this show up where discussions of climate refugees enter the picture and where the fate of low-lying states in the face of rising sea levels is addressed. If mass migration is portrayed as a threat to national security, then the possibilities of military responses loom (Smith 2007). Modern geopolitical assumptions of stable state arrangements and in situ political solutions to complex security problems are directly challenged by environmental change in the new period of the Anthropocene (Hommel and Murphy 2013). Just as the territorial fixity norm has become hegemonic, climate change threatens the existence of some members of the United Nations quite directly and challenges the assumptions of state solutions to global problems too. Building fences to stop migration, as numerous governments are now doing, especially in areas where economic discrepancies across boundaries are dramatic (Jones 2012), runs directly counter to the most basic ecological adaptations to environmental change, which are for species to move to more suitable circumstances.

Sources of these migratory species, whether human or otherwise, are often specified in terms of the dangers of failed or failing states.

This matters because labelling a country as a failed state is more than merely a rhetorical exercise. It delineates the acceptable range of policy options that can be exercised. States called 'failed' are therefore primarily those in which such crises are perceived to threaten Western interests; in other cases, conversely, these features of state (mal)functioning are not only accepted, but sometimes almost encouraged. (Boas and Jennings 2007: 483)

With this goes the implicit assumption that sovereign authority has effectively been suspended in a 'failed state', which by definition cannot provide order and is not effectively occupying its territory. Sovereignty here is, in Elden's (2009) terms, contingent; the absence of effective sovereignty invites interventions from abroad to provide order; the international community now has a 'responsibility to protect'. The implicit, although frequently misleading, assumption in the notion of a failed state is that internal causes lead to failure, but in the case of climate change, and the extreme case of state extinction due to rising sea levels, this is not an appropriate way to frame the issue. The causes are nearly entirely external. Insofar as state failure leads to an exodus, then responsibility cannot easily be assigned to the origin state. But, at least so far, the 'responsibility to protect' doctrine does not apply to people set in motion by climate disruptions.

Discourses of invasive species and migration threats reproduce the territorial fixity assumption in terms of security precisely where innovation to adapt to changing sea levels and weather patterns is needed. Ironically in human terms, the elegant formulation of fixed boundaries is now, even more than in the past, running directly into the simple fact of contemporary environmental transformation (White 2011). For those in need of sustenance, health care, the opportunity for employment and housing the borders and fences of the current order are the security problem. For those, like Ioane Teitiota, faced with impending inundation of their homelands, these difficulties are especially acute. How does the international system, premised on a precise and fixed cartography deal with the fact that anthropogenic climate change is rendering that fixed cartography something at best temporary? At least so far the answer is 'not very well'. The Montevideo convention may need an update!

SOVEREIGNTY IN THE ANTHROPOCENE

Quite what sovereignty might mean in the face of disappearing territory is a fraught question in the climate discussion, not least because as globalization seems to be leading to a diminishment of sovereign control, states are ironically sometimes responding precisely by building walls (Brown 2010). As the Montevideo convention made clear, states have territories. While India, China and the United States all face considerable coastal inundation issues in coming decades, it is the small island states built on coral reefs that face the immediate prospect of elimination from the system of states, and hence have been the focus of a rapidly growing literature on climate adaptation and international law (Gerrard and Wannier 2013; Yamamoto and Esteban 2014). These are also those states that have the least material capabilities in terms of the traditional measures of power, financial, diplomatic and military capabilities. They cannot physically protect their territorial integrity from rising seas despite the growing popularity of the slogan 'we are not drowning we are fighting' with its explicit refusal on the part of those facing inundation to be treated as victims and refugees. Insisting on their collective rights as citizens of states raises the crucial questions of how they might be understood once their territory disappears under the waves. If not drowning, at least some of these people will indeed become 'lives adrift' as they take to the seas in search of dry land. What is to be done about the elimination of these states in future decades? What legal remedies might apply, and with what implications for the implicit assumptions within the state system about the persistence of states?

None of these questions can be answered by simple invocations of state sovereignty; power and political practices have always operated in complicated patterns that evade neat encapsulation in theories of state sovereignty. That said, the geography of transboundary issues, and the so-called new security agenda dealing with non-traditional threats usually start with the invocation of statehood in some form even if much of the discussion is about the limited capabilities of individual states have for dealing with the problems identified as new ones for security (Hameiri and Jones 2015). Understanding these as global phenomena usually quickly follows. The point is made that the larger political economy of globalization emphasizes that economic policy is key to security (Stiglitz and Kaldor 2013). But such formulations usually require a very considerable amnesia concerning earlier historical situations, the migrations implicit in imperial colonial practices of the nineteenth century in particular. Indeed the migratory patterns that currently reflect the anxieties of globalization are fears about what might happen if 'they' come 'here'. The historical consequences for 'their' societies when, uninvited, 'we' went 'there' earlier are not to be remembered much less considered as part of the globalization discussion.

When it comes to questions of who is subject to what treatment at contemporary borders, or points of immigration, the questions of jurisdiction remain tied to matters of location and citizenship even as the rights and responsibilities of states for non-citizens have become more complicated by United Nations arrangements regarding human rights and the refugee convention, and the larger overarching rationales of the responsibility to protect. This is especially the case where matters of forced migration are in play even if not the outright political persecution for which the refugee regime was initially established (Mountz 2010). There is a long-standing argument about whether a category of environmental refugee is appropriate in dealing with current transformations (White 2011).

The distinction is also frequently made between voluntary and involuntary migration, the latter being a matter of necessity as a result of persecution or imminent danger. But, Ioane Teitiota discovered that in New Zealand the refugee convention does not apply to many people who are forced to move but who are not directly persecuted. There is it seems a need for some additional category of 'survival migration' (Betts 2010). However the distinction between someone forced to move because of poor crop results caused by climate change, and poor rural economic performance because of matters of political economy is not easy to sustain; migration, especially from rural to urban areas, is a key part of the contemporary changes of the human condition even if much of it happens within national boundaries. It is playing out in spaces changed by the practices of the global economy, and agricultural transformations and the consequences of global property markets in particular (Parenti 2011).

All of this becomes even more complicated when state building enterprises force people to relocate due to rising waters. National development was frequently linked to the infrastructure of big dams in the second half of the twentieth century when they were built in huge numbers and in most states. In Anna Tsing's (2005: 223) terms:

> Big dams are symbols of human mastery over nature; they are among the most high-profile international development packages. In the second half of the twentieth century, big dams became a standard of national sovereignty. Every nation wanted its own dams, and multilateral development banks wanted every nation to have them. In Indonesia in the 1970s and 1980s, big dams were seen as monuments of national development. Opposing them hit a nerve.

Thus state efforts often set people in motion, and hence, understanding them as environmental refugees runs into state development policies quite directly. At the heart of this debate is the frequently implicit recognition that assumptions of a stable geographical situation, wherein people are supposedly capable of gaining sustenance in the territory in which they reside, is no longer tenable, given environmental changes, some at least of which originate from outside the state that is generating out migration. Climate change and rising sea levels are a loose global analogy to the specifically national displacements by rising water levels caused by development. Rising sea levels are also consequence of 'development' even if a somewhat less direct one.

The larger literature on current transformations, encapsulated in the discussion of the Anthropocene is challenging the modern state cartographic assumptions of a place for everyone and everyone in their place (Dalby 2014). Clearly species are in motion, either autonomously in search of more conducive ecological conditions or being moved by gardeners, pet owners and agricultural corporations. New modes of 'conservation' are attempting to 'rewild' spaces in part to facilitate adaptation to Anthropocene conditions (Lorimer 2015). Such movements do not apply to humans who are bound not by the ecological niches they need for sustenance but by the cartographies of power that is the contemporary geopolitical system of state territorial jurisdiction. Thus the palpable contradiction whereby the floating fences used to allow the structures to rise and fall with the changing dune patterns on the Mexican–American border allow the landscape to change quite literally while preventing the border crossing by people and presumably at least some other terrestrial species.

These complicated and contradictory geographies are the context for discussing climate migration; simple assumptions of either stable material circumstances or stable institutional arrangements are no longer useful premises for trying to grapple with the questions of migration. While there are many difficulties with suggesting that climate change in particular is setting migrants in motion as a result of environmental transformation, there is one case where this is very clearly and obviously what is happening. This is the situation of low-lying island states where rising sea levels are in some cases either, already or soon will be threatening states with extinction. If they are to live, citizens of these states will have to move and live in the jurisdiction of other states. What then matters of sovereignty as a principle for organizing human affairs?

The admittedly limited number of cases of impending state inundation does pose key questions for sovereignty in the Anthropocene: bluntly put, the issue is simply, 'What happens when states are permanently failed?' In the case of island state inundation the failure comes from abroad, from the failure of advanced industrial states to address climate change and by their explicit failure to live up to their implied responsibilities to at least not harm others if not actually protect citizens of other states. Related to that is the question of whether principles of compensation or rights of the internally displaced inform discussions of what happens when sovereignty is extinguished. What then does all this mean for post-sovereign politics if some notion of global justice prevails rather than brute force, and if some notion of a human collectivity is seen as a necessary entity to which rights continue to be extended even if the territory is inundated (Nine 2012)? Can humans be understood as such first and foremost, rather than only in terms of their territorial state-defined citizenship?

DISAPPEARING STATES, MOVING PEOPLE

All these questions relate to the key matter posed in the second epigraph to this chapter regarding the scientific basis of sovereignty, and its long-held presuppositions of a stable context within which autonomy operates (Elshtain 2008). This is now being undercut by new understandings of the interconnectedness and contingencies of ecology, and at the largest scale by the rethinking of the human condition in the discussion about the Anthropocene. Rising sea levels challenge the assumptions of stable physical contexts; the implicit geography of modernity can no longer underpin adaptation to climate change and other Anthropocene phenomena. This chapter is not the place to engage the finer points of legal argument on these issues; nonetheless, a few key points are germane not least because they raise crucial matters about whether sovereignty can be disconnected from territorial states; and if that is done in the case of say Kiribati and Tuvalu, it might have implications elsewhere too for the new geopolitics of the Anthropocene. 'The mortality of a state is no longer a far-fetched hypothetical: the "theoretical" possibility of state extinction via emigration of its entire population and the complete loss of territory may come to pass in the foreseeable future' (Wong 2014: 44). What then sovereignty?

Obviously only a few states face complete inundation, although many face partial territorial loss in coastal areas, but the case of the small island states emphasizes the key point that geographical change is upon us and the premise of stable territorial entities as basic units of governance can no longer be accepted as applicable to all state situations (Vidas, Zalasiewicz and Williams 2015). Migration is a necessity for survival for some people, but sovereignty in terms of territorial fixity does not imply an obligation to receive those who have to move. There is as yet no clear path forward in resolving these tensions, but some thoughtful suggestions have been forthcoming in contemporary scholarship that highlight the dilemmas posed by migrants from failed states in a world where sovereign territory is still the key governance arrangement.

The questions posed most starkly by the prospect of rising sea levels inundating existing states relates to whether states have obligations to either the endangered state as a legal entity or some kind of ontological entity, and who has the responsibility to accommodate the people moving from the former state. Are there circumstances whereby territory will be granted to migrants, or is it the case that they may do little better than purchase property in states to which they migrate without the transfer of legal powers that go with claims to territorial sovereignty? In such cases, if the destination state grants citizenship to the immigrants, then the specific identities of the migrants and their claim to sovereignty will presumably, at some point, be extinguished, unless some innovations are made that perpetuate sovereign claims among descendants of migrants.

Vaha (2015) ponders whether states can be disconnected from territory, whether a state's right to exist as part of the system of states rather than just as a territorial entity might be formulated, given the likely inundation of some island states. Nine (2010) emphasizes that states are mere institutions; it is the political collectivity that matters, but can it persist in the absence of territory? This would obviously require a rethinking of the Montevideo convention, and much international law since, but the point about the relation of members of the system suggests an ontological status not dependent on the continuity of territory in perpetuity. 'One might ask whether and to what extent international community of states has a duty to prevent or react to such state-extinctions, in the same manner as individual morality and duties require us to help the dislocated people' (Vaha 2015: 207). The argument leads to a formulation that 'suggests that there might be a duty on behalf of the members of the international state-system to take measures that guarantee the continuing existence of these states – although this does not (necessarily) amount to a duty to provide them with a new territory' (Vaha 2015: 208). To do so, however, requires invoking notions of ontological and state identity rather than territorial sovereignty as usually understood: 'By relying on the concepts of ontological security and state identity, one can now argue that what is essential to the state is not mere physical existence, but rather ontological existence as an entity, as well as a continuing sense of "the self" as a state' (Vaha 2015: 215–216). This is important because states do not intend to renounce sovereignty. 'The intention of island states is not one of renouncing sovereignty, but rather *reflective of the reality that movement is necessary*' (Wong 2014: 16; emphasis added).

Wong (2014) comes at this point by starting explicitly from the Montevideo convention premise. Crucially she points out that the extinction of states is not something that will come as a surprise; it is entirely predictable and something that needs to be planned for.

> Climate change is not a sudden phenomenon and loss of territory will not occur instantaneously. There are therefore two periods which require consideration. The first is when the people migrate due to the effects of rising sea levels. Crucially, there is still territory but issues relating to abandonments of sovereignty may arise. The second period commences with the complete loss of territory. Here, the question is whether extinction automatically follows from a complete loss of territory. (Wong 2014: 6)

An additional solution, not discussed by either Wong (2014) or Vaha (2015) would seem to be state amalgamation, an extension of one state to encompass the citizenry of the soon-to-be-inundated area, one that might give the uninundated part of the new state access to fishing rights and seabed resource access too if these are perpetuated after the first wave overruns the last rock, a matter that may yet provide imperial temptations and promises of extended protection in various neo-colonial arrangements. But insofar as law of the sea arrangements for territorial seas and exclusive economic zones are premised on measurements that work outwards from shore baselines, extinguishment of territory suggests that waters surrounding land that has been inundated will revert to the status of high seas, thus removing the temptation for amalgamation. Where this is avoided it is entirely feasible to suggest that sovereignty for sale, in exchange for migration and citizenship, opens up as a possibility. This is effectively an extension of the practices that already provide for tax havens and financial services based on extra-territoriality. The alternative, probably most likely in the Pacific Ocean cases is that many of these people will end up either as immigrants in New Zealand or Australia or living in some updated neo-colonial arrangement whereby they have residence rights but not full citizenship rights as is the case with existing American-administered islands in the Pacific.

If such strategies fail to give citizens of inundated states effective agency to relocate or find ways to keep their territories above the waves, then questions of compensation and liability for lost territory arise. Given that, at least roughly, the responsibilities for climate change can be allocated to specific states in terms of the amount of fossil fuel burnt historically, or at least since 1990 when clear warnings about the consequences of greenhouse gas accumulation in the atmosphere were widely circulated, and hence the proportion of the sea-level rise attributed to a particular state can be ascertained, then the possibilities of territorial compensation beyond mere land rights emerges (Dietrich and Wundisch 2015). Compensation for land lost can be imagined in terms of financial measures approximating the value of the lost real estate. Rights to relocate and the obligation of other states to make possible modes of earning a living for migrants are also possible formulations that deal with polluters' obligations. But territorial rights, and with them matters of self-determination and the ability to operate a recognized separate political identity, require more than financial recompense or the provision of new land rights in a new location (Nine 2010).

Dietrich and Wundisch (2015) suggest that the particular loss of the ability to operate as an autonomous territorial polity can only be compensated by the provision of that ability on some other territory. Clearly the worst carbon polluters have the largest obligation to replace the territory that their actions have indirectly inundated. Most discussions of climate justice and responsibility do not include this in kind compensation, not least because this is not so easy given the current absence of any vacant unclaimed territory where displaced people could relocate. Hence territory will have to be transferred in some manner, one that Dietrich and Wundish (2015) suggest must meet at least three criteria, those of 'cultural identity', 'appropriate size' and 'population majority' conditions. In other words, the compensatory territory must allow the migrant population to continue living in ways analogous to those of its former homeland and not be faced with a situation where it becomes a political minority in its new territory.

All of which suggests a sense of, in Nine's (2010) terms, 'nested', territorial arrangements, but one that challenges simple cartographic assumptions of mutually exclusive sovereign spaces. These are all requirements for appropriate restitution of lost territorial rights. These go beyond normal measures of compensation related to relocation within states as a result of mining or such development projects as dam building and resultant flooding. The mechanisms by which these might be done are not going to be simple, and Dietrich and Wundisch (2015) have various ideas about communities, auctions and state obligations, none of which are easy to administer and all of which will require international transparency if obvious invidious practices are to be avoided in the process of sovereignty transfer. They argue that states that concede sovereignty over parts of their territory are not obligated to accept displaced islanders as immigrants, a situation that would require migrants to give up their territorial rights, for which they argue there is no possible non-territorial compensation.

Dietrich and Wundisch (2015) do not expect culprit states to respond positively to their suggestion, but the normative claim of territorial rights and in-kind compensation requiring territory transfer puts the questions of sovereignty and security at the forefront of how climate change is now to be rethought. The reallocation of sovereign territory to a migrant state also causes doubts about how the territorial fixity norm will subsequently be adjusted in international practice. Crucially xenophobic invocations of migrants as threats suggest that invoking security understood in terms of territorial sovereignty in the face of environmental change are likely to make everything worse.

RETHINKING GEOPOLITICS

Politics as a matter of territory thus first raises key questions of political responsibility and the ability of states to act as independent autonomous authorities. In short, the case of territorial compensation and the difficulties that inevitably arise quite fundamentally challenge the modern geopolitical assumptions of separate territorial entities as the most effective mode of political action. In Ulrich Beck's (2008: 78) terms regarding European response to contemporary difficulties:

> While the world faces a host of problems – from climate change, global economic interdependence and migratory movements through to issues of regional

and global peace keeping – nation-based thinking has lost its political capacity to deal with any of them. Ironically enough, every issue that has helped to fuel nationalism in Europe – the transfer of jobs to other countries, refugee flows, wars, terrorism – is an international issue.

Assumptions of a given geographic context and separate containers for politics are no longer tenable as the premise for either scholarship or policy advocacy, and yet their elegant resolution of the difficulties of universal claims and political particularity have no obvious replacement as of yet.

The frequency with which the question of 'why do people move?' is posed in discussions of migration presupposes that this is an aberration, a departure from the norm of stationarity. The history of humanity is one of movement and adaptation, but this is implicitly denied by political actions reaffirming the fixity of boundaries and the presuppositions of a simple cultural geography of nations in particular places. While this provides a principle for international politics, the mobility of people and the rapid environmental changes wrought both directly in terms of development projects and indirectly by the changing climate, as well as the rapidly enhanced patterns of connection between particular places that is globalization, all operate counter to the simple assumptions of a stable geographic order.

Where authority has shifted from divinity to state and now to individuals as Elshtain (2008) has suggested, the question posed by the rapidly changing environmental circumstances of the present is how notions of authority and legitimate politics are to be disconnected from increasingly untenable geographical premises. Beck (2008) suggests that coordinated action among states is part of what needs to be done, because without the coordination then states are increasingly ineffective. Cerny (2010) suggests that the sources of effective action are dispersed through numerous actors, a neo-pluralist arrangement, not all of which can be specified in geographical terms. It is clear that attempting to deal with such things as climate change and migration is leading to a transformation of many states as cooperation and unilateral measures begin to reshape many state agencies (Hameiri and Jones 2015). Or at least they do so in the absence of nationalist and xenophobic responses to supposedly external threatening 'migrants'.

What is inescapable now is the simple fact that climate change, which is no respecter of territorial boundaries, makes clear that the geographical fixity assumption on which territorial jurisdiction operates is literally being eroded as sea levels rise. The complicated interconnected global geophysical reality that science has been elucidating in the last few decades, now under the label of the Anthropocene, reinforces the point that the political ontology of territorial states, human collectivities, Lockean notions of property rights and the modern assumptions of autonomous sovereign entities are increasingly ill-suited categories for grappling with contemporary transformations.

The extreme case of territorial extinguishment thus emphasizes the point that global politics is premised on territory and citizenship, not on humanity. Despite the frequent invocation of a universal humanity, a key ontological premise for modern international relations and one that justifies interventions under the responsibility to protect (Mitchell 2014), people in motion are still administered, granted access or not, dependent on the paperwork related to their citizenship, not on the basis of belonging to the species. While the refugee convention was an attempt in the 1950s to deal with this problem, the designation of a refugee and the resultant obligation on the part of states to accommodate such persons does not apparently, as the case of Ioane Teitiota shows, extend to those who are not persecuted.

Security understood in terms of protecting territorial sovereignty is not appropriate for a situation where adapting to changing circumstances and quite literally to changing geographies is what is needed. What needs to be secured for many marginal peoples in particular but increasingly also for all the rest of us is the ability to adapt. In many circumstances this is quite simply the ability to move out of harm's way. But securing the ability to move is precisely the opposite of insisting that the geographical order of territorial states is the bedrock principle for contemporary governance. Hence the fate of island peoples facing inundation is both tragic in the sense that their future is being determined by forces beyond their control that make them vulnerable, and ironic in that territorial fixity, the solution to one key former set of security problems, that of aggressive warfare for territorial gain, is precisely what presents security problems to those now forced to move to ensure their survival.

ACKNOWLEDGEMENT

Thanks to Masaya Llavaneras-Blanco for much useful research assistance in assiduously tracking down key sources in a diverse scholarly literature, to Silvia Maciunas for helpful suggestions and to the Social Science and Humanities Research Council of Canada for support through a Partnership Grant on 'Borders in Globalization'.

REFERENCES

Archer, K., et al. 2007. "Hegemony/Counter-Hegemony: Imagining a New, Post-Nation-State Cartography of Culture in an Age of Globalization". *Globalizations*, 4(1): 115–136.

Beck, U. 2008. "Climate Change and Globalisation are Reinforcing Global Inequalities: High Time for a New Social Democratic Era". *Globalizations*, 5(1): 78–80.

Betts, A. 2010. "Survival Migration: A New Protection Framework". *Global Governance*, 16(3): 361–382.

Boas, I. 2015. *Climate Migration and Security: Securitisation as a Strategy in Climate Change Politics*. New York: Routledge.

Bøås, M. and K. M. Jennings. 2007. "'Failed States' and 'State Failure': Threats or Opportunities"? *Globalizations*, 4(4): 475–485.

Brown, W. 2010. *Walled States, Waning Sovereignty*. New York: Zone.

Buxton, N. and B. Hayes (eds.). 2016. *The Secure and the Dispossessed: How the Military and Corporations are Shaping a Climate Changed World*. London: Pluto Press.

Cerny, P. G. 2010. *Rethinking World Politics a Theory of Transnational Neopluralism*. Oxford: Oxford University Press.

CNA Military Advisory Board. 2014. *National Security and the Accelerating Risks of Climate Change*. Alexandria, VA: CNA Corporation.

Dalby, S. 2002. *Environmental Security*. Minneapolis: University of Minnesota Press.

———. 2013. "The Geopolitics of Climate Change". *Political Geography*, 37: 38–47.

———. 2014. "Environmental Geopolitics in the Twenty First Century". *Alternatives: Global, Local, Political*, 39(1): 3–16.

Dauvergne, P. 2008. *The Shadows of Consumption: Consequences for the Global Environment*. Cambridge MA: MIT Press.

Dietrich, F. and J. Wundisch. 2015. "Territory Lost – Climate Change and the Violation of Self-Determination Rights". *Moral Philosophy and Politics*, 2(1): 83–105.

Elden, S. 2009. *Terror and Territory: The Spatial Extent of Sovereignty*. Minneapolis: University of Minnesota Press.

———. 2013. *The Birth of Territory*. Chicago: Chicago University Press.

Elshtain, J. B. 2008. *Sovereignty: God, State, and Self*. New York, NY: Basic Books.

Gerrard, M. B. and G. E. Wannier (eds.). 2013. *Threatened Island Nations: Legal Implications of Rising Seas and a Changing Climate*. Cambridge: Cambridge University Press.

Hameiri, S. and L. Jones. 2015. *Governing Borderless Threats: Non-Traditional Security and the Politics of State Transformation*. Cambridge: Cambridge University Press.

Hommel, D. and A. B. Murphy. 2013. "Rethinking Geopolitics in an era of Climate Change". *GeoJournal*, 78: 507–524.

Jackson, R. 2000. *The Global Covenant: Human Conduct in a World of States*. Oxford: Oxford University Press.

Jones, R. 2012. *Border Walls: Security and the War on Terror in the United States, India and Israel*. London: Zed Books.

Lorimer, J. 2015. *Wildlife in the Anthropocene: Conservation after Nature*. Minneapolis: University of Minnesota Press.

Mitchell, A. 2014. *International Intervention in a Secular Age: Re-enchanting Humanity?* Abingdon: Routledge.

Mountz, A. 2010. *Seeking Asylum: Human Smuggling and Bureaucracy on the Border.* Minneapolis: University of Minnesota Press.

Nine, C. 2010. "Ecological Refugees, States Borders, and the Lockean Proviso". *Journal of Applied Philosophy*, 27(4): 359–375.

Nine, C. 2012. *Global Justice and Territory.* Oxford: Oxford University Press.

Parenti, C. 2011. *Tropic of Chaos: Climate Change and the New Geography of Violence.* New York: Nation Books.

Smith, P. J. 2007. "Climate Change, Mass Migration and the Military Response". *Orbis*, 51(4): 617–633.

Stiglitz, J. E. and M. Kaldor (eds.). 2013. *The Quest for Security: Protection Without Protectionism and the Challenge of Global Governance.* New York: Columbia University Press.

Thomas, C. 2014. "What does the Emerging International Law of Migration Mean for Sovereignty?" *Melbourne Journal of International Law*, 14(2): 76–104.

Tsing, A. L. 2005. *Friction: An Ethnography of Global Connection.* Princeton, N.J.: Princeton University Press.

Vaha, M. E. 2015. "Drowning Under: Small Island States and the Right to Exist". *Journal of International Political Theory*, 11(2): 206–223.

Vidas, D., J. Zalasiewicz, and M. Williams. 2015. What Is the Anthropocene – and Why Is It Relevant for International Law? *Yearbook of International Environmental Law*, 25(1): 3–23.

Walker, R. B. J. 2010. *After the Globe, Before the World.* London: Routledge.

White, G. 2011. *Climate Change and Migration: Security and Borders in a Warming World.* Oxford: Oxford University Press.

Wong, D. 2014. "Sovereignty Sunk? The Position of Sinking States at International Law". *Melbourne Journal of International Law*, 14(2): 1–46.

Yamamoto, L. and M. Esteban. 2014. *Atoll Island States and International Law: Climate Change Displacement and Sovereignty.* Heidelberg and New York: Springer.

Zacher, M. 2001. "The International Territorial Order: Boundaries, the Use of Force and Normative Change". *International Organization*, 55: 215–250.

Chapter 4

Dead in the Waters[1]

Brad Evans

THE GLOBAL TIDES

On Wednesday September 2, 2015, the body of a young and helpless refugee washed up on the shores of the Mediterranean. His name was Alyan Kurdi – a three-year-old child, whose family was fleeing the conflict and violence tearing apart the place he once called home. The devastating image of this disturbing tragedy reverberated across social media, particularly in the United Kingdom and Western Europe. The hash tag 'Flotsam of Humanity' accompanied the painful image of this singular child lying face down at the water's edge. Whilst it is always difficult to measure the scale of impact from such moments, it was no doubt evident to many commentators that something was beginning to change in public attitudes and broader political discourse. Alyan thus became a potent 'symbol' around which various humanitarian claims coalesced, concentrating in the process the unnecessary suffering endured by so many who suffered a similar fate and ended up dead in the waters. Alyan seemed to speak, in death, to the sacrificial weight of recent history.

Alyan's water-soaked body, laid face down and lifeless on the beach, resonates with what has previously been called the 'intolerable' as a way to disrupt the aesthetic field of perceptions, namely a fundamental rupture or breakthrough in how we come to know and see the world (Evans & Henry, 2015). A shattering if you like of what Jacques Rancière (2004) has termed the 'distribution of the sensible'. It captured a truly intolerable moment – its portrait was something too difficult to bear, yet impossible to ignore. It certainly wasn't as vivid as other images of the crises, which have been circulating around the Internet for some time. Maybe that's the point? In an age of the global media spectacle, where lives are continuously rendered disposable, where the extreme parades as entertainment, while the graphic echoes the pornographic, forced witnessing to tragic events often work by harvesting our attentions but for only a moment's brief reflection. It's all about looking, without *seeing* the wider political context. It is arguable that what then becomes more powerful in this overtly politicized and mediated settings are 'image-events' that don't always follow some sensational scripting. Rather the depictions unsettle because their intimate portrayals foster humane connections. This is not about abstract questions of death. It is to face the raw reality of its presence.

Whilst Alyan's image undoubtedly sparked more sombre political reflections and mobilized a certain ethical awakening in terms of the crisis, there is a fundamental question which still remains: Why did the image of this particular boy, amongst all others, have such a notable political and emotional effect? It certainly broke new ground in terms of the media's approach to the crisis. As Hugh Pinney, vice president at Getty Images, noted: 'The reason we're talking about this photograph is not because it's been taken or not because it's been circulated, but it's because it's been published by mainstream media'.[2] Adding, 'The reason we're talking about it after it's been published is because it breaks a social taboo that has been in place in the press for decades: a picture of a dead child is one of the golden rules of what you never published'. Pinney's comments invariably invoke memories here of Nick Ut's image of Kim Phuc, whose naked and burned body became an iconic symbol of the Vietnam war, remaining one of most enduring images of conflict in the twentieth century.

It is difficult however to explain the media event surrounding Alyan's death by simply pointing to some shared empathy, as if the pictures, which exposed us to horrifying and radical contingencies of this particular tragedy, perfectly resonated with the sensibilities of picture editors and media alike. No image can be afforded such a universal status. Just a few days prior, for example, the artist Khaled Barakeh published a series of equally tragic images of dead Syrian and Palestinian children, whose boat on this occasion sank off the coast of Libya in a mournful and devastating series titled *Multicultural Graveyard*. Such images also spread across the Internet and social media, though on this occasion Facebook quickly shut them down, as they apparently contravened its rules on the publishing of 'graphic content'.

So, did the image of Alyan just happen to take us over the tipping point? Did it actually expose the limits of censorship and the mediation of aesthetic regimes of suffering? Or, was there something more relatable about the composition? Hence it resonated as a direct assault upon some shared humanness because it was all too relatable to our normal, albeit disrupted images of the world? How many tourist pictures are after all taken of children smiling, dancing and rolling around on the beaches of the Mediterranean? As Peter Bouckaert, a director at Human Rights Watch, reflected, 'What struck me the most were his little sneakers, certainly lovingly put on by his parents that morning as they dressed him for their dangerous journey. . . . Staring at the image, I couldn't help imagine that it was one of my own sons lying there drowned on the beach'.[3] Further adding with tragic honesty, 'This is a child that looks a lot like an European child. . . . The week before, dozens of African kids washed up on the beaches of Libya and were photographed and it didn't have the same impact. There is some ethnocentrism [in the] reaction to this image, certainly'.[4] Such relationality is often seen as an explanation for empathy.

Aesthetics are crucial to any understanding of power relations. How we narrate images is in fact crucial to the authentication and disqualification of the meaning of lives. Images alone, however, offer no sure guarantee for immediate or lasting impact and change. Why certain images resonate draws upon a number of complex and competing political, social, cultural, emotional and religious investments, which defy neat explanation or blueprinting in terms of perfectible formulas. That is not to say they are incapable of being manipulated. On the contrary, the affective currency generated by aesthetics can often connect to well-established tropes in order to produce generalizable visceral reactions. Images are selected for public consumption to reinforce narratives and agendas, which, in the process of revealing well-rehearsed formulaic tendencies and recurring motifs, function in politically contrived ways such that proscribed change is regulated and policed.

Let us compare, for instance, the image of Alyan to other deeply unsettling images headlining and in widespread circulation at the time of his tragic death. A day before Barakeh's images appeared, another refugee story dominated the media landscape in continental Europe. On this occasion, some seventy badly decomposed bodies were discovered packed into an airtight cooler lorry, which was left abandoned on the roadside in Eastern Austria. A number of the victims were again children. Whilst the image of the suffering was more regulated and hence less explicit in terms of being confronted with bodies of the victims – though no doubt such images do exist, the tragic potency of this event was all too apparent, as the Slovak truck's intended produce was processed meats for public consumption.[5] The symbolic nature of this supplementing of disposable cargo seemingly eluded news and media outlets. Something biopolitical theorists would have readily appreciated and rightly critiqued in terms of its evident neoliberal resonance.

Such differing fortunes in terms of mobilizing a response raise fundamental questions regarding the power of images, and their capacity to bring about genuine political change. It is worth remembering that Alyan's image resonated powerfully in its singularity. The other eleven who died when the boat capsized don't feature in the frame. So, how are we to make sense of this? In a particularly insightful commentary, which specifically connects to previous analysis on the political function of images and their iconic antecedents,

Nicholas Mirzoeff refocuses our attention on the preferred mainstream media image depicting the young child cradled in the arms of a Turkish policeman. Why this composition impacted, as Mirzoeff suggests, might be explained in terms of Christian iconography:

> We can open our eyes to this photograph because it reminds us of images we know well. Such iconic images carry the power of the sacred. The posture of the policeman, Sergeant Metmet Ciplak, who carries Aylan's body, unconsciously echoes one of the key icons of Western art. Known as the Pietà, meaning 'pity', this frequently explored motif depicts the Virgin Mary holding the body of Jesus, after he was taken down from the Cross.[6]

It is worth remembering that it was this representation of the tragedy that was deemed most appropriate by media outlets. As Ian Jack observed, in the British context at least, 'News editors thought to moderate our distress by omitting an earlier picture in the sequence that shows the dead child lying face down on the sand with his head in the sea. . . . Among national newspapers, only the Guardian and the Independent published this image unaltered. The websites of the Mirror, the Express and the Mail used versions that pixelated the body or (in the Daily Star's case) obscured the head. The Telegraph and the Financial Times made the same decision as the BBC and omitted the image from their selection'.[7] For Jack, this is explainable as it suits a 'finer idea of humanity', for the alternative 'represents the less comfortable proposition that death reduces even the liveliest child to a heap of flesh and bone'.

Having been confronted with this intolerable scene, what does it mean for critical thinkers and pedagogues to reproduce the image, mediate upon it, write about its presence, in the company of our own children and loved ones, while remaining ethically sensitive to the senselessness, devastatingly intimate and terrifying contingency of its occurrence? That is to say, how do we deal with the burdens of this image without becoming parasitic to the violence, latently dwelling upon its horror, normalizing its reception through repetition, curiously gazing at its macabre content, which at best points to banalization and at worse reduces it to yet another spectacle of violence? As Kent Brintnall warns while commenting on the body in pain:

> Representations of the suffering body per se are a screen, a surface burnished by history's erasure, that can reflect the viewers and the victims shared capacity for pain, trauma and suffering. Of course, representations of violated bodies do not always function this way – cruelty, humor, voyeurism, and indifference often intervene. Mirrors warp. But histories of violated bodies, which are only another manner of representing them, also misfire – the desire to explain is often a desire to explain away, to justify, to diminish the horror. (Brintnall, 2011)

One thing is clear. Aesthetics should not be theorized for the sake of any discipline. Nor should we engage with aesthetics so that we might glean something of the political out of modes of representation to authenticate some sovereign gaze. The world is already too full of sovereign thinkers who claim some privileged access to the world. As Rancière argues, *politics is aesthetic* insomuch as it is inextricably bound to the creation of images of thought – images of the world – though not always according to some universal blueprint that paves the way to the castle of pure reason. As Georges Bataille (1994) observes, for aesthetics to be meaningful, 'It is necessary to give words the power to open eyes. . . . To use words . . . no longer [to] serve the ends of knowledge but sight. . . . As if they were no longer intelligible signs but cries'. It is to connect the aesthetic with the poetic, the image with the discourse, such that the intolerable is always confronted and apprehended.

Alongside images such as Alyan, we also find emerging from this crisis a number of complementary aesthetic themes, which are no less iconic and theological in terms of narrating tales of political salvation and earthly redemption. Take, for example, the image of Antonis Deligiorgis, a Greek Army sergeant who was captured saving a twenty-four-year-old Eritrean refugee, Wegasi Nebiat. This particular image from April 2015 again went viral and featured on the front pages of many news outlets, including The *New York Times*. It was narrated as part of a heroic effort by the topless soldier Deligiorgis, who in the process of rescuing some twenty refugees (who were often omitted from the media spotlight) was subsequently awarded the Cross of Excellency. And yet the latent racial and gendered dimensions of this image are all too apparent. It speaks directly to militaristic valour, and as many commentaries subtly and explicitly mentioned, the notable beautification of both figures in the heroic scene.

Time Magazine's[8] special edition on the crisis, accompanied by the headline 'Exodus', also returns us to the theological. Biblical stories are bound up with tales of human flight from persecution, so often used by political regimes, leaders and campaigners to galvanize support for particular causes. None more than Martin Luther King Jr, whose 'I've Been to the Mountaintop' speech from Memphis, Tennessee, April 3, 1968, just before his death, connected the tale to the civil rights struggle in the United States. Whilst King's religiosity is well established, what concerns me here are its subtle and apparent secularized adaptations, which remain loaded with political and theological significance. Indeed, we might argue, the recurring motif of images connecting redemption and salvation to racial and sexualizing grammars have been borne of the Benjaminian logics of mythical and divine forms of violence and its demands for obedience and the recreation of relations of power.

Taken together what we are beginning to uncover here is an intimate portrait of the encounter with contemporary forms of violence, which speaks directly to the questions of human sacrifice, the political humanization of the victim, notions of militaristic valour, onto the aesthetic mediation of suffering – including political expediency, cultural and theological resonance, and beautification. They point in fact more specifically to the complex relationship between sacrificial violence and the authentication of a meaningful life. For our concerns here, it is worth reminding ourselves of Francois Laruelle's important contribution from his *General Theory of Victims*, in which he explains the need for a more ethically astute engagement with those who needlessly suffer from the catastrophic weight of historical forces:

> The victim's overrepresentation is the forgetting of its origin, its necessity, and its contingency. Like any term that sees its media moment arrive, the victim passes through a stage of expansion and then of nausea, of ascendance, and of decline. By the time we grasp it, it is already perhaps too late; it is theoretically dubious, eroded by the media and buoyed by the securitarian and juridical rise of crime. As though it were miming and fabricating an artificial unconscious, media corruption has made the victim a new ethical value, a point of condensation and effervescence, of the exacerbation of ideological conflicts. (Laurelle, 2015)

Nowhere has this been more apparent than with the recycling of image of Alyan to further the calls for the mobilization of war in order to eventually bring about lasting peace, along with the need to bring about justice by displacing the history of the conflict, especially our complicity, by focusing instead on the new demonic figures of this human crisis – the people smuggler. If there is a crime to be put on trial, it is not the continued recourse to violence, which on all sides works by violently exacerbating the catastrophe through various technologies, in order to ultimately control the crisis; it is those who are ultimately part of the clandestine processes of human migration. The complex and often-hidden biographies of the smugglers are inconsequential.

The political hijacking of the Mediterranean crisis has been predictable and deplorable. Syria itself, the region from which many of the current refugees have been fleeing, brings together a toxic mixture of competing factions from the Assad family dictatorship that has historically been a useful proxy in wider political agendas (not least to tame Islamic organizations), to ISIS, which can be directly linked to the failed interventions and bombing campaigns in Afghanistan and Iraq – all of which have been produced, armed, funded and manipulated by outside forces. Following the media attention on the plight of Alyan, the very day British Prime Minister David Cameron addressed parliament to pledge support for the refugees, it was also announced that for the first time the country had used drone technologies for targeted strikes against British-born jihadists fighting in the country. The right-wing media's 'about-turn' on the refugee problem, which evidenced a notable change in the narrative as it moved away from outright demonizing to a more sympathetic embrace, also became clearer. As the headline from Rupert Murdoch's *The Sun*, on September 6, 2015, demanded, there was now a justification for violence *in the name* of the child victim. Alongside a poll showing how 52% of people now say 'Bomb Syria Now', it featured an image of the child's face circled with the words 'For Alyan'.

To use the child's image in this way is deplorable and fascistic in the way Wilhelm Reich (1970) understood the term. That is to say, it is all about manipulating the desire for violence such that an intolerable image of a dead child is appropriated, repackaged and strategically redeployed to sanction further violence and destruction. And so, once again, like Afghanistan, Iraq and Libya, to name a few, the drumbeats to war start by showing apparent sympathy with an all-too-human crisis, but fail however to provoke serious political and philosophical discussion on violence and disposability of populations, in the end punishing instead those in whose name we claim to be acting for in the first place. Such is the cyclical nature of violence in our times. Devoid of a critical valence, it merely points to ongoing processes in which Western societies have culpability, responsibility and continue to show a profound failure of the political and ethical imagination.

NEW VIOLENT GEOGRAPHIES

So, how are we to make sense of the spatial implications to such violence and human disposability? And, how might we connect this to the concerns raised in this anthology with climatic conditions? While the modern political imagination has been colonized by a material foundationalism, which invariably gives rise to grounded imaginations, there is also a rich history to the phenomenology of the waters, which is often forgotten. The Roman Empire, for instance, always understood the political importance of all the elements. This was witnessed through their identification and imperial reworking of earlier Greek forms of deification, which were invoked in order to emphasize their relevance to social order and forms of human mobilization and population control. The oceans in particular had a special meaning and were seen as essential to its vision of the world. Mare Nostrum – literally 'our sea' – was feared and tamed. Westernized topographies of the sea have since appeared embodied in one way or another. Indeed, if we take the famous frontispiece to Thomas Hobbes' *Leviathan* treatise ('leviathan' itself was a term previously used to describe the beast of the oceans), the presence of the waters in the far right corner of the illustration does suggest that the sovereign king, who also embodies in this work the body politic, might in fact be emerging from the planetary waters.

We owe it to Carl Schmitt (2006) for showing how the embodiment of space and the eventual cartographical and phenomenological separation of the oceans from the land were pivotal in the development of those key order-ing principles that have come to define worldly affairs. Indeed, just as we may write a violent history of the earth, as familiar biological terms such as 'dis-section' have been applied with equal force to populated spaces, so too the planetary waters tell their own stories of violence and oppression. However, whereas the scars of suffering often leave permanent marks and traces upon geographical landscapes, so integral to the memory of loss, tragedy, separa-tion and ruination, the body of water, like the desert plains, retains its capacity for disappearance. Centuries of mariners and migrants have been lost at sea often to vanish without a trace.

Contemporary stories regarding the unnecessary suffering of bodies at the mercy of the oceans resurrects the wretched ghosts of the transatlantic slave trade, wherein the commodification of life resulted in the genocide of millions of Africans. The oceans are in fact a veritable graveyard of human disposabil-ity. They speak to the untraceable histories of those violently uprooted from their homes, whether as slaves sold like cattle, or today's migrants putting themselves in a truly perilous position since at least it appears more secure than what was being fled. In doing so, the ocean points to a spatial genealogy of violence, though for its victims, forms of remembrance and biographical reckoning are much more difficult to locate. We need to keep hold of the idea here that space (oceans) is always embodied as far as politics is concerned. Geographical demarcations would prove to be completely insignificant were they not underwritten by political and philosophical claims of habitus. It is life that bestows particular meaning upon the otherwise empty signifiers of spatial integrities and habitual residency. Space in this regard is always occu-pied and overlaid with certain meanings and attributes, which point directly to assumptions made about its inhabitants. But such meanings are never static as much as the ground itself upon which they are inscribed is always in the process of ecological transformation.

And yet, the altogether more fluid – or to use Zygmunt Bauman's (2000, 2006, 2007) terms, 'liquid' – nature of the ocean continuously defies any attempts to colonize the imaginary.[9] However much we try to chart the waters, they still remain, like the desert plains, difficult to map and attri-bute fixed meanings without returning to old-fashioned cartographic ideas. Take Google Earth as the obvious example. Whilst this sophisticated digital platform offers the most detailed multilayered mapping of the world's bio-sphere, its image of lifeworld systems still retains a notable commitment to territoriality, which conforms to foundational designs. Indeed, whilst the platform has been complemented by a Google Ocean extension, what matters here is the mapping of ocean beds as a means of gaining some tangible purchase on oceanic cartographies. Even so, what makes Google Earth significant, politically, remains its policy of including people within its scenes – only to depersonalize them in ways which speak less to questions of liberty, than removing the vexed question of agency from practices of stereotypical profiling and spatial determinism.

Oceans and deserts are the final frontiers in a world assumed to be full. People are quite literally being pushed to the *ends of the earth*. What is therefore demanded is a logical inversion of spatial politics, not in ways that continue to prioritize geographical demarcations over its human content, thereby concealing pre-existing biopolitical assumptions about the human condition; rather this inversion would entail looking at the way the body itself provides critical insight into new violent geographies, which have long since abandoned centuries of topographical awareness. Such insight was always a mask of mastery for containing and mapping out the body politic, setting in train biopolitically determined configurations of oppression and subjugation, whose markings are still evident today. Inversion requires a foregrounding of the life of the subject in ways that are attendant to those forces, which are overwhelming logics of containment. Or as Herman Melville would write, 'It is not down on any map; true places never are'.

The new violent geographies being confronted today add new drama and insight to the logics of space purposefully theorized by Gilles Deleuze and Felix Guattari (2004).[10] Drawing upon a range of sources, they explained how the history of the modern human condition has been marked by the notable tension between nomadic and sedentary ways of living, which invoke particular understandings of spatial awareness in terms of its smooth versus striated qualities. Modernity, they argued, represented a mammoth exercise in the sedentarization of mass populations for the purpose of productive needs and appropriations. We might nuance this history of spatial design and the manner in which it is underwritten by human perceptions, by recalling Schmitt's continuously influential analysis of the *Nomos of the Earth*, showing how the ordering principles for world incorporation was originally conceived by the attempts to map the world's oceans. And it was following these circumnavigating processes that subsequent mappings of the earth and its peoples became a possibility. We have now gone, quite literally, full circle, so to speak. Perhaps it was no coincidence then that the body of Osama Bin Laden was dropped into the oceans instead of being laid to rest in an unmarked grave, which used to be the hallmark in the secret burial of monsters and evildoers.

That is not, however, to say that our concern with spatial integrities should decrease. It would certainly be tempting here to return to the work of

Giorgio Agamben and see how 'the camp' is once again becoming a defining feature of the present moment. The Syrian refugee is certainly exposed to the violence of the camp, which in terms of scale alone seem to deny meaningful political and ethical responses. Of the 1.8 million registered refugees to be officially documented since the start of the conflict in March 2011, the Zaatari refugee camp situated in the middle of the Jordanian desert, for example, homes some 80,000 refugees, all living in makeshift tents within a five-mile radius, making it the fourth largest city in the country.[11] We have also been exposed more recently to the forced encampments of refugees in Eastern parts of Europe, who boarded trains in the false hope that they would be granted freedom, only to be interned; while confronting the viciousness of state brutality and the shameful pictures such as the Hungarian camerawomen Petra Laszlo kicking and tripping a fleeing refugee with a child in his arms, comparisons with twentieth-century fascism are readily made.[12]

It has been common to write of 'Fortress Europe', which more broadly speaking might be seen as a form of subsidiary to a broader 'Wall Around the West' (Huysmans, 2006). Populations have been routinely *contained* in order to better manage the life chance divide separating the Global North and South (Duffield, 2007). Such divides of course are never geographically fixed. Rather, they are determined by the individual biographies of those requesting passage. Borders in this regard have always been embodied and biopolitically authored. Whilst there is a broader genealogy to consider that goes back to the Palestinian crisis of 1947, it is important to situate contemporary *en mass* displacements in a global neo-liberalized context. Nobody has understood the plight of the refugees better than Bauman. As he has explained, what has defined the recent condition of the refugee is a 'frozen transience', where the preferred method of encampment means 'they are catapulted into a nowhere' (Bauman, 2002). Such enclosures, however, should not be interrogated by simply relying upon security or legal rights-based discourses. They demand ethical critique, which, appreciative of the history of the violence of the camps, looks directly into the ethical distancing they create amongst people, as its inhabitants are reduced to a problem population stripped of agency. As Bauman reminds:

> Contemporary menaces, and particularly the most horrifying among them, are as a rule distantly located, concealed and surreptitious, seldom close enough to be directly witnessed and very rarely accessible to individual scrutiny – for all practical purposes invisible. Most of us would never have learned of their existence were it not thanks to the panics inspired and boosted by the mass media and their alarming prognoses composed by experts and swiftly picked up, endorsed and reinforced by cabinet members and trade companies – hurrying as they do to turn all that excitement into political and commercial profit. (Bauman, 2013)

What the refugees evidence today, however, is the crisis of containment, whether that refers to the desire to flee war-torn situations instead of waiting for some international response that in the end will seek a local solution in order to maintain the integrity of borders or to actively resist the policies of encampment. That many prefer to make the treacherous journey across the Mediterranean, instead of seeking refuge in the camps of a neighbouring Arab state, speaks volumes in this regard. As the poet Warsan Shire wrote of *Home*, 'No one puts their children in a boat unless the water is safer than the land'. Indeed, whilst some policymakers and theorists write of this in terms of economic opportunism, as images from mainland Europe have shown, the refugee is fully aware of the political function of the camp, and how its humanitarian ascriptions are merely illusionary. Containment is therefore in crisis, as the camps are now being overwhelmed physically, politically and ethically.

This should come as no surprise, for, as argued elsewhere, in today's radically interconnected world, defined and shaped by global imaginaries of threat, the camp is subsumed within broader logics of power (Evans, 2013). This adds further depth to Peter Sloterdijk's idea of living in a world interior (on Sloterdijk, see Saldanha, this volume). Brian Massumi has force-fully articulated the significance of this in the context of thinking about catastrophic overspills:

> The complexity of the interlocking systems we live in, on the social, cultural, economic and natural levels, is now felt in all its complexity, because we're reaching certain tipping points, for example, in relation to climate change and refugee flows. There is a sense that we're in a far from equilibrium situation where each of the systems we have depended upon for stability is perpetually on the verge of tipping over into crises, with the danger that there will be a sort of cascade of effects. . . . And there's no vantage point from which to understand it from the outside. We're immersed in it. (Massumi, 2015)

This notion of immersion brings us directly to the problem of climatic conditioning. Human life has always been affected and its politics transformed by the elements. Or, to put it another way, Aeschylus' Oresteia onwards, the elements have always been of metaphorical and phenomenological signifi-cance to the political order of things.[13] Avoiding, however, the all-too-common reductionist tendency here to directly correlate climatic change with the causes of war and violence, such that once again a self-validating moral imperative allows for the demonization of illiberal ways of living; following Sloterdijk, it is more meaningful to situate the manipulation of climatic conditions within a military diagram for power. In this regard, it is not that changes to the climate lead to social and political collapse. It is, rather, to understand the ways in which a transformation in atmospheric conditions is made real through forms of environmental militarism, which allow for the bypassing of racially coded determinism. Such theorization after all is seldom applied to the way peoples in metropolitan areas of the world might respond to environmental transformation! Thus understood, the environment does not simply relate to biospherical conditions. It is *bios*-spherical as it points to an always and already politicized notion of active living space, which necessary to the sustenance of life, demands appreciating how its catastrophes are resultant of a failure of the political and ethical imagination that needs to be increasingly framed in planetary terms.

A WORLD WITHOUT REFUGE

In a world that is effectively full – one where there are no spaces left to territorially claim, mark out and subsequently demarcate – those without citizenship are caught in a global no man's land of being physically cast out and yet globally included within imaginaries of threat and endangerment (see Dalby, this volume). Such a fugitive status is a world apart from the nomadism compellingly theorized by post-structuralists. Indeed, while there is still much to be taken from Deleuze's insistence that oppression is less about the denial of rights than it is to do with the restrictions placed upon the movements of those seeking flight, there is a need to address today the powerlessness experienced by those without political citizenship. As the refugee flees from those conditions of urbicide and the wanton destruction of their lifeworld systems, at every stage their movements are incorporated within competing military diagrams for power, publicly narrated through narratives of security, such that the term 'climate of fear' shows itself to have many different points of origins, situational meanings, and yet continued atmospheric resonance from the perspective of its victims, borne of the all-too-real sense of vulnerability and insecurity that war produces and continually recreates.

It is tempting perhaps to argue here that the refugee will become one of the defining political problems of the twenty-first century. They certainly overwhelm our physical, political and ethical registers in ways that are demanding a rethink on the relationship between humans and the world to which they are 'inclusively-abandoned'. This becomes all the more pressing with the realization that changing environmental conditions – whether understood through the immediate catastrophe of hard militarism or the slower catastrophe of environmental degradation – in all likelihood will result in population displacements and flight from such devastation. To reiterate, it is not being suggested here that changes in local environmental conditions will necessarily produce the conditions that give rise to future wars and violence. Such violence is more likely to be borne of the response, including the containment of those who have every right to mobilize flight from devastation and through the denial of the most basic of human freedoms – namely the right to live with dignity and in the hope that their families can find more peaceful habitation. It is to recognize the prospect for future human displacements brought about by changes in environmental conditions and the poverty of contemporary political and ethical responses so inevitable due to their *reactionary* nature.

So, how might we begin to rethink this problem in more affirmative ways? Much has been made of the distinction between the migrant and the refugee in terms of their political framing and significance. The migrant in itself should not be seen as problematic, as we are all, ultimately, born of human migrations. The designated term 'refugee', however, is significant, as it demands affording 'refuge', that is, forms of protection. Etymologically it is also supplemented by the 'refusal' as a clear political act of denial by those who may ultimately be complicit in the oppression. The word also draws us to the tensions presented by the word 'refuse' that oscillates between the negation, that is, to refuse somebody something, against the production of something worthless that can be thrown away, that is, refuse as a category of disposability. Despite its more overt political conations, over the past two decades international organizations and governments have actively used the term 'refugee' as the favoured device for containing populations in sites, which have become permanent residences. A space of what Bauman calls 'permanent temporality' (Bauman, 2002). Refugees, in short, have appeared as a problem to be solved, not persons demanding an ethical welcoming based on friendship and hospitality on account of their shared humanity. Hence what matters here is precisely the ethics informing discursive labels.

Here the plight of the contemporary refugee becomes particularly instructive. It is important to recognize that taking flight across the treacherous oceans is another example of what might be termed a 'non-decision decision'.[14] Faced with violent conditions, wherein the only wager is competing promises of a terrifying encounter, the capacity for acting freely is fully denied save giving oneself over to a *less certain* alternative. The only certainty to be written of here is 'certain death'. It is to respond to something truly intolerable. Ethically speaking, however, it is important to hold onto the notion here that regardless how desperate the situation, the flight is an *affirmation* of the people's humanity. It is impossible to imagine what it must be like to have to watch your family board a small dingy, setting out onto the waters you know have taken so many lives. What we can do is approach the issue with ethical sensitivity, foregrounding the agency of those facing such a predicament. That is not to say we should hold them *responsible* for what happens. Where after all is any choice ultimately being made? Instead it is to recognize the humanity of the victims, and their desire for freedom and dignity. This takes us some way into understanding Laruelle's point that the victim is more than a problem to be solved and that they might be seen as a site for rethinking resistance.

A DEATH WITHOUT SACRIFICE

The concept of the intolerable has been previously used as a way to highlight and interrogate the mediation of suffering by contemporary neoliberal regimes of power (Evans & Giroux, 2015b). In doing so, attention has also been drawn to the ways in which groups such as ISIS mimic the nihilistic logic of the times by utilizing the intolerable for devastating political effect (Evans & Giroux, 2015a). Indeed, if the violence of the twentieth century pointed to clear and normalized forms of dehumanization to bring about the slaughter of millions, the foregrounding of 'the human' as a disposable category in the performance of beheading forced us to reflect more purposefully on the relationship between intolerability, the performance of killing and the ethical question of sacrifice.

Building on from the work of Walter Benjamin, amongst others, Agamben has pushed forward our thinking on the idea of sacrifice as a fundamental political category in the context of the wilful, calculated and systematic killing of human lives. As he purposefully articulates throughout his politically and philosophically rich *Homo Sacer* series, the dehumanized subject – what he terms 'bare life' – refers precisely to those lives 'killed without sacrifice'. Such lives, he claims, provide a key entry into understanding the organizing principles of sovereignty (albeit in a way that remains for the most part a hidden secret). Hence, unlike Schmitt's well-established idea that the political is all about demarcating who is the friend and who is the enemy, for Agamben the history of sovereignty is all about determining which lives are worthy of political qualification against those who may be killed without any crime being committed. Sacrifice as such retains something of a positive value.

In our attempts to bring these categorizations into the orbit of the intolerable violence we are forced witness to today, with the purpose of developing and moving beyond some of the structural limits of Agamben's important work, it is important to ask: Who constitutes those lives killed without a crime being committed from a systemic perspective? How are we to understand the political function of sacrifice from the perspective of power, as it points to the appropriation of tragic events for the furtherance of violence and enactment of justice, while providing further insight into the mediation of those terrifying moments of human disposability many are continually subjected to on a daily basis? And in what ways does this allow us to further our understanding of the intolerable, while interrogating with renewed purpose and ethical awareness the order of politics in the contemporary moment, not least its forms of intellectual violence?

My understanding of the sacrificial is worth clarifying from the outset. If the question of the intolerable (as already argued) designates a political category, which provides critical insight into the threshold between acceptable and unacceptable forms of violence, it is the sacrificial which nuances our understanding by foregrounding human qualities of the victims. It asks what exactly is being inscribed upon the bodies of the victims? In this regard, the sacrificial refers precisely to those deaths, which, in a symbolic order of things, are intended for public consumption. Hence, from the perspective of power, the problem of sacrifice requires a great deal of mediation in the spectacle of violence as the narrative dominates the message of the medium, that is, which deaths are recorded and appear rightful casualties of systemic oppression. This we might argue is opposed to forms of counter-spectacle in which the sacrificial is consciously exposed and disrupted in order to address more fully the human qualities of its victims.

As mentioned above, sacrificial tropes proliferate across the contemporary political moment. In doing so, they connect the theological with the secular in ways that demand sustained and considered critique beyond claims of institutional separation. And yet, like violence, the term 'sacred' proves very difficult in respect of clear definition and working description. Nobody understood this better than Bataille, who theorized in dense and challenging ways the links between intolerable representations and their sacred qualities. As he wrote, 'Across time, the blood sacrifice opened [our] eyes to the contemplation of the vexing reality completely outside daily reality, which is given in the religious world this strange name: the *sacred*. We can give no justifiable definition of this word. But some of us can still imagine (try to imagine) what *sacred* means. . . . [and] try to relate this meaning to the image of what the bloody reality of sacrifice represents to them, the bloody reality of the animals death in sacrifice'(Bataile, 1999).

Alyan embodied the sacrificial victim. The image of his body concentrated in the most intimate way our attention on the bloody reality of the situation, as his tragic death brought about the calls for a more ethically sensitive and humane response to the crisis. But what would have happened to the body of Alyan had this image, like so many others, eluded public attention? What if the body of the image hadn't captured the attentions of picture editors at that particular moment in time? What if his body, like so many others, perished at sea and vanished without a trace, instead of being washed up on the shores? What if another story grabbed our attentions? Hence the death of this young innocent child simply registered as yet another statistic in the ongoing production of nameless and faceless victims. Could we then use the term 'sacrifice' to describe the violence if, in death, there was no notable crime attached or subsequent cause attributed?

A death with sacrifice requires the sacrificial victim to assume certain symbolic importance. The death appears to be worthy of something. However tragic, there is value attributed to the singular loss of life. Here, then, we encounter a fundamental difference between the wider tragedy of human disposability, whose numbers continue to be written and yet whose biographies remain forgotten, and those who come to embody certain tolerable and intolerable conditions, through which we learn to attribute a metaphysical meaning to the suffering and the sheer fact of their witnessed death. Unwittingly or not, sacrifice demands some connection to a 'greater good' or that it is worthy *because of the sacrifice.* While the sacrificial in these terms may concentrate our attentions on intolerable conditions, there is an evident danger to the symbolism, as the complex nature of their killing is overlaid with authenticating narratives and definitive truths about the event, which, rather than putting systemic forces on trial, ends up precluding serious critical attention. Once the sacrificial makes its entry into political discourse, complicity is easily written out of the script, as the need for new thinking is displaced by the intellectual violence of rehearsed orthodoxy that continues to reveal theological traces.

A NATURAL HISTORY OF VIOLENCE

What is being outlined here is the need to rethink the disposability of life and its environmental cartographies such that the politics of the human in the twenty-first century can be rethought. New geographies of violence are forcing us to confront the brutalities of the world interior. Every surface holds the potential to appear problematic, just as our very understandings of spatial integrities and belonging are being radically altered. Nature as such – the waters most certainly included – appears more important as ever in terms of political insight and critical awareness. Its embodied forms are also demanding a force change in the ongoing conceptualization of political terms such as 'freedoms', 'liberties', 'rights' and 'justice', in ways that are more attendant to human occupancy in an endangering global lifeworld system. The intellectual dangers of this broadened worldly focus are however painfully evident, demanding more vigilance to the creation of fascistic earths.

Naturalism and Social Darwinism have been rightly discredited from both a political and a philosophical perceptive. Perniciously underwriting a history of racial prejudice, naturalized and embedded through discourses of survivability, its centrality to colonial subjugation has been purposefully exposed. Despite the force of these critical histories of violence, however, many of its logics still appear in sophisticated in troubling ways. For example, theories of survivalist aptitudes are often detected in the associated pathologization of neoliberal casualties that often focus on individual failures, while popularized academics such as Richard Dawkins often fall back upon theories of natural selection in their intellectually violent crusades. Naturalism has also made a comeback in the theatres of war today, as representations of environmental inhospitability are often invoked to designate the inhospitability of peoples. The environment in such terms is being increasingly drawn into war paradigms, such that questions of bad environmental stewardship (excluding corporate) are increasingly tied to the causes of conflict and instability in zones of crisis already blighted by chronic poverty and suffering. The allied response is new forms of environmental militarism giving rise to a development–security–environmental nexus that is finding new reasons to govern planetary life.

As nature increasingly appears central to political and military deliberations and concerns, there is a need to rethink the politics of nature in ways that allow for more purposeful critique. Mindful of the dangers associated with naturalism and its all too racial heritage, often reworked in the contemporary moment under the zeitgeist of new forms of positivism, there is a need to be attentive to the overt politicization of the natural world, especially the advent of environmental militarism and the absorption of environmental tropes for the continuation of violence and interventionism. Moving beyond asking then what is natural, and how the natural realm appears endangered, our task is to look at the ways in which the elements of nature function politically – thereby conducting what can be termed a 'natural history of violence', which is crucial to understanding the new violent geographies of today.

To conclude, it is worth turning to Bill Viola's *Martyrs* installation, permanently on display in the South Quire Aisle of St Paul's Cathedral, London, which offers a remarkable example of the representational interplay between, violence, sacrifice, mediatized victims and the elements of nature. The title itself – *Martyrs* – immediately invokes political and theological connotations. Depicting four figures on large rectangular plasma screens, visibly overwhelmed as they are submitted to an intense physical trial, the work speaks directly to human suffering. Each of the bodies in the installation is exposed to the violence of the elements, as earth, air, fire and water gradually place intolerable pressures on the powerless and immobile subjects. The overall sequence lasts several minutes. Aside from the fact that the work follows a familiar historical tradition of the spiritual commissioning of artworks for prominent religious sites across the world, the religiosity at play is all too apparent.

The biblical significance of four figures would be striking to theologians and students of the gospel. Violas work however demands a more secularized and contemporary reading. Something is invariably intended here by this digitalized and humanized performance piece. This is not about the four horsemen of the Apocalypse, whose genocidal violence signifies the End of Times. Viola's four martyrs, in contrast, appear as victims (albeit ambiguously as the video's time sequence develops) who are subjected to a slower earthly catastrophe. And yet the interplay between violence, sacrifice and redemption through suffering offers less a departure than a contemporary reworking of theological themes, which explicitly emphasizes their continuous political relevance. Viola's martyrs thus embody, it might be argued, the foregrounding of life, which is *enduring suffering* in full physical gaze, so that through a forced witnessing, finally we are able to appreciate the physical and temporal predicament of earthly catastrophe and the time of its crisis.

Alongside the insertion of life into the violence of the frames, what makes Viola's work compelling is his ability to concentrate the imagination by consciously slowing down the viewer's experience. This demands a certain reflection borne of acute awareness of the passing of time. Agamben has noted this temporal significance, writing, 'If one had to define the specific achievement of Viola's videos with a formula, one could say that they insert not the images in time but time in the images. And because the real paradigm of life in the modern era is not movement but time, this means that there is a life of the images that is our task to understand' (Agamben, 2013). Agamben's attention here to what we might properly describe as being the *psychic life of images* as a means for opening up new critical discussions on the political places it in direct confrontation with the inscriptions of 'spectral destiny' (Agamben, 2013). It is not about constructing 'the image of the body but the body of the image' (Agamben, 2013), liberating its wider political significance – the life of the image. As Viola explains in a passage cited by Agamben: 'The essence of the visual medium is time . . . images live within us. At this moment we each have an extensive visual world inside us. . . . We are living databases of images – collectors of images – and these images do not stop transforming and growing once they get inside us.' (Agamben, 2013)

How those images are mobilized becomes key to how the intolerable is confronted and the political reimagined to the creation of better futures, and how those images are mobilized becomes key to how the intolerable is apprehended in the present moment. It is to write of the politics of disposability, long before the bodies end up washed on the planetary shores. It is to reimage the art of the political, harnessing the power of aesthetics to the liberation of the oppressed. And it is to rethink the ethical subject of violence in ways that is mindful of the need to engage in more reciprocal relations amongst the world of peoples. As Jacques Derrida (1993) powerfully writes, 'I would say there is no politics without an organization of the time and space of mourning, without topolitology of sepulchre, without an unconscious and thematic relation to the spirit as ghost, without an open hospitality to the guest as ghost, whom one holds, just as he holds us, hostage'. This requires liberating the spectacle of violence and its intolerable depictions from the scene of the sacrificial, for it is here that the memory of violence is inscribed with the logics of violence to come.

NOTES

1. This article owes considerable debt to a number of people who helped shaped its focus. I am particularly indebted to the audiences at NYU, Columbia University, New York, University of California at Irvine, and McMaster University, Ontario, who offered incisive and critical comments during lectures I gave with the same title. This article will be part of a wider book project I am currently working on that looks at the links between the concept of humanity and the question of sacrifice.

2. Quoted in Oliver Laurent, "What the Image of Alyan Kurdi Says About the Power of Photography," *Time Magazine*, 2015. Online at: http://time.com/4022765/aylan-kurdi-photo/

3. http://news.nationalgeographic.com/2015/09/150903-drowned-syrian-boy-photo-children-pictures-world/

4. http://time.com/4022765/aylan-kurdi-photo/

5. https://www.rt.com/news/313603-migrants-dead-austria-lorry/

6. https://theconversation.com/dont-look-away-from-aylan-kurdis-image-47069

7. http://www.theguardian.com/commentisfree/2015/sep/04/images-aylan-kurdi-syria?CMP=fb_gu

8. http://time.com/4022765/aylan-kurdi-photo/

9. The term 'liquid' has become a defining metaphor for much of Bauman's later work. See in particular, Bauman (2000, 2006, 2007).

10. See in particular Deleuze and Guattari (2004).

11. http://www.huffingtonpost.com/2013/07/18/zaatari-refugee-camp-photos_n_3618761.html http://www.telegraph.co.uk/news/worldnews/middleeast/jordan/11782770/What-is-life-like-inside-the-largest-Syrian-refugee-camp-Zaatari-in-Jordan.html

12. http://edition.cnn.com/2015/09/09/europe/hungarian-camerawoman-migrant-firing/

13. In the Orestia, for example, we encounter the very first example of political sacrifice, which takes places in Western literature with Clytaemnestra's killing of Agamemnon (which sets in place the very idea of the cycle of violence/revenge). Significantly, it invokes directly a metaphor of the oceans as it connects to the flow of blood . . . to quote: 'There is the sea, and who will drain it dry? Precious as silver, inexhaustible, ever-new, it breeds the more we reap it – tides on tides of crimson dye our robes blood-red'.

14. This concept was initially put forward concerning those who had to jump from the Twin Towers on September 11, 2001. See Evans (2013).

REFERENCES

Agamben, Giorgio. 2013. *Nymphs*. Seagull Books.
Bataile, Georges. 1999. *Tears of Eros*. San Francisco: City Lights.
———. 1994. *The Absence of Myth: Writings on Surrealism*. London: Verso.
Bauman, Zygmunt. 2000. *Liquid Modernity*. Cambridge: Polity Press.

————. 2002. *Society Under Siege*. Cambridge: Polity Press.

————. 2006. *Liquid Fear*. Cambridge: Polity Press.

————. 2007. *Liquid Times: Living in an Age of Uncertainty*. Cambridge: Polity Press.

————. 2013. *Collateral Damages: Social Inequalities in a Global Age*. Cambridge: Polity Press.

Brintnall, Kent. 2011. *Ecce Homo: The Male Body in Pain as Redemptive Figure*. Chicago: University of Chicago Press.

Deleuze, Gilles and Felix Guattari. 2004. *A Thousand Plateaus*. London: Continuum.

Derrida, Jacques. 1993. *Aporias*. Stanford: Stanford University Press.

Duffield, Mark. 2007. *Development, Security and Unending War: Governing the World of Peoples*. Cambridge: Polity Press.

Evans, Brad. 2013. *Liberal Terror*. Cambridge: Polity Press.

Evans, Brad and Henry A. Giroux. 2015a. "Intolerable Violence". *Symploke* 23, no. 1 & 2: pp. 197–219.

————. 2015b. *Disposable Futures: The Seduction of Violence in the Age of Spectacle*. San Francisco: City Lights.

Huysmans, Jef. 2006. *The Politics of Insecurity: Fear, Migration and Asylum in the EU*. London: Routledge.

Laurelle, Francois. 2015. *General Theory of Victims*. Cambridge: Polity Press.

Laurent, Oliver. "What the Image of Alyan Kurdi Says About the Power of Photography". *Time Magazine*, September 4, 2015. Online at: http://time.com/4022765/aylan-kurdi-photo/

Massumi, Brian. 2015. *The Politics of Affect*. Cambridge: Polity Press.

Rancière, Jacques. 2004. *The Politics of Aesthetics: The Distribution of the Sensible*. London: Continuum.

Reich, Wilhelm. 1970 [1933]. *The Mass Psychology of Fascism*. trans. V. Carfagno. New York: Farrar, Straus, Giroux.

Schmitt, Carl. 2006. *The* Nomos *of the Earth in the International Law of the* Jus Publicum Europaeum. New York: Telos.

Chapter 5

Unsettling Futures

Climate Change, Migration and the Obscene Biopolitics of Resilience

Giovanni Bettini

INTRODUCTION

Tragedy *and* farce. Both aptly describe the political climate that currently sur-
rounds migration. Thousands of lives are sacrificed while crossing seas and
deserts to circumvent borders and reach safer shores – in the Mediterranean,
along the Mexico – US border, in the Sahara, in the Bay of Bengal and in
many other places. At the same time, mounting waves of right-wing populism
agitate xenophobic sentiments against migrants and push the coordinates of
whole political landscapes to the right. In an atmosphere of generalized 'moral
panic' (Bauman 2015), time after time new 'migration crises' are produced;
barbwires and militarized border enforcement are cast at the centre of the
political stage and the 'spectre of invasion' conjures up in public debates. The
fences erected around Europe and the deployment of NATO vessels to patrol
the Aegean Sea spring to mind, as well as the openly xenophobic tones that
characterized both the Brexit referendum campaign in the United Kingdom
and the 2016 US presidential election. While both the dire predicament many
migrants face and the right-wing racism that gesture in a number of political
scenes are tragic, the political conjuncture shows farcical connotations. One
suspects that the calls to enforce borders on which right-wing populisms build
their fortunes owe more to the spectacular mode of politics within which
they are staged, than to an actual design to block migration. While it added a
powerful signifier of racism, regressive closure and misplaced rage in a viru-
lent campaign, I doubt that many (including the president) seriously believe
the 'Trumpian wall' will be a 'solution' to govern the complex migration
systems that link the United States, Mexico and the whole Central American
region. The aggressive propaganda against migrants, the display of a will to
control migration at any costs and the ever more frequent promise to protect

a country's perceived integrity by erecting walls, all have markedly theatrical traits; at a closer look, they appear as vain attempts to reaffirm a waning
state sovereignty (Brown 2010). The humanitarian responses to the 'crises'
deploy in a homologous if not coincident register, with similarly theatrical
traits. We could say they are part of the same spectacle, most immediately
because of the blurring of distinctions between the logics, scope and practices
of humanitarian, security and military interventions (Reid 2010, Duffield
2007, 2012). In this respect, the Mediterranean case is exemplary, with rescue
and capture of migrants operated by same actors, the military, and administered by the same departments that regulate the allocation and disciplining
of migrants once they are on European soil. But also because the scene of
the (militarized) humanitarian rescue is a key moment of the same 'migration crisis' staged at the border; it contributes to the production of specific
subjectivities for those who move, and disciplines their movement into the
very specific channels provided for by the rescue machine, even beyond
the moment of rescue (Pallister-Wilkins 2015, De Genova 2013, Tazzioli
2015a, b). According to several studies that have explored the strong 'spectacular' traits of contemporary politics of migration, one of the crucial phases
of the governance of mobility is indeed the modulation of the (in)visibility of
(violent) border enforcement as well as of humanitarian tragedies and rescue
(Tazzioli 2015a). Another key insight is that the 'spectacle of border' – the
noise of the weapons, barbwires and walls, humanitarian rescues, hecatombs
in the seas and desert, the rabid right-wing anti-migration propaganda – is
functional to the creation and normalization of 'illegality'(De Genova 2013).
Both militarized borders and humanitarian interventions are functional to the
harnessing of migrant flows through a very thin comb: while the few qualify-
ing are disciplined through ever-narrower channels, most migrants are made
into 'illegal', 'undocumented' bodies. As noted by Nicholas De Genova,
the migration crisis' scene is accompanied by an obscene side not framed in
the show. The crisis is in effect a normal(ized) device part of a complex of
operations, and the spectacular alternation of the scenes of death, rescue and
capture at borders go hand in hand with the ordinary inclusion of 'illegal'
migrants into the workforce. Scene and obscene are part of the same story,
staged and hidden at and through the border (De Genova 2013). A number of
critical studies offer similar vistas, by highlighting the productivity of borders
and proposing to understand them, rather than as mere places of exclusion,
as sites of selective inclusion and of the production of subjectivities (Jansen,
Celikates and de Bloois 2015, Mezzadra and Neilson 2012, 2013).

In the brief introduction to the dramatic 'spectacle of border' proposed
above, those readers familiar with debates on climate change and migration surely recognize various traits of the narratives on 'climate refugees'
and the crises they are said to represent. Drawing from and expanding on

these similarities, this chapter 'looks awry' at climate and migration. Taking inspiration from existing work on the 'spectacularized' character of borders and migration, it sketches the scenes that mainstream discourses on climate migration enact, what they put under the spotlight and the connections they consider. Various scenes are identified, noting how alarmist narratives on climate refugees co-exist with the neoliberal phantasy of the docile adaptive climate migrant – both highly evocative and 'spectacular', as well as depoliticizing. I then contrast these scenes with their obscene, what is left out, ignored or not narrated. What is negated from these scenes is the very political kernel of climate migration: the scenes of dangerous 'climate refugees' and of docile 'climate migrants' are staged as part of complex geopolitical and economic relations that regulate population and labour mobility in the postcolonial present. In the name of resilience, the 'majority world' is trained to be docile in front of the series of crises and disasters through which planetary capital thrives and expands (Chaturvedi and Doyle 2015).

THE SPECTACLE OF CLIMATE MIGRATION

The starting point of this chapter is the spectacular character that competing discourses on climate migration (for a recent overview, see Ransan-Cooper et al. 2015) share, in spite of the markedly different scenes they stage. The question of climate change and migration has gone through various transitions: from being a narrow and rather marginal debate on ecological displacement that took place in environmental agencies and scholarship in the late 1970s, it has become a well-established policy field that poses climate migration as a bouquet of mobility responses and involves an array of key mainstreaming actors and institutions (Bettini 2014, Felli 2013, Methmann and Oels 2015). Confusion, inconsistencies, polarizations, as well as quick turns of direction have been constants in debates on climate change and migration. Important actors have also changed their positions – the International Organization for Migration (IOM) and the UN High Commissioner on Refugees (UNHCR), initially among the most hostile to posing the question of climate and displacement, have become some of the most active players in today's policy and advocacy arenas (for a very detail account of this transition, see Hall 2016). Over a few years, for sure since the publication of the UK Foresight Report (2011), the idea of 'migration as adaptation' gained momentum while the figure of the climate refugee apparently lost its traction. But suddenly, with the outburst of the 'refugee crisis' in Europe, the figure of climate refugees underwent a renaissance in a dramatic turnaround (e.g. Gemenne 2015), with fears of mass international displacement caused by 'climate crises' back at centre stage.

These inconsistencies, turns and revolutions can confound the discussion and result distracting. In effect, recent debates have mostly been structured around a reified notion of climate migration as an entity to dissect, with an incessant quest for its essence. A lot of effort has been directed towards debating whether a number of cases are 'specimens' for climate migration. Were the migrants choking in the dust of the American plains in the 1930s environmentally displaced persons? Will inhabitants of Tuvalu become climate refugees, if/when anthropogenic sea-level rise submerges their island? Or, can we consider a worker from one of the many ecologically fragile valleys in the mountains of Nepal, who moves to a Gulf state to sell their labour, a proto-example of the virtuous climate migrant? Attributing those movements to the impacts of environmental or climate change would be simplistic or incorrect, and there are many examples of attempts to naturalize imperialist expansion or political conflicts behind the screen of climate change – including the outrageous idea that Syrian displaced are climate refugees, or the blatant false explanation of the conflict in Palestine, undeniably rooted in the Israeli occupation, as caused by ecological pressure and a drier climate. At the same time, in many of the situations mentioned above, ecological vulnerability and socio-economic marginalization conjure up to limit the freedom with which the concerned persons do (not) move. This chapter, rather than delving directly into these questions or attempting to reconstruct the trajectory followed by the debate, explores the scenes (the affective, economic, geopolitical, relations represented) conjured up by competing discourses.

We can get a vivid illustration of the scenes represented by different discourses on climate migration if we compare an 'old' and a 'new' account of environmental displacement in Bangladesh. The choice of country is not random: one thing that has not changed over the last several decades is the identification of Bangladesh as key hotspot of vulnerability to environmental and climate change, in reason of its low-lying territory and fragile coastal ecosystems, as well as for its history of political economic vulnerabilities. Year after year, cyclone after cyclone, Bangladesh has been identified as one of the places on earth most vulnerable to the wraths of climate change, one of the 'sure' sources of mass climate-induced displacement. We can, for instance, compare Norman Myers' work on Bangladesh (Myers 1997, Myers and Kent 1995) and the study by Lu and colleagues (Lu et al. 2016). Both studies were published in the aftermath of violent cyclones causing serious damages and numerous casualties (the 1991 cyclone and Cyclone Mahasen), and in their backdrop lie the concerns over the combined effects of intensifying extreme weather events and slow-onset degradation, in particular land erosion and sea-level rise. But there are key differences symptomatic of profound changes reconfiguring the scene on which climate migration is represented.

FIRST SCENE: CLIMATE REFUGEES

Myers' work was firmly situated in the wake of the Northern discourses on global environmental challenges and on planetary stewardship that arose in the 1970s (for more detail, see Bettini 2017), as were the other key interventions launching the concept of 'environmental refugees' in the late 1970s and early 1980s (e.g. Jacobsen 1988, El-Hinnawi 1985, Brown 1976). The nexus was framed in terms of mass displacement and international security, based on an evocative but simplistic idea: over a certain threshold, the impacts of climate change (land degradation, sea-level rise and coastal erosion, droughts, extreme weather events) will force vulnerable populations into displacement. The result is a series of 'environmental displacement crises', menacing to undermine regional, national and international stability and security. All the ingredients of the 'classic' (and colonial) environmental discourse of the 1970s and 1980s are present, such as the alarmist narrative on a planet on the verge of a catastrophe; the identification of (over)population (metaphorized here by waves of environmental/climate refugees) and 'inappropriate' environmental management in the Global South as main threats to the prospects of sustainable development; the idea that international and multilateral institutions and law would 'solve the problem' (on these aspects, see Bettini and Andersson 2014). While the concept of environmental and climate refugees has been heavily criticized (for some early examples, see Findley 1994, Suhrke 1994, Kibreab 1997), this framing has been very influential and at times dominant in academic (Stern 2007, Reuveny 2007, Westra 2009, Myers 2002), advocacy (Environmental Justice Foundation 2009, Christian Aid 2007) and policy (Council of the European Union 2008, WBGU 2008) arenas. The resonance of this scene with the 'spectacle of borders' introduced above is clear on a number of levels. For instance, a lexicon drawn from the military and often associated to warzones is mobilized both in the concept of 'hotspots' of vulnerability in the field of climate change (e.g. WBGU 2008) and in the current hotspots approach to migration in the EU (Neocleous and Kastrinou 2016). More deeply, common traits include the invocation of securitized tones, the alarmism and the spectre of invasion, but also the inextricable interconnection between the humanitarian and the military/securitized response – the climate refugee is both a victim to be protected and a security threat to fear (on this ambivalence, see Bettini 2013). It should be of little surprise that, at a time such as now when the 'spectacle of borders' and anxieties around migration are in the ascendant, the figure of climate refugees – discredited among a vast majority of scholars – resurfaces in media[1] and even academia (Gemenne 2015).

SECOND SCENE: DOMESTICATING THE DISASTER

As anticipated, a more moderate 'scene' has gained ground in recent years. The aforementioned study by Lu and colleagues (2016) is illustrative. To begin with, the tone of the article, presented as an investigation of 'migration and mobility patterns in climate stressed regions' is nowhere close to Myers' alarmism and dramatic emphasis. The recent study by Lu and colleagues understands migration as a complex, multidimensional and multicausal phenomenon (contra the environmental determinism of the 'old' monocausal models). The focus is also on temporary internal rather than international mobility, the type of movement most contemporary studies expect climate change to influence in the first instance (Foresight 2011). Moreover, the study – rather than distant satellite images and heuristic maps – draws on anonymized mobile phone data, which allow it to trace, at a very fine resolution, patterns of micro-mobility in the aftermath of a cyclone. The innovative 'smart' methods employed raise concerns though, as they come dangerously close to the many existing high-tech surveillance mechanisms that detect and track migrants. In any case, the nexus is understood as a 'problem' of *risk management* at the individual or household level, building on the idea that individuals can and should have a key role (not least by optimizing their mobility patters) in securing themselves against the wraths of climate change. Resonating with the resilience discourse (more on this later), the framing underlying the study by Lu and colleagues is in line with that of most organizations currently engaged with the climate and migration nexus – such as the IOM, UNHCR and UNFCCC. This framing, whose momentum dramatically increased with the publication of the Foresight Report on 'Migration and Global Environmental Change' (Foresight 2011), is nuanced, holistic, reassuringly 'technical', with little room for the alarmism and simplistic understanding of mobility of the 'old' discourses on climate refugees. Seeing migration as a complex phenomenon, it presents the nexus as a matrix of mobility responses, namely displacement, planned relocation, reduced mobility and migration as adaptation. These different forms of mobility interpellate different agendas and actors. There has been a tendency – clearest at least until the 'crisis' in Europe – to move the issue away from the alarmist and politically tricky terrain of displacement and security (Warner 2012), and towards fora concerned with disaster risk reduction, resilience and development (cfr. Bettini and Gioli 2016). One finds references to this register and forms of mobility in the dedicated section on IPCC's last Assessment Report (IPCC 2014, ch. 12); in the Cancun Adaptation Framework (UNFCCC 2010), in several of the Intended Nationally Determined Contributions (INDCs), countries submitted as basis for the Paris Agreement[2], as well as in the final decision taken at the Paris summit itself (see Preamble and Paragraph 49, UNFCCC 2016).

Forced displacement is still on the table, although not with the heavy baggage of alarmism that the term 'climate refugees' carries. International displacement is, for instance, the way in which the Warsaw International Mechanism for Loss and Damage addresses mobility, and was the focus of various very high-level initiatives such as the Nansen Initiative and the recently launched the Disaster Displacement Platform (DDP)[3] – both state-led and both involving IOM and UNHCR. However, also the idea that climate change could lead to a reduction of the mobility of vulnerable populations is included in the framework launched by the UK Foresight Report (2011), and has generated its own subfield of research (Adams 2016, Afe et al. 2015, Black et al. 2013).

In parallel, a number of actors have been advocating the idea of planned resettlement or relocation as a last-resort option to avoid displacement and/or losses when adaptation proves unsuccessful or unfeasible (e.g. de Sherbinin et al. 2011, Warner et al. 2013, Bronen and Chapin 2013). Mentioned in the text of the Cancun Adaptation Framework (UNFCCC 2010), relocation was discussed in the Sanremo Consultation (UNHCR 2014). The tone of the latter's outcomes clearly mirrors the 'new' understanding of the climate–migration nexus introduced above.

The growing momentum of the idea that (governed) migration can represent a strategy of risk management and adaptation (ADB 2012b, Warner et al. 2012, Warner and Afifi 2014, Black et al. 2011) was somehow halted by the European 'refugees crisis'. This framing, which also appears in the Cancun Adaptation Framework (UNFCCC 2010) and in several of the Intended Nationally Determined Contributions (INDCs),[4] marks the appearance of a new scene, dominated by the figure of the 'climate migrant'. The assumption is that labour migration can be a way to mobilize the 'human capital' of individuals or households in order to generate virtuous feedback loops enabling 'spontaneous' resilience (or development), not least by generating remittance flows, expected to provide a buffer during environmental stresses and to become self-financed adaptation funding. This scene is profoundly different – apparently at the antipodes – of that conjured by narratives on climate refugees: (governed) migration is predicated as a positive response to climate stress, and the vulnerable are not represented (only) as passive victims (to be protected or to fear), but as virtuous 'agents of adaptation'. This is not a dramatic representation, and is in many ways reassuring. But even the idea of migration as adaptation is spectacular or theatrical: it casts at the centre stage a figure (the docile, resilient migrant) that is idealized and evocative and that, as we will see, orients the gaze in a very selective dimension, overlooking a number of crucial aspects of the story.

THE (OB)SCENE: EVACUATING THE POLITICAL

If we continue taking inspiration from De Genova's work (2013, 2016) after having appreciated the various forms of the 'climate–migration spectacle', the obvious question becomes: What is left out of the scene? What relations are pushed out of the frame by the dominant discourses?

These are very pertinent questions in the case of climate migration. Addressing them also allows us to better grasp how the apparently contradictory discourses are related, and even produce combined effects. The scenes described so far – the catastrophic spectre of mounting waves of climate refugees, the virtuous climate migrant or the technocratic idea of resettlement – share strong depoliticizing effects: their 'obscene', what is removed from the 'scene', is the political kernel of the relation of climate change and migration. The emerging discourses foreclose the political by sterilizing the radical questions associated to a warmer planet. The dominant discourses on climate migration respond with 'more of the same' (through securitized, humanitarian or economized approaches), making sure that nothing changes even in the face of epochal changes that global warming will bring about. What is lost is the possibility to question dominant relations, to carve out space for their reimagining mobility in progressive directions. To appreciate this important trait, a useful tool is offered by Erik Swyngedouw's (2009, 2010, 2013) diagnosis of the de- and post-politicization of environmental politics, which in turn draw on work by political theorists such as Slavoj Žižek and Jacques Rancière. One of the key aspects that such contributions highlight, and which stands out in the debates on climate change and migration, is the apparently paradoxical but very productive co-existence of apocalyptic narratives and mild, technocratic governance routines and tools. How can the apocalyptic image of hordes of climate refugees co-exist with the glossy rhetoric on mobilizing migrant's human capital pushed by organizations such as IOM or the Asian Development Bank (ADB 2012a)? Žižek provides an illuminating illustration of how apocalyptic narratives have contributed to the '(re)normalization' of the ecological crisis in mainstream policy circles (Žižek 2010), while Swyngedouw has proposed a convincing account of the way in which the compulsive waving of the spectre of the climate catastrophe can paradoxically contribute to 'business-as-usual' – basically to doing nothing about it (Swyngedouw 2010). In a nutshell, the emotive investment channelled through the spectre of the apocalypse contributes to the normalization of a 'traumatic' phenomenon, contributes to making 'the unacceptable' acceptable, to inscribe the 'unthinkable' in the fabric of ordinary governance and policy (Swyngedouw 2010, Žižek 2010). The solution to the catastrophe is to be found in moderate, governance mechanisms.

This displacement of the political in favour of the 'rule of technocracy' is evident in the idea of planned relocation and resettlement (e.g. UNHCR 2014, de Sherbinin et al. 2011), a problematic policy avenue in a number of respects (McDowell 2013, Schade et al. 2015). The prospect of whole communities forced to abandon their homes and relocate because of the impacts of climate change is tragic, as tragic is the fact that relocation can be the only possible solution. Moreover, the large number of past failures with (development-related) relocations and resettlement demands caution (Wilmsen and Webber 2015). But what I'd like to focus on is another angle: What is the response envisioned to the catastrophic prospect of habitat loss contained in 'planned relocation' proposals? The highly political questions involved – concerning the root of the problem, that is, the failure to avoid climate change; the degree of investment in adaptation measures up to which relocation is deemed to be avoidable; the destination and conditions for relocation; the identification of who should bear its costs – are devolved to experts, technocratic protocols and top-down interventions.

The palatable technocratic scenes and the apocalyptic, ticklish figure of climate refugees together facilitate the removal of the political kernel embedded in the climate–migration relation. They favour the normalization of the imagined catastrophe (the climate exodus), which becomes an 'ordinary' issue, to be dealt with, governed (and when necessary, curbed) with the instruments and mechanisms of governance. Through protocols and consultations on planned relocation, by fostering/harnessing docile labour migration, by generating remittance flows. The prospect of unprecedented changes is dealt with through mundane measures.

This also shows that catastrophic narratives on hordes destitute climate displaced threatening international security (the spectacle of climate displacement) are not necessarily leading to 'radical' responses or measures. Contrary to what supporters of the concept of climate refugees hope(d) for, the spectre of climate exodus has not pushed towards more radical mitigation measures or more generous financial support for the adaptation of the vulnerable. Even less, these apocalyptic narratives have not led to any affirmation of climate justice in the name of the incredible *vulnus* to justice or human rights that displacement would represent. Apart from reinforcing sentiments against migrations which already have quite some currency in contemporary European and American politics, it seems to have contributed to the normalization of the catastrophe that climate change will represent. In a process that at the end of the day ensures that dominant relation (and in particular capital accumulation and its need to discipline labour) will be able to survive in spite of (maybe even thanks to) the extreme impacts climate change will have on a planetary scale.

OBSCENE BIOPOLITICS

Once we have described how the various scenes of the 'spectacle of climate migration' depoliticize and renormalize the question of climate change and migration, we can look closer at that which is evacuated from the scene. This obscene can be brought to light by examining the docile climate migrant, who self-finances his/her trajectory towards resilience. As we will see, this is a neoliberal phantasy, an expression of the logic of resilience and the individualization of climate adaptation. Before delving into this, it's important to notice that while the idea of migration as adaptation entails the extension of the neoliberal rule and a re-proposition of 'old' ideas on the beneficial impacts of migration on development, it should not be seen as only 'more of the same'. It also produces new spaces and new subjectivities and makes climate change (migration) into a site for new experiments – although not very progressive.

Going back to the idea of migration as adaptation: its effects become fully intelligible only if we read them in the context of the disciplining and reproduction of labour in the so-called 'global south'. Let us reiterate a few important aspects already mentioned. First, the idea that migration can be an adaptation strategy is no plea for free migration. It is rather a mechanism for selecting, harnessing and or curbing flows. Second, the new discourses are not very new. Although written in the name of climate change, the idea that vulnerable populations should manage risk by mobilizing their human capital and financing their adaptation through remittances is in effect a reworking of mainstream recipes circulated for decades within debates on the 'migration–development' nexus (Bettini and Gioli 2016). This should also remind us of the role that development and sustainable development have both played in the way docile populations are made available to the neoliberal rule in the so-called Global South in the aftermath of decolonization (Duffield 2007, 2001). Third, and not something to underestimate, the mainstream discourses on climate migration, and in particular the idea of migration as adaptation, are conducive to or at least part of the production of novel empirical realities, subjectivities, relations, such as the extension of insurability, and the market rule in new spaces (Bettini 2014, Baldwin 2016).

Indeed, when examined in light of recent studies on the discourse of resilience, narratives on 'migration as adaptation' do not appear as benign as they might seem. If we look at the subjectivities envisioned by the idea of migration as adaptation, we encounter the neoliberal phantasy of the docile migrant, who, in order to survive, is expected to mobilize his/her human capital, follow the signals of labour markets and thereby be rewarded with the possibility to self-fund his/her household's or community's adaptation through the remittances generating by selling his/her labour. As shown elsewhere (Bettini 2014), this figure signals a further biopoliticization of climate change policy and mirrors the debased entrepreneur of himself/herself that is the subject of neoliberal discourses on resilience, as described by Julian Reid and others (Reid 2012, Evans and Reid 2014, Chandler and Reid 2016). The debased character of this subjectivity in our specific case emerges in the fact that climate adaptation is individualized and depoliticized (Felli and Castree 2012). This is an important shift in the discursive landscape of climate change, as resilience 'naturalizes' the condition of continuous danger to which the impacts of climate change expose us – in particular, those marginalized. Resilience is not about securing from danger, pre-emption or precaution, but about adaptive risk management. This brings us closer to the cores of 'obscenity' of climate migration. Not only the spectacle of the 'climate refugee' goes hand in hand with the more moderate inscription of the issue in the realm of governance (in the field of labour migration, as well as in increasingly converging areas of development and climate adaptation). Also, the inscription of climate migration in the discursive wake of resilience points in the direction of an abdication of climate action – with those vulnerable left alone, expected to be prepared to confront environmental shocks and ecological degradation, required to learn 'the art of living dangerously' (Evans and Reid 2014) under the intertwined pressures of socio-economic marginalization and environmental degradation. Even the theoretic notion of a responsibility at some collective level to avoid the occurrence of climate change at all, to support adaptation or to protect those displaced, fades away, undermining the very possibility to pose climate change as a problem of (in)justice (Bettini, et al. 2016).

CONCLUSION

As we move towards a conclusion, we can turn the rather abstract reflections developed so far into more 'practical' propositions. If we agree that the options on the table are far from promising, what is next?

For instance, should we advocate for 'solutions' to be put forward within the context of UNFCCC? There were expectations about this in the run-up of the Paris summit, which some hoped would delineate a strategy to deal with climate migration. For instance, earlier drafts of the text off the Paris Agreement mentioned the creation of a 'coordination facility' on climate-induced displacement. But the roaring mountain gave birth to what apparently is a rather small mouse as the facility disappeared from the text in the last days of the summit and the outcome was the established an ad hoc task force that is currently gathering evidence from research and policy initiatives carried out so far on the nexus (UNFCCC 2016). This is not nearly as substantial as the institution of a facility that was advocated for by many. This is not too surprising, given that the goal of Paris summit was the signature of a treaty, after the big Copenhagen fiasco in 2009. Expecting an issue as ticklish as displacement to be included in any substantial degree in such a context was very optimistic.[5] But looking ahead, should we hope and struggle for some facility or protocol, or 'solution', coming from the UN or UNFCCC?

A simple and pragmatic answer: this is not very realistic. Given how difficult it has proved to spur effective climate action (in terms of real emission reductions and financial commitments), it is hard to see UNFCCC finding the mandate to 'rule' on issues directly linked to migration.

A more substantial answer is that there is and can be no single solution. Of course. Climate migration is not a problem that should be 'solved'. This formulation stems from the 'spectacle' of borders and migration and mirrors an understanding (currently widespread, unfortunately) of migration as pathological, seen as the result of a failure to develop, to adapt to climate change or to be more resilient. Of course, it would be naive to overlook the divisive questions that migration brings to the surface. And we should always remember that people on the move (or stuck somewhere they don't want to be) can suffer and are often exposed to many wrongs. However, relying on the UN's climate governance machinery to sort these matters out only obfuscates their inherently political character. To make a provocative comparison: Would we ever expect the UNFCCC to 'solve poverty'? Hoping so entails a reification of the relations coagulated in the nexus and their depoliticization, a combination that in turn facilitates the unchallenged (re)production of hegemonic relations.

Finally, I would like to argue – for the same reason – that we should not either embark in a search for a new, progressive, revolutionary articulation of the climate change–migration nexus. Looking for an alternative, radical or revolutionary figure (some sort of 'climate rebel') means looking for something that does not exist. Not only because climate change – as political object – is currently a neoliberal, depoliticized and (post)colonial discourse (Chaturvedi and Doyle 2015), but because placing hope in such a figure means reifying climate vulnerability and assuming it is possible to articulate climate struggle and migration in one single, progressive way, which is far from given. The only way forward, I would argue, is to continue looking awry at the question of migration and climate change, pushing an understanding of it as a relation that has to do with climate justice, rather than security. That is not a contingent problem to be solved (or that can be solved) by some technocratic protocol – but rather a metaphor carving out space to pose, contest and struggle for the highly political questions about the climate, mobility, economy and society we want.

NOTES

1. See, for instance, articles in *The Independent* (Bawden 2014), *The Guardian* (2015), *The National Observer* (Dinshaw 2015) and *Time* (Baker 2015).
2. For a detailed mapping of the mentions of migration in the INDCs, see https://environmentalmigration.iom.int/migration-indcsndcs.
3. See DDP's webpage, disasterdisplacement.org.
4. See https://environmentalmigration.iom.int/migration-indcsndcs.
5. See this commentary I wrote before the summit http://www.transre.org/en/blog/what-can-and-should-we-expect-cop21-climate-migration/.

REFERENCES

Adams, H. 2016. Why Populations Persist: Mobility, Place attachment and Climate Change. *Population and Environment*, 37, 429–448.

ADB. 2012a. *Addressing Climate Change and Migration in Asia and the Pacific.* Mandaluyong City. Philippines: Asian Development Bank.

———. 2012b. *Addressing Climate Change and Migration in Asia and the Pacific.* Mandaluyong City: Asian Development Bank.

Afe, W. A. Nigel, B. Richard, D. Stefan, G. Andrew & S. G. T. David. 2015. Focus on Environmental Risks and Migration: Causes and Consequences. *Environmental Research Letters*, 10, 060201.

Author. 2014. Official Prophecy of Doom: Global Warming will Cause Widespread Conflict, Displace Millions of People and Devastate the Global Economy. *The Independent* [online], 18 March.

Author. 2015. Prepare for Rising Migration Driven by Climate Change, Governments Told. *The Guardian* [online], 8 January.

Baker, A. 2015. How Climate Change is Behind the Surge of Migrants to Europe. *Time*.

Baldwin, A. 2016. Resilience and Race, or Climate Change and the Uninsurable Migrant: Towards an Anthroporacial Reading of 'race'. *Resilience*, 1–15.

Bauman, Z. 2015. The Migration Panic And Its (Mis)Uses. Retrieved from https://www.socialeurope.eu/2015/12/migration-panic-misuses/.

Bettini, G. 2013. Climates Barbarians at the Gate? A Critique of Apocalyptic Narratives on Climate Refugees. *Geoforum*, 45, 63–72.

———. 2014. Climate Migration as an Adaption Strategy: De-securitizing Climate-Induced Migration or Making the Unruly Governable? *Critical Studies on Security*, 2, 180–195.

———. 2017. Archaeologies of the Future – Tracing the Lineage of Contemporary Discourses on the Climate-migration Nexus. In *On the Move: Environmental history of Modern Migrations*, (eds.) M. Armiero & R. Tucker. London: Routledge.

Bettini, G. & E. Andersson. 2014. Sand Waves and Human Tides: Exploring Environmental Myths on Desertification and Climate-Induced Migration. *The Journal of Environment & Development*, 23, 160–185.

Bettini, G. & G. Gioli. 2016. Waltz with Development: Insights on the Developmentalization of Climate-induced Migration. *Migration and Development*, 5, 171–189.

Bettini, G., S. Nash & G. Gioli. 2016. One Step Forward, Two Steps Back? The Changing Contours of (in)justice in Competing Discourses on Climate Migration. *The Geographical Journal*, doi:10.1111/geoj.12192.

Black, R., N. W. Arnell, W. N. Adger, D. Thomas & A. Geddes. 2013. Migration, Immobility and Displacement Outcomes following Extreme Events. *Environmental Science & Policy*, 27, S32–S43.

Black, R., S. Bennett, S. Thomas & J. Beddington. 2011. Climate Change: Migration as Adaptation. *Nature*, 478, 447–449.

Bronen, R. & F. S. Chapin. 2013. Adaptive Governance and Institutional Strategies for Climate-induced Community Relocations in Alaska. *Proceedings of the National Academy of Sciences*, 110, 9320–9325.

Brown, L. 1976. *World Population Trends: Signs of Hope, Signs of Stress*. Worldwatch Paper 8. Washington, DC: Worldwatch Institute.

Brown, W. 2010. *Walled States, Waning Sovereignty*. New York: Zone Books.

Chandler, D. & J. Reid. 2016. *The Neoliberal Subject: Resilience, Adaptation and Vulnerability*. London: Rowman and Littlefield International.

Chaturvedi, S. & T. Doyle. 2015. *Climate Terror: A Critical Geopolitics of Climate Change*. New York, NY: Palgrave Macmillan.

Christian Aid. 2007. *Human Tide: The Real Migration Crisis*. London: Christian Aid.

Council of the European Union. 2008. Climate Change and International Security – Report from the Commission and the Secretary-General/High Representative. Brussels.

De Genova, N. 2013. Spectacles of Migrant 'illegality': The Scene of Exclusion, the Obscene of Inclusion. *Ethnic and Racial Studies*, 36, 1180–1198.

———. 2016. The Incorrigible Subject of the Border Spectacle. In *Public and Political Discourses of Migration: International Perspectives*, (eds.) A. Haynes, M. J. Power, E. Devereux, A. Dillane & J. Carr. London: Rowman & Littlefield.

de Sherbinin, A., M. Castro, F. Gemenne, M. M. Cernea, S. Adamo, P. M. Fearnside, G. Krieger, S. Lahmani, A. Oliver-Smith, A. Pankhurst, T. Scudder, B. Singer, Y. Tan, G. Wannier, P. Boncour, C. Ehrhart, G. Hugo, B. Pandey & G. Shi. 2011. Preparing for Resettlement Associated with Climate Change. *Science*, 334, 456–457.

Dinshaw, F. 2015. This is What a Climate Refugee Looks Like. *The National Observer* [online], 4 September.

Duffield, M. 2007. *Development, Security and Unending War – Governing the World of Peoples*. Cambridge: Polity Press.

———. 2012. Challenging Environments: Danger, Resilience and the Aid Industry. *Security Dialogue*, 43, 475–492.

Duffield, M. R. 2001. *Global Governance and the New Wars: The Merging of Development and Security*. London: Zed Books.

El-Hinnawi, E. 1985. *Environmental Refugees*. Nairobi: UNEP.

Environmental Justice Foundation. 2009. *No Place Like Home – Where Next for Climate Refugees?* London: Environmental Justice Foundation.

Evans, B. & J. Reid. 2014. *Resilient Life: The Art of Living Dangerously*. Cambridge: Wiley.

Felli, R. 2013. Managing Climate Insecurity by Ensuring Continuous Capital Accumulation: 'Climate Refugees' and 'Climate Migrants'. *New Political Economy*, 18, 337–363.

Felli, R. & N. Castree. 2012. Neoliberalising Adaptation to Environmental Change: Foresight or Foreclosure? *Environment and Planning A*, 44, 1–4.

Findley, S. E. 1994. Does Drought Increase Migration? A Study of Migration from Rural Mali During the 1983–1985 Drought. *International Migration Review*, 28, 539–553.

Foresight. 2011. *Final Project Report – Foresight: Migration and Global Environmental Change*. London: The Government Office for Science.

Gemenne, F. 2015. One Good Reason to Speak of 'climate refugees'. *Forced Migration Review*, 49, 70–71.

Hall, N. 2016. *Displacement, Development, and Climate Change: International Organizations Moving Beyond Their Mandates*. New York: Routledge.

IPCC. 2014. *Climate Change 2014: Impacts, Adaptation, and Vulnerability. Part A: Global and Sectoral Aspects. Contribution of Working Group II to the Fifth Assessment Report of the Intergovernmental Panel on Climate Change*. Cambridge (UK) and New York (NY, USA): Cambridge University Press.

Jacobsen, J. L. 1988. *Environmental Refugees: A Yardstick of Habitability*. Washington: World Watch Institute.

Jansen, Y., R. Celikates & J. de Bloois. 2015. *The Irregularization of Migration in Contemporary Europe : Detention, Deportation, Drowning*. London and New York: Rowman & Littlefield.

Kibreab, G. 1997. Environmental Causes and Impact of Refugee Movements: A Critique of the Current Debate. *Disasters*, 21, 20–38.

Lu, X., D. J. Wrathall, P. R. Sundsøy, M. Nadiruzzaman, E. Wetter, A. Iqbal, T. Qureshi, A. Tatem, G. Canright, K. Engø-Monsen & L. Bengtsson. 2016. Unveiling Hidden Migration and Mobility Patterns in Climate Stressed Regions: A Longitudinal Study of Six Million Anonymous Mobile Phone users in Bangladesh. *Global Environmental Change*, 38, 1–7.

McDowell, C. 2013. Climate-Change Adaptation and Mitigation: Implications for Land Acquisition and Population Relocation. *Development Policy Review*, 31, 677–695.

Methmann, C. & A. Oels. 2015. From 'fearing' to 'empowering' Climate Refugees: Governing Climate-induced Migration in the Name of Resilience. *Security Dialogue*, 46, 51–68.

Mezzadra, S. & B. Neilson. 2012. Between Inclusion and Exclusion: On the Topology of Global Space and Borders. *Theory, Culture & Society*, 29, 58–75.

———. 2013. *Border as Method, or, the Multiplication of Labor*. Durham: Duke University Press.

Myers, N. 1997. Environmental Refugees. *Population and Environment*, 19, 167–182.

———. 2002. Environmental Refugees: A Growing Phenomenon of the 21st Century. *Philosophical Transactions: Biological Sciences*, 357, 609–613.

Myers, N. & J. Kent. 1995. *Environmental Exodus. An Emergent Crisis in the Global Arena*. Washington: Climate Institute.

Neocleous, M. & M. Kastrinou. 2016. The EU hotspot – Police War against the Migrant. *Radical Philosophy*, 200, 3–9.

Pallister-Wilkins, P. 2015. The Humanitarian Politics of European Border Policing: Frontex and Border Police in Evros. *International Political Sociology*, 9, 53–69.

Ransan-Cooper, H., C. Farbotko, K. E. McNamara, F. Thornton & E. Chevalier. 2015. Being(s) Framed: The Means and Ends of Framing Environmental Migrants. *Global Environmental Change*, 35, 106–115.

Reid, J. 2010. The Biopoliticization of Humanitarianism: From Saving Bare Life to Securing the Biohuman in Post-Interventionary Societies. *Journal of Intervention and Statebuilding*, 4, 391–411.

———. 2012. The Disastrous and Politically Debased Subject of Resilience. *Development Dialogue*, 58, 67–80.

Reuveny, R. 2007. Climate Change-induced Migration and Violent Conflict. *Political Geography*, 26, 656–673.

Schade, J., C. McDowell, E. Ferris, K. Schmidt, G. Bettini, C. Felgentreff, F. Gemenne, A. Patel, J. Rovins, R. Stojanov, Z. Sultana & A. Wright. 2015. Climate Change and Climate Policy Induced Relocation: A Challenge for Social Justice. Recommendations of the Bielefeld Consultation (2014). *Migration, Environment and Climate Change: Policy Brief Series*, 1.

Stern, N. 2007. *The Economics of Climate Change: The Stern Review*. Cambridge: Cambridge University Press.

Suhrke, A. 1994. Environmental Degradation and Population Flows. *Journal of International Affairs*, 47, 473–496.

Swyngedouw, E. 2009. The Antinomies of the Postpolitical City: In Search of a Democratic Politics of Environmental Production. *International Journal of Urban and Regional Research*, 33, 601–620.

———. 2010. Apocalypse Forever? Post-political Populism and the Spectre of Climate Change. *Theory, Culture & Society*, 27, 213–232.

———. 2013. The Non-political Politics of Climate Change. *ACME*, 12, 1–8.

Tazzioli, M. 2015a. The Desultory Politics of Mobility and the Humanitarian-military Border in the Mediterranean. Mare Nostrum Beyond the Sea. *REMHU: Revista Interdisciplinar da Mobilidade Humana*, 23, 61–82.

———. 2015b. The Politics of Counting and the Scene of Rescue – Border Deaths in the Mediterranean. *Radical Philosophy*, 192, 2–5.

UNFCCC. 2010. The Cancun Agreements: Outcome of the Work of the Ad-hoc Working Group on Long-term Cooperative Action under the Convention.

———. 2016. Report of the Conference of the Parties on its twenty-first session, held in Paris from 30 November to 13 December 2015. Addendum. Part two: Action taken by the Conference of the Parties at its twenty-first session.

UNHCR. 2014. Planned Relocation, Disasters and Climate Change: Consolidating Good Practices and Preparing for the Future. In *Final report of the Expert consultation on Planned Relocation, Disasters and Climate Change: Consolidating Good Practices and Preparing for the Future*. Sanremo, Italy, 12–14 March 2014.

Warner, K. 2012. Human Migration and Displacement in the Context of Adaptation to Climate Change: The Cancun Adaptation Framework and Potential for Future Action. *Environment and Planning C: Government and Policy*, 30, 1061–1077.

Warner, K. & T. Afifi. 2014. Where the Rain Falls: Evidence from 8 countries on how Vulnerable Households use Migration to Manage the Risk of Rainfall Variability and Food Insecurity. *Climate and Development*, 6, 1–17.

Warner, K., T. Afifi, K. Henry, T. Rawe, C. Smith & A. De Sherbinin. 2012. *Where the Rain Falls: Climate Change, Food and Livelihood Security, and Migration – Global Policy Report*. Bonn: UNU-EHS (United Nations University Institute for Environment and Human Security).

Warner, K., T. Afifi, W. Kälin, S. Leckie, S. Ferris, S. Martin & D. Wrathall. 2013. *Changing Climates, Moving People: Framing Migration, Displacement and Planned Relocation*. Bonn: United Nations University.

WBGU. 2008. *Climate Change as a Security Risk*. London: Earthscan.

Westra, L. 2009. *Environmental Justice and the Rights of Ecological Refugees*. London: Earthscan.

Wilmsen, B. & M. Webber. 2015. What Can We Learn from the Practice of Development-forced Displacement and Resettlement for Organised Resettlements in Response to Climate Change? *Geoforum*, 58, 76–85.

Žižek, S. 2010. *Living In the End Times*. London: Verso Books.

Part II

ANTHROPOCENE: ON THE TWILIGHTS OF HUMAN MOBILITY

Chapter 6

Parting Waters

Seas of Movement

David Theo Goldberg

The environment has become an increasingly significant force in the move-ment of people from more resource challenged to more economically privi-leged societies. As the planet has warmed and environmental events have become more dramatic, the threat to already fragile lived environments has grown exponentially. And while climatologically induced migration is not new (consider Dust Bowl migration westward from Oklahoma in the 1930s), more people are displaced of late by storms, rising sea levels, earthquake induced tsunamis, tornadoes and other weather-related events. In addition, even more have moved as economic life has become challenged, living con-ditions less amenable, life prospects increasingly in question as a result of climatically impacted ecosystems. Living in a critical condition has prolifer-ated, from the coastlines of Bali to downtown Manhattan.

I will be engaged in these pages with a preliminary exploration of the play of the Sea in migratory movements of people. I will accordingly seek broadly to map the agency of the Sea and its impacts on the colouring of prevailing patterns of contemporary migrations.

Some prefatory observations: First, all environmental disasters are the complex product of what, following Donna Haraway (2008) and Bruno Latour (1993), I call natureculture (note no hyphen). Most have tended overwhelmingly to think of environmental disasters – earthquakes, tsunamis, droughts and land aridization, famines, floods, mudslides, etc. – as naturally caused. On this view, nature is taken to act on humans whose agency is, at most, considered that of victims to the unpredictable contingencies of such natural events. But, at the least, the experience of disaster very much impli-cates human beings. Wooden homes are built on spindly stilts well within the high tide mark on beaches prone to high surf, tidal surges and beach erosion, when they could be sited more or less easily further back.

Pretty much all environmental disasters, consequently, are a function of human 'contribution'. The large-scale climatological shifts are deeply entangled with environmental and so human social, political, economic and cultural forces. There is no environmental disaster – least of all those a product of climate change – in which human agency, oversight, blinkers, arrogance, greed, carelessness and ignorance are not centrally implicated.

Second, risk emerges in relation to and helps to produce a specific notion of society, as Diren Valayden (2013) has demonstrated. The welfare state from its 1930s expansion on sought to vest itself in the secularization of the pastoral, of the state as caretaker. On this understanding, risk – in the face of wars and natural disasters – was taken up as a social responsibility. Under the caretaker state, risk was considered collectively shared by ensuring that state resources would alleviate the effects more or less evenly across the population. Franklin Roosevelt articulated the conception as well as anyone in putting it to Congress in the lead up to passage of the *Social* Security Act of 1934 (my emphasis), that this would 'safeguard' against 'misfortunes which cannot be wholly eliminated in this man made world of ours' (Valayden 2013, ch. 4, p. 7).

The welfare state undertook to spread the individual and social risks across its members. Natural disasters were still, well, natural, the work of 'God's hand', at least as conceived and comprehended. Caring for the impacted and bearing the costs, which included reaching out to and ultimately welcoming in the stranger, was presumed a collective responsibility, at least in principle.

This began to change as the expressed social commitment from roughly the 1980s onwards. Collective responsibility increasingly gave way to the individualization of self-caring. One increasingly found oneself bowling alone, expected more and more to self-insure. Caretaking became the cause of private groups, from religious charities to costly bought care. Insurance companies want us to think of them as our best friends (television commercials in the United States make this sensibility explicit). Those unable to afford the coverage are left largely to fend for themselves, dependent less on social welfare than on charitable, mainly religious, handouts. 'Social security' is increasingly pressured to give way to private self-investment.

Compare the prevailing policy responses to the post–Second World War *Empire* Windrush (my emphasis) to today's boat people. Windrush migrants were greeted with a mix of welcome and concern, taken in but distributed in small numbers across the country to prevent the 'overburdening' of any one community. Racial dilution was clearly a driving concern. Post-Thatcher, if there is still such a thing as society, it applies only to those already inside its orbit, and then subject more and more to the citadel of securitization than to social welfare. Migrants and refugees are taken in, if at all, only under extreme duress, and left largely to fend for themselves. The rest, as the securitizing state would have it, are barbarians at or already inside the gate.

Third, historically, migration has long travelled across land and water (often in combination). The Sea connects land to land, placing both lands in relation to each other but also sea to sea – as passageway, as medium, less noticed as substance in and of itself, as life form(s) and life source(s), each cultivating its own general and locationally specific habitus(es). Travel and traversal, migration itself, are made possible by virtue of the fact that the Atlantic, the Indian and the Pacific flow into each other, the Atlantic into the Mediterranean, North and Baltic Seas, the China and Japan Seas into the Pacific, the various Indonesian Seas into the Indian Ocean and so on.

It follows quite obviously that the boundary lines articulated in the names of these waterways are human artifices, shaping the connecting flows. Seas, it might be said, connect worlds otherwise divided by geographies and politics. Seas put these worlds in play with each other, tend to undercut if not altogether to undo nations and states. They intersect if not blur cultures disposed to guard their presumed homogeneity. The Sea thus is a key source of intense heterogenizing and hybridization of mixture and metissage. It is the carrier in its flows of pollutants, both material and cultural, of ecological and political, conflicting and consorting bodies.

Air travel comes to the story obviously late in the game and remains the least dramatic and least noticed mode of migration even now. Perhaps because so many fly today as a matter of course, we attend to air-mediated migration only when security is compromised or violated. But 'the paperless' – those lacking the required credentials – have a better chance entering their state(d) destination of choice by sea (or land, where possible) than by the funnelling surveillance of airports.

Seawater, in any case, comprises more than two-thirds of the earth's surface, and creeping upwards annually. That said, the more or less central role of the Sea (including oceans), both in dramatic aspects of climatic conditions and in migrations' traversals, makes it a key intersecting factor in thinking about the relation between environmental/climatic transformations and their impacts on major movements of people globally.

The Sea by 'nature' bounds but intrudes upon the landed, intimating that boundaries and borders have blurred edges, even if they are intended as materialized resistances to those blurrings. Tsunamis are the most violent intrusions, though hurricanes, perhaps less like tornadoes, come off the sea too, gathering strength as they cross the ocean, pulling up water and becoming faster and more furious the warmer the water gathers up. Yet the drama of these violent events tend to eclipse from view the less immediate chaos and conditional concern caused by the erosions of salted mist, rust and sea breeze at the coastline.

This suggests in turn that the Sea deeply and more broadly shapes our social and even scientific imaginaries. Consider waves: of history, of electricity, of nausea, of a military campaign. Or currents of electricity and of culture. And *sea*sons, sea of love or nausea, a sea of people. Or the metaphors trading on inhabitants of the sea: whale of a good time, capitalist sharks, sea monsters and so on. The Sea more or less silently suffuses our lives, materially and culturally, often deeply impacting life with little realization.

In all of this, then, we tend to think of the Sea as surface and medium of movement, and perhaps only secondarily as causal agent. But the Sea (ocean) is a key moving agent as much in climatic conditions as in migrating forces. For one, constituting such a large proportion of the planet's surface and volume, seas serve as a key hinge in the rising volatility and eventful effects associated with climate change. However, it also shapes our social imaginaries at the interface of natureculture.

Storms emanate from low-pressure systems, gathering volume, speed and power across the vast stretches of water they traverse. As the planet has warmed – nearly 1degree C (1.4 degree F) in the last century, two-thirds of that since 1980 sea temperatures have heated up as well, by up to a couple of degrees (hence the melting ice caps in the Arctic and Antarctic). Storms accordingly are taking up warmer air off the sea surface, enlarging their reach and deepening their power and volatility as colder higher air comes into contact with warmer lower air spiralling off the Sea. Winds are stronger, more readily reaching hurricane strength, stormy seas achieving wave heights hitherto beyond experience. Storms are becoming more frequent and violent, whipping densely populated shorelines.

When last the planet's carbon levels approached today's levels in the Pleistocene (on mobility and geologic time, see both Clark and Colebrook, this volume), seas were 17 feet higher than they are now. Hurricane Sandy's storm surge in the mid-northeast United States in late October 2012 averaged 6–11 feet, and in some neighbourhoods reached 14 feet. The tidal surge, in short, was greater than the average height of a person standing straight backed. This was enough to wipe out three to five blocks of beachfront property and flooded the cityscape as much as a mile north of Manhattan's southern tip.

Storm surges recede. And while sea levels rise and fall as a matter of course over time (the El Nino effect in 1997–1998 added 10 mm, while in 2007 it fell by 5 mm), the longer-term overall rise in sea levels has far more lasting effects. Sea levels rose 6 cm in the nineteenth century and 19 cm in the twentieth, and the rate is accelerating (between 1 and 2 feet over two centuries). So a 17-foot rise will be super slow (not least in digital time today) and will show far slower effects with much larger permanent impacts. This is what the Maldives and other island and low-lying nations are fearing (the Dutch are in half-denial, half retro-engineering mode). Slow devastation, to twist Rob Nixon's (2013) characterization. (I sometimes joke with my colleagues that it will place the California beachfront much closer to the Arizona border, horror upon horror.) Just to join the melancholia to future projections, estimates are that in this century global surface temperatures will increase 1.1–2.9 degree C (2–5.2 degree F) for low emissions and 2.4–6.4 degree C (4.3–11.5 degree F) for high emissions. The consensus is that anything over something around a 2 degree C increase will exhibit increasingly devastating impacts.

To bring this closer to my prevailing concern here with racial implications in and through migration, a recent report predicted the top twenty cities in the developing world with the greatest number of inhabitants are likely to be most largely affected by rising sea levels and storm surge (assuming a modest 1 m/3 feet surge as a result of one in 100-year storm intensity – actually increasingly frequent). These cities included: Manila, Philippines; Alexandria, Egypt; Lagos, Nigeria; Monrovia, Liberia; Karachi, Pakistan; Aden, Yemen; Jakarta, Indonesia; Port Said, Egypt; Khulna, Bangladesh; Kolkata, India; Bangkok, Thailand; Abidjan, Cote d'Ivoire; Cotonou, Benin; Chittagong, Bangladesh; Ho Chi Minh, Vietnam; Yangon, Myanmar; Conakry, Guinea; Luanda, Angola; Rio de Janeiro, Brazil; and Dakar, Senegal.

As tragic as the situation more immediately facing the likes of the Maldives (the canaries in the appropriately proverbial coalmine), the potential disruption and devastation to the vast numbers across the global and globally networked population defies the imagination (*The Day after Tomorrow*, notwithstanding). Note that, but for Rio at #19, every one of these cities is in Africa/North Africa or Asia/South Asia. They all include densely populated urban regions of overwhelmingly diverse people who are largely poor and of colour (Hicks 2013).

Any good Gary Becker-inspired rational choice theorist would conclude that if one were going to disrupt one's own life and move from these threatened lower-level living environments to higher ground, one might as well do it all at once. The point on this account is to get to where resources and the chance to make a reasonable living are more readily available, if not sewn into the cultural expectation. Today, this may as much be Shenzhen or Australia, Hong Kong or Singapore, Brazil (well, maybe not Rio) and Chile as North America or Europe. Living in critical conditions for so long requires that those subject to such conditions become resourceful simply as a matter of survival, as Hegel pointed out two centuries ago in the master–slave dialectic.

Coastline living has been attractive to the affording for its beauty and recreational draw (until relatively recently seaside living had an artisanal and unskilled working culture long associated with it). Yet it has also pulled (or lured) in those with little if any means because of the opportunities more likely available. Coastlines likely have any number of ports, funnelling goods and services into narrowed corridors offering opportunities not available elsewhere. Besides the activities associated directly with ports, industries often concentrate close at hand to diminish delivery costs. Ports, then, are ready stepping-stones to elsewheres where imagined living is (more) appealing. And coastlines offer a source of cheap and nutritious, even if increasingly threatened, food supply less (readily) available at a distance from the Sea. So coastlines pull migrants, internal and external, into their orbits, exacerbating conditions, further threatening fragile habitats and pressuring seafood supplies.

Ports have long been the crossroads of hybrid, rebellious, transgressive and mobile people, departing and arriving, as well as servicing the departing and newcomers. It is as if the sea-ness of the Sea is nothing but the interacting and intersecting sum of these marginalizations, these representations of its edges, surfaces and boundaries. This may have to do with why most people so largely ignore the impact of human pollutants on the very sea about which most of us have so rich a fantasy life. In this focus on the margins and surfaces, the Sea is readily turned into a site of copious and capacious fantastical investment as Mick Taussig (2000) has commented. It – they, really – are sites, suppositories, and 'substances' of fantasy.

Much of the cultural production of the Sea is predicated in each instance around the specificity of the particular seaside with which the cultural producer is familiar, and thus the character of which the producer tends to presuppose, to naturalize as universal. The visible coastline is the border of our perceivable comforts, beyond which we project fears and foreignness. The 'Great Wave off Kanagawa' (1830–1833), the image of the iconic woodcut, perhaps reaches more broadly for a universalization (understandably, given its island formation). In *The Years of Rice and Salt*, Kim Stanley Robinson (2002) is almost unique in taking seriously the Sea's globalizing relationalities and relationalizing globalities (with all their attendant violence). He is joined by the writers Amitav Ghosh (in his epic *Ibis trilogy,* 2008–2015), if in a more historically specific set of contexts, and Michael Ondaatje (2011), both migrants as they are. These three authors sew race into the stories they convey in which the Sea constitutes a combining – attracting and repelling – substance, an agent, a historical actor.

The Sea here, beyond the coastline and surface – the seeable and more or less knowable – becomes increasingly the unknown, the opaque, the dark, the threatening. It has made the site of monsters and monstrosity the racial of the natural world. And the bearer, the bringer, the transporter of the racial, of the outsider, the stranger, the strange, the necessarily unbelonging, the naturally culturalized and the culturally denaturalized. As the racial of nature, the Sea's other side, its underside, represents all the built up fears about those racially characterized from the not-here: monsters from elsewhere, shadows from places unknown and threatening in their unknowability.

Those from beyond the Sea, from out of the Sea, embody the fears and threats of the unknown, novel embodiments, Mary Douglas's polluting unclean and uncouth (Douglas 1966). They are, from the viewpoint of the dominating 'host', prehistoric, transformable if at all only to the extent that they leave behind their 'natural' – birthright – culture, shed it as they dry off, dry out, washing away their legacy condition for a modernizing reach, if they can in the final analysis (some do, some cannot). The tension exactly between presumptions of racial naturalism and historicism (Goldberg 2002).

The Sea has always signified in terms of the dialectics of surface and depth. Until the technologies of submersion began to alter the imaginative disposition towards the Sea after the 1930s, depth tended to represent the unknown, threat, mystery, the dangers of monsters. The surface was considered merely mode of delivery, more easily tamed or at least predicted and negotiated. One could actually see the perils before one. With the technological thrust of the Second World War and its aftermath – submarine technology, sensors, tele-communications cables, etc. – the secrets of the deep started to give way bit by bit. The dangers became calculable, transforming uncertainties and their imaginaries into calculable risks. More recently, the genetic profile of the Sea is increasingly being fathomed, its microbial make-up mapped (Helmreich 2009). We have come to know more and more of the Sea in all its depth.

As depth became more manageable and knowable, surface became increasingly unpredictable. The Sea surface brought strangers, waves of migration and rivers of blood, boatloads of pirates and containers of pirated goods, heightened weather patterns and storm surges. The hitherto hidden from view became more transparent, knowable. The more readily visible became more dangerous, more invasive. It represented the unkempt hordes, the harder to grasp and control, and so all the more threatening, imaginatively as readily as materially. This was 'alien ocean', to use Stefan Helmreich's (2009) pressing notion, from a different if related context.

Colonial migration at its height tended to be north to south and east to west. The former consisted largely of colonial administrators, henchmen, military forces, entrepreneurs in search of raw materials, those fleeing Europe's repressions, Europe's social dregs exported to the outlying netherworld or seeking opportunities in new worlds. The latter were labouring slaves and indentured servants though some indentured too were driven south in the wake of abolition. The Sea here operated in the imaginary as surface on which personal, nation state and indeed imperial interests got to be imposed. The weather was one of the elements of the natural conditions that needed to be, well, weathered in the passage, part of the adventure, challenge or threat of raw survival. Climate cured from social ills to asthma and other diseases. Fixed seasonally, climates were to be favoured or endured, asset or liability.

Postcolonial migration, by contrast, turned face, Global South to Global North. Migrants now seek employment and educational opportunity, sustained life prospects (recall the Windrush, an apposite metaphor for the then to come). Interestingly, there is a small but notable wave of retiree migration from Global North to South, overwhelmingly white, seeking a cheaper more unplugged sunset, la pura vida. The point is to make dollars, pounds and euros go further in the face of deteriorating economic conditions and more challenged retirement accounts at home. With the spacetime compressions of globalization, these movements have also led to hastened movement and diminished inhibition.

So there is no exactly privileged direction, with far more voluminous comings and goings, going and working and perhaps resting before moving on again. Migrations have become part of the circulating flows of capital, financial and human. Even if an initial migration or wave is prompted by non-economic conditions, labour-on-demand now more or less determines the rate of picking up again and moving along. Stays are tending to become less permanent, less lifelong, more intermittent. They last only until the next opportunity elsewhere lures them to move on. Unsurprisingly, the prevailing trend tends overwhelmingly to be migrant movement from poorer parts of the world to the wealthier, seeking service work or small-scale trade.

These movements have become increasingly climactically indexed: as weather patterns produce more violent effects, everyone in their wake is made to march, if often temporarily. The wealthier of course are able more readily to return and rebuild, to leave behind heightened securitization of property as they flee and to use the moment to purge the intermittently abandoned place of supposedly undesirable elements (post-Katrina New Orleans augured the near-future in this regard). And yet, given the intricacies of naturalcultural entanglements, as well as the suddenness of cataclysmic eruptions, predictability and control are tenuous at best.

The upshot is that we have gone from stable social conditions to the more and more vulnerable. Irruptive events have become more frequent and spectacular. The populations effected are now more numerous and often more densely concentrated in urban areas. Social infrastructures are less and less able to cope. The flows of people – prompted by wars, climatic and terrestrial events, as well as by political unsettlements and poverty – are more immediate, intense and seemingly incessant. The Sea's role in all of this is multiple: cause or multiplier, medium of movement or formidable barrier to it, beckoning horizon or daunting dampener to the sea of dreams.

In turn, the vulnerability of the conditions places those with less means predictably at greater risk of permanent loss than those with means. It likely means that the vulnerable move more readily, seeking opportunity wherever it might eventuate. Where the wealthier and better connected might be able to fly out on an as-needed basis, the more impoverished often see the Sea less as overriding disvalue in the calculus of (im)possibility than as just another challenge in the reach for a tolerable life.

The global economy of labour-on-demand is new, although less in conception than in its now ubiquity, scale and circulation. After all, it marries its post-abolition antecedents in conception to the proliferation of modernizing migrant labour regimes. Unlike these earlier regimes, though, they are now denuded of any modicum of social support systems such as health care 'benefits' that drive up the costs. Today, migrant workers from the Philippines, Sri Lanka or Romania show up in the Middle East and Israel. But domestic and factory labour from Indonesia can just as readily be found in significant numbers in Hong Kong, leaving the likes of Bali in the wake of devastating sea flooding in search of a (barely) living wage. Their lives of course change. Their networks of association are reshaped, their experience not quite like home, as constraints on their lives accumulate (one day a week to themselves). They are faced also by freedoms not anticipated, unhindered by immediate family expectation or religious imposition.

Wealthier states and their populations tend to produce a disproportionate amount of the world's waste and polluting agents. Americans make up 5–6% of the world's population but produce fully 40% of global waste and nearly as much in pollution. The wealthier consume more and therefore also discard more: replaceable culture is at once the culture of the discard (for one example among many, consider the vast continent of discarded plastics floating across broad swaths of the Pacific). If one can afford it, why fix when the new, the next best or bigger, faster or design-appealing thing is so much sexier and priced for affordability and replaceability. In low-end stores in disprivileged parts of town, cheap plastic shopping bags are readily discarded because they are not useable more than once and there are less likely to be convenient garbage or recycle bins close to hand. The bags float about streets, as likely to end up against a wind-blown fence as in the garbage disposal, in the ocean as on the beach.

The Sea has long been the world's toilet, its garbage dump. Only now the polluting materials are even more toxic and perilous: in addition to plastics, seeping oil as well as nuclear waste and leakage. Sea life is increasingly under duress (Donovan 2011). The Sea stands as the barometer of the planet's slow suffocation.

This index of asphyxiation embeds the logic of spiralling unsustainability. It wasn't so long ago that resource reproduction outstripped resource depletion: we were renewing resources faster than using them up or destroying them. Then a half-century or so ago, resource depletion started outstripping, and increasingly so, resource renewal. Today, however, there has been another dramatic turn, a qualitative rather than quantitative development in resource management. No longer is it 'merely' the case that depletion is out-stripping reproduction. Rather, the natural infrastructure and conditions that make resource reproduction even possible are now being undermined. It's not just that the rate of reproducibility is dangerously debilitating. It is now that the conditions of possibility for reproducibility themselves are being under-mined. And those eroding conditions of possibility further exacerbate exist-ing climatological conditions in ways destined to heighten the challenges.

Fifty years ago, the Kalahari Desert was expanding by a couple of inches a year. This, like all major global deserts, has accelerated. Currently 8% of Africa's land mass is desert, and some projections have this doubling over time, given deforestation, aridization and shrinking rainfall in the region. There is an analogous – perhaps commensurate – condition with the world's water bodies. Their 'revenge' is to expand the zones and scapes of destructive impact, to erode coastlines, to drown islands, but to do so seemingly without agency.

The Sea, supposedly, has no subjectivity (the seemingly perfect 'post-modern' condition). Left to its own devices – its own 'natural' forces and patterns, flows and energies, it would be more or less predictable. Its pre-dictabilities, however, are the outcome of human technological intervention, at once undermining the very predictability it was supposed to enable. The Seas' expansions, elasticities, assertions and exertions, so to speak – their periodic calmness, turbulence, anger, pacificity, wildness and so on – are pure effects of the combination of natural and human forces, of naturaliz-ing human forces and desubjectified natural ones. It is, as Donna Haraway might say, both effect of and causal loop in the forces of natureculture. In the absence of agency, responsibility recedes, if not evaporates. And given the profound changes afoot, interlockingly and indiscernibly natural and cultural (naturalcultural/culturalnatural), we no doubt are coming to imagine the Sea and ourselves in relationally different terms.

James Joyce, thinking of something else, writes in *Ulysses* (1922) of the 'snotgreen' and 'scrotumtightening sea', striking characterizations in the wake of what we are experiencing today. To bring the effects gobsmack-ingly home, the first interdisciplinary International Report on the State of the Ocean (IPSO) (2013) recently noted that if we take together global warming, pollution, acidification, overfishing alongside hypoxia and anoxia (low and no oxygen), ocean degeneration is occurring much more quickly than any previous prediction: massive and accelerating extinctions (all coral could be gone by 2050), oceanic dead zones (the Gulf of Mexico dead zone will be the largest it has ever been due to the Mississippi run off bringing massive amounts of fertilizer into a fragile ecosystem) and so on (Donovan 2011).

As the Mississippi River flowing across a couple of thousand miles out into the Gulf of Mexico makes evident, those producing sea pollution are mostly at a remove from the Sea: the sources of pollution are distant from their visible effects. It is telling, in this context, that there are so few hit pop songs about the Sea. Just as drones make war impersonal and so irresistible because failing to witness their effects directly, face-to-face, so pollution at a remove fails to be seen as consequential: if I can't see it, it must not exist (the return of Moorean common sense, a century on). This is the sort of reductive empiricism in denial that constitutes the 'logic' of global warming/climate change deniers like James Inhofe, US Senator from Oklahoma, and other politicians blind to the impacts of their own legislative (in)action.

So, we all live *by* the Sea, even those who do not in any immediate sense. We are all impacted by the Seas' climatological effects, their shifting 'moods', increasingly angry as they heat up. Too few know this, living at the seaside or afar. (How many living at the Sea do more in and with the Sea than look at its view and eat its source of mercurized protein?)

When we ask in the banalities of our daily greetings about the weather, we are in fact also asking about the state of the Sea. And, I have been suggesting, we are also registering concern about what the sea may be hiding, its secrets and secreting, the scavengers not just within but skating across, the cultural currencies out to pollute the pristine nature of our own. The ruins of nature – in this case, the Sea, about which Beckett's *Endgame* (1957/2009) is so harrowing – remain hidden in plain sight. Neo-liberally, we have to be bribed to attend to them, as Hamm must bribe Nagg to listen to his tale, to think there is something in it for ourselves. The trouble is that the instrumentalizing and self-interested bribes of capital and its supporting forces to remain inattentive and silent far outweigh those to attend and act or refrain from acting appropriately. This is as much the case about migration as about the devastating of our deeply networked environments.

Seasickness is a condition of the Sea, of our larger planetary ecology, just as it is of those at some point who are migrating by its means. But increasingly seasickness has become more generally experienced, a virus, perhaps one attacking the immune system. It is as applicable inland, on the plains and high ground, as at the coast, desert and mountainside as waterside and sea level, as Kim Stanley Robinson (2000) intimates. Increasingly, we are finding ourselves fleeing to high ground to escape high seas. We are abandoning static location for migrating process, constraints of the local for the affordances of the global, containers for networks. And in doing so we take the worlds we have fashioned and their environmental ecologies with us.

There is a curious oversight in all of this. We tend to think of migration in terms of sending sites and their immediately visible causes along with the receiving destination and its immediately obvious impacts. The presumptions of plurality to singularity, outsider heterogeneity to the homogeneity of hosting singularity are immediately evident here. But what of the in-between, the materialities of getting from there to here, or here to there? And of the agency, effect, and affect of that in-betweenness on the transitional life, on the life of transition itself? That transitional life has become increasingly the mark of the life of work, of seeking work, procuring possibility, of life itself at all now.

The prevailing disposition towards the Sea, then, critical and otherwise, as Steinberg (2001) notes, is instrumental: it is overwhelmingly predicated upon the presumption of the Sea as a set of resources. Dominant views tend to calculate how to control these resources. Critical views tend to worry about resource distribution or redistribution, and perhaps more recently about their sustainability. The latter, after all, is both logical and political implication of the worry about (re)distribution. Theoretical views in the register with which humanists and interpretive social scientists are concerned tend to consider the Sea as surface across which social, political and legal determinations (more often than not historically understood) are played out: histories of Middle Passage and wars of control, colonial and postcolonial narratives, extensions of sovereignty through law and force and so on.

How then to think about the implications of all this for racial migrations, which might be to say migrations as such? Consider Charles Olson's (1947/1998) claim in his classic book about Moby Dick, that there are 'three seas': the Atlantic, the Mediterranean and 'now' the Pacific. In this parochial, extended-Euro provincialism, there is embedded here obviously the invisibilizing of the Indian Ocean. We find reproduced once more the refusal of the East, the occlusion even of 'the Orient', and so a profound de- if not disorientation (cf. Gunder Frank 1998).

This begins to suggest that Seas and oceans have unique 'characters'. These characters are likewise shaped by the landscapes at their edges as they lap on and over land. The 'character' is a function of how it is taken to 'behave', its projected agency, but also as a reflection of the land masses and the perceived nature of their populations it connects, between which it mediates. The one is a presumed mirror of the other. The presumptuous otherness of the population is a function for and implication of its sea-'source'.

The Indian Ocean is projected as warm but prone to violent eruptions, interventions, events. The Pacific is supposedly a reflection of its name, 'majestic', inviting recreationality, but also conjuring the opacity and inscrutability of its 'rimming' land bases (South Asian and the Western Americas). The Atlantic, cold, wild and dangerous, is bounded by the Global North, Eastern Latin America, the Caribbean, West Africa and North America; hence one might say also 'the Black Atlantic'. The Atlantic and Indian meet at Africa's most southern point, just as the Atlantic and Pacific meet at Latin America's. These are points of coastal wildness and wilderness both, the metaphor for mixture, for mongrelization, the Atlantic perhaps polluting the character of its pairings (the aesthetic analogy may be Casta paintings). The Indian and Pacific have no landed meeting *point*, blending rather indistinguishably into each other, reflecting their relative porousness, colonially and postcolonially.

The Black Atlantic is often thought the alter-condition of the Atlantic, its constitutive outside. And this is often how it is addressed, taken up almost invariably as the Atlantic's underside. But the point could be pushed that the Atlantic *is* constitutively the Black Atlantic, the Black Atlantic nothing less than the Atlantic as such. As such, Atlantic Europe in fact marks a margin of the Atlantic, its provincialized and by extension its provincializing determinant, not its centre, not its crown, destination rather than emanating point, receptacle rather than fountain. Weatherwise, Europe – continental and islandic – is the dumping ground of the Atlantic's wrath, its piss pot.

To Europe, by analogous extension, migrants go to imbibe – take in – and relieve themselves, to replenish, ablute and take leave. Some get stuck, falsely lured; some take anchor, lured by the new life; some return to homeland, refusing the lure beyond the instrumental possibilities for a better life at home (Nakache and Toledano 2014); and some simply turn into the circulating global migrant disanchored from all constraining moorings, shedding homeland of any and all kind. The new cosmopolitical raced subject.

The Sea, it could be said, is variously source of labour, life and the recreational. It is not that most now experience the Sea only though the commodities brought in the hulls of ships, as Taussig (2000) puts it, but more mediatedly through cultural expressions (television series like Pamela Anderson's *Baywatch*, *Hawaii Five-O*, HBO's *Boardwalk Empire*, films such as *Titanic*, video games, news reports about tsunamis and terrorist actions, etc.). The Sea itself has become commodified in a wide variety of ways. It is, as a consequence, imaginatively enlarged through its cultural enablement and prostheses while incorporating the prevailing semantic stereotypes. In contrast to these examples, in thinking about the sea-ness of the Sea (following Sarah Nuttall's exhortation to think about the thingness of the thing, and not just its cultural expressiveness or affect), consider *The Perfect Storm* (Peterson 2000) and much more interestingly Pieter Schoendorffer's *Le Crabe Tambour* ('The Drummer Crab', 1977), based on his novel a year earlier. This suggests that the life of the Sea and life at sea (in both senses) are co-constitutive. The sea-ness of the Sea comes to life, the lead character itself, as much agent as acted upon.

Seas have long been the mediums/media of racial relationality. Examples include the passage to European 'discovery', wars of colonization followed by settler colonial histories, migrations and counter-migrations. Oceans and the major seas at once undercut any isolating imperative of whiteness/Europeanness (or more recently of attempts at Euro-self-fortressing). At the same time, they mirrored and indeed reinforced conditions of mastery and slavery, domination and subjugation, repression and resistance. Historically, transport across the Sea to a new beginning, or an interlude in life, an adventure or familial and economic necessity has offered a period of reflective transition. Far more readily than air transport or travel by foot, if for differing reasons, it offered the chance to contemplate the left behind and expectations, to shed part of what one may be fleeing from while looking to a future not yet cast in stone, to lose and acquire raciality. Michael Ondaatje's *The Cat's Table* (2011) captures something of this metamorphosis.

Today, that sense of temporal transporting is less readily available. The crossings tend to be more fraught: in smaller, older vessels sardine packed, often open to the elements, barely above the waterline, creaking across straits and sea crossings – North Africa to Southern Europe, Caribbean or Central America to the United States, Indonesia to more or less mainland Asia and so on. Or, risking life alternatively, packed into cargo containers, reduced at least momentarily to commodities. The wealthier (al)luring destinations tend to be those elevated on the racial scale, respecting the lives only or largely of their racial and/or class equals. The migrants, from sites historically identified as racially challenged, are extended raciality by their hosts, fitting them into existing racial schema, perhaps modestly revised consistent with contemporary racial expectation and conceptualization in the metropole (consider as but one example Indians or Malaysians in Singapore).

In any case, recent changes in Australian law signal a new racially indexed development. Even though international norms and law recognize that those arriving by boat are more likely to be genuine refugees from repression in contrast to more self-serving air travellers, Australian law now determines *how* one arrives at the border is more important than *where* one arrives, one's port of call. Boat arrivals are shorn of rights air travellers are taken to have. This may have to do with the funnelling effect of air travel arrivals mentioned earlier. By contrast, pirate boats bearing migrants and especially refugees are generally less visible to local metropolitan populations. Race is indexed in the mode of travel itself, while foregoing the need for explicit racial reference now regarded as unbecoming to governmental practice. The Australian migration law offshores migrants arriving by boat to island incarceration (Jones 2013). Migrants have become today's infectious threat, confined to the current-day version of the leper colony. Race, in short, evaporates from explicit postracial referentiality (Goldberg 2015).

Postraciality is the prevailing conception regarding race in the metropole today (Goldberg 2015). I end accordingly by asking what relation exists, if any, between migrancy and postraciality. The 'post' in 'the postracial' is to the racial as the 'post' in 'the postcolonial' is to the colonial. Each conjures different or renewed ways of racial articulation and coloniality respectively ordering and fashioning the global. They embed how raciality and coloniality today are lived and lived out. Given this, postraciality – like postcoloniality – makes for the disappearance of the racial by removing its language of referentiality. The racial does not so much disappear as it gets displaced to less legible sites of social expression, denuded of explicit racial annunciation. Migrants, it might be said, lose their explicit racial characterization en route, only to be silently re-racially configured as they come ashore as new arrivals, as refugees, strangers, new welfare recipients or (potential) terrorists.

Regions more vulnerable to coastal flooding or storm surges, to more violent weather events and higher seas, to mudslides and especially to political ignoring in their aftermath are those that tend overwhelmingly to be inhabited by the traditionally conceived racial poor. They are far less well prepared for environmental disasters as a result of climatological events, more likely to be permanently displaced, and as a consequence to be overlooked or criminalized.

In disappearing, race reappears under other, less recognizable terms of reference. Migration is thought to have no racial dimension today because the terms of recognition, of identification, of reference themselves have been made to disappear. But as the terms of characterization fade to the point of transparency, of being 'seen through', and the phenomena become unrecognizable in those terms, if not in themselves as such, resort to the public sphere becomes increasingly insistent and persistent. In the face of their traditional invisibility and illegibility, large-scale demonstrations in central public areas of major cities, on social media, and so forth become more assertive. They break out perhaps where least expected. Their raciality becomes enigmatically self-evident in its non-referentiality.

Raciality has long been known for its capacity to morph, to assume terms other than the predictable and readily recognizable ones. Where migrations are thought to embody no racial dimension, let alone definition, the terms of the racial reappear. They become insistent and persistent even while shed of their explicit referentiality. Where fear eating the soul twenty-five years ago was Moroccan migrant worker Ali's (Fassbinder 1974), today it is Alan's, Alain's, Alfonse's, Aleks's, Alexi's. That shift, not least, is linked to the changing face and fact, function and presumptuous familiarity of migration, it's now silently racial but not silenced sense of threat.

The fear about the racially characterized migrant is at once the fear of a planet perceived to be climatologically out of control; and the fear of a planet climatologically run amok is the fear of racial invasion. *Melancholia* (as Lars von Trier, 2011, suggests) is nostalgia for this lost control, a recall for a world resettled racially and predictable climatologically. As with melancholia more generally, such nostalgia is for an object in both instances permanently and interactively lost and at a loss. And in the case of climatologically prompted migrations, alas, the unsettled at both initiating and landing sites are unlikely to be left (or found) to rest in peace.

REFERENCES

Beckett, S'amuel. 1957/2009. *Endgame: A Play in One Act*. London: Faber and Faber.

Donovan, Travis. 2011. "State of the Ocean: 'Shocking' Report Warns of Mass Extinction from Current Rate of Marine Distress". *Huffington Post*, June 20. http://www.huffingtonpost.com/2011/06/20/ipso-2011-ocean-report-mass-extinction_n_880656.html.

Douglas, Mary. 1966. *Purity and Danger: An Analysis of the Concepts of Pollution and Taboo*. London: Routledge and Kegan Paul.

Fassbinder, Rainer. 1974. "Ali: Fear Eats the Soul".

Frank, Andre Gunder. 1998. *ReOrient: Global Economy in the Asian Age*. Berkeley, California: University of California Press.

Ghosh, Amitav The Ibis Trilogy. 2008–2015. New York: Farrar, Strauss and Giroux.

Goldberg, David Theo. 2002. *The Racial State*. Malden, Massachusetts: Basil Blackwell.

———. 2015. *Are We All Postracial Yet?* Malden, Massachusetts: Polity Press.

Haraway, Donna. 2008. *When Species Meet*. Minneapolis, Minnesota: University of Minnesota Press.

Hicks, Jonathan P. 2013. "Report: Blacks are Disproportionately Connected by Natural Disasters". *BET*, May 24. http://www.bet.com/news/national/2013/05/24/african-americans-are-disproportionately-affected-by-disasters.html.

Helmreich, Stefan. 2009. *Alien Ocean: Anthropological Voyages in Microbial Seas*. Berkeley, California: University of California Press.

International Report on the State of the Ocean (IPSO). 1913. *Marine Pollution Bulletin*. http://www.stateoftheocean.org/science/state-of-the-ocean-report/.

Jones, Michael. 2013. "What Does 'excising the mainland from the migration zone' Mean?" http://migrantlaw.blogspot.com.au/2013/05/what-does-excising-mainland-from.html.

Joyce, James. 1922. *Ulysses*. Paris: Sylvia Beach.

Latour, Bruno. 1993. *We Have Never Been Modern*. Cambridge, Massachusetts: Harvard University Press.

Nakache, Olivier and Toledano, Eric. 2014. "Samba".

Nixon, Rob. 2013. *Slow Violence and the Environmentalism of the Poor*. Cambridge, Massachusetts: Harvard University Press.

Olson, Charles. 1947/1998. *Call Me Ishmael*. Baltimore: Johns Hopkins University Press.

Ondaatje, Michael. 2011. *The Cat's Table*. New York: Knopf.

Peterson, Wolfgang. 2000. "The Perfect Storm".

Robinson, Kim Stanley. 2002. *The Years of Rice and Salt*. New York: Bantam Books.

Steinberg, Philip. 2001. *The Social Construction of the Ocean*. Cambridge: Cambridge University Press.

Taussig, Michael. 2000. "The Beach (A Fantasy)". *Critical Inquiry* (Winter): 248–278.

Valayden, Chandiren. 2013. *Outbreak Racism: The Embrace of Risk after Structural Racism*. Dissertation. University of California Irvine.

Von Trier, Lars. 2011. "Melancholia".

Chapter 7

Transcendental Migration

Taking Refuge from Climate Change

Claire Colebrook

The November 13, 2015, terrorist attacks in Paris generated, perhaps predictably, intensely xenophobic responses from US Republican Party candidates for the 2016 presidential nomination. When challenged Donald Trump did not offer an answer as to how a database for Muslims would differ from the monitoring of Jews in Nazi Germany; Ben Carson defended screening procedures by drawing an analogy between refugees threatening the border and a rabid dog threatening one's children.[1] One might want to respond to such alarmist scare-monger tactics by pointing out that those seeking refuge are fleeing *from* terrorism and ought not to be targeted and demonized. The more considered move, and the one I will pursue here, would be to think deconstructively. If one is really to be hospitable and to consider a world in which one would offer genuine refuge, then such openness and promise would necessarily require accepting risk and threat. If I only accept those who offer no threat whatsoever to my way of life, and if I define hospitality and the offering of refuge as something that is completely humanitarian and *not* a challenge to my way of life, then I am not really opening my borders, my self or my future at all. In this respect Barack Obama's response that the refusal of Syrian refugees was 'not American' sustains the notion of a homeland that may open itself to unfortunate others and yet all the while (ideally) remain the same.

SPECIES REFUGE

In this chapter I want to undertake three manoeuvres. First, there has been much debate about the legitimacy of the category of climate refugees: Is this really a distinct category, or are we once again blaming broad, inhuman and climactic factors to cover over the brutal political forces that displace individuals (Lister 2014)? Here, rather than argue for the inclusion of climate refugees within the category of the modern refugee (whose position of appealing for refuge in a nation other than that of his citizenship already seems to require modern geopolitical conditions), I want to deconstruct the concept of the refugee. What appears to be parasitic and accidental – the displacement of persons who then have to seek refuge elsewhere – is the condition for what appears to be proper. Rather than seeing climate change refugees as an unprecedented disturbance and sign of how 'we' have destroyed nature, it would be more accurate to see the production of 'nature' and 'climate' *and* the epoch of stability as violent interruptions of a life that is migratory and in constant search of refuge. What called itself 'humanity' was formed by way of a suspension of migration and the attainment of sovereign stability for some living beings, eventually producing 'the refugee' as its necessary counterpart.

When, today, we see both popular culture and high theory placing all of humanity in the condition of refugees it might seem that we have reached an unprecedented point of despair. A series of recent films (such as *Interstellar* [2014]) has presented the human species as a whole in the condition of seeking refuge, while Giorgio Agamben (2000) has argued that 'we' are all now potentially bare life – exposed and vulnerable without the bordered protection of the polity. Such a way of conceiving the present, as a loss of home, is part of a broader rhetoric of sustainability that grants a prima facie value to holding on to an epoch of stability and that has already embarked upon preliminary mourning where the 'end of the world' is really the end of the world of nations and sovereignty.

Climate change, and being a climate change refugee, would seem to render questions of hope and futurity imperative: one seeks refuge not just because one is fleeing a past, but because one is searching for a home. Whether or not the earth will be able to provide an ongoing home seems to be a question – if not *the* question – of the future. If, however, one turns hope to the past, and considers refuge and migration to be the conditions *from which* hope and home emerge, one would generate the following thought. Climate change and migration are the way of the world, the very conditions of life. In this respect the dominant figure of entwined hope and refuge are symptoms of a period of civilized barbarism that produced national borders and stability for some (very few) living beings. The production of nature as a stable and unchanging home *and* the generation of life as oriented towards hope (an always better and more fruitful future) are the necessary conditions for what has come to be known as the Anthropocene. The world as we know it – a world that is 'our' stable home – was progressively constituted by way of (first) migration, and then stabilization (always at the expense of some other mobile mode of life). I would suggest that we think about hope, *not* as the future attainment of a stable home for all but as a relation to the past that would not reduce all that has taken place as nothing more than the precondition for what has become 'our' futurity (Allen 2016). What other worlds might have been?

As climate change becomes increasingly undeniable, volatile and intractable, dreams of finding a home elsewhere abound, and are coupled with an anticipatory mourning of the humanity and home of the present. Humanity as a whole (insofar as there is such a unity) has begun to imagine various forms of species migration and refuge, from colonization of other planets (in *Elysium* [2013], *Interstellar* [2014]) to being colonized by others seeking refuge from their depleted worlds (*Colony* [2016-], *Oblivion* [2013]), and has done so in the manner of preliminary mourning. One interesting variant of this imaginary that couples future displacement (or being reduced to the status of refugees in our own world) with anticipated mourning is *Mad Max: Fury Road* [2015]. In this narrative it is not techno-science or straightforward humanist inclusiveness that guarantees that there will be a future that is just like 'our' present; it is a romanticized pseudo-feminist Indigenous ecological attunement. And yet, what is mourned in *Mad Max* is the world of the present – the world of hyper-consumption, resource abundance, available fossil fuels and an owned and stabilized homeland. In a sleight of hand the film turns to a pseudo-feminist and pseudo-indigenous culture, *not* to contemplate a truly different counter-humanist counter-factual world that might not have fetishized nation and homeland, but to provide hope for 'our' apparently doomed present. These supposed post-apocalyptic or 'end of world' narratives are ultimately about the end of 'our' world of progress, fruition, hyper-consumption, stability and futurity. More specifically, a 'we' is constituted by a supposed new condition of a species united by the seeking of refuge. The means of attaining this refuge (especially in *Mad Max*) are given by the very forms of living (such as indigenous lifestyles) that were obliterated in order to achieve the 'humanity' that is now facing its end.

MIGRATING LIFE

Life, as such, *is* displacement in the face of one's milieu becoming hostile; the origins of organic life from single-celled organisms can be traced to the movement towards metabolism of oxygen. It is not that there are individuals, with a proper place and intentionality, who embark upon movement. Rather, it is from movement and migration that relative stabilities are formed – *not* in a stabilization of 'ownness' but in a relation among forces, such as the first single-celled organisms relying on light and oxygen for outside energy. It is movement from insufficient to energizing milieus that then allows for the boundedness or relative stability of life forms. Human life is an intensification of a process that might be referred to as transcendental climate refuge: if a milieu were to satisfy the energy demands of a body completely, then there would be no need for increasingly complex systems to emerge. One might think of 'civilization', or the development of polities that colonize and displace others, as a consequence of finding one's own milieu to be insufficient at the level of energy, with this displacement then involving the displacement and harnessing of energy from elsewhere. What appears as the proper condition from which the modern refugee has fallen away – citizenship, nation, sovereignty – is actually an intensification (and then annihilation) of a broader horizon of displacement and migration. The stable polity and nation state generate a milieu where the general conditions of transit, transposition and migration become parasitic and secondary. In short, imperialism and colonization transform a world of movement to a world of fixity, where the condition of being exiled, stateless and in need of refuge becomes possible. There can be proper sovereign nations, blessed with the conditions of justice and rights *only after borders have been secured, or relatively closed*; not only is such enclosure a contraction from a milieu of ongoing migration and displacement, one might say that a history of colonization, appropriation and enslavement allowed certain nations the luxury of declaring themselves to be independent republics of rights and freedoms. After a history of colonizing, enslaving and appropriating energy from elsewhere, such nations could *then* declare themselves to be universally human and open themselves to only the very deserving few who might be genuine refugees (rather than supposedly opportunistic migrants). In short, the sovereign nation is the privileged extraction from a condition of migration and refuge that – broadly speaking – enabled a stable climate and benevolent nature at the expense of others who had to contend with volatility.

One might think of the history of colonization that embarked on intensive nature-stabilizing agriculture by enslaving others, and then by taking over more and more territory to fuel the demands of the host nation, as an exceptional hiatus in a history of the world that has always been one of climate change, migration and refuge. (Dumping and exporting waste are the twenty-first century's continuation of this practice that achieves pristine stability by way of displaced unsustainability.) The creation of certain clean and stable spots of nature, and the blessed security of nations, require a halting of general patterns of flux and migration, and do so by generating dead zones elsewhere.

To deconstruct an opposition is not to favour one term over another – this is how Deleuze and Guattari's nomadology (1987) was misread, as a naïve celebration of what ought to be considered a position of vulnerability. Just as 'the schizo' becomes a sad and parasitic form in a milieu that produced the stable bourgeois individual, so nomadism becomes a desperately pitiable condition in a world that makes political personhood the only mode of a livable life. Taking a broader historical and inhuman timeline would allow the fetishized attachment to 'man' and his accompanying 'world' to be seen as contingent events in a broader life of movement. Deconstruction would locate the seemingly parasitic effect in the supposed origin: nomadism is the condition for what would subsequently become nationhood. Furthermore, the condition of transcendental migration does not go away with the birth of nations. To take just two examples: US imperialism – this land that is our land and your land, and that would become the refuge for so many – achieved its grandeur by way of slavery (capturing and halting the movement of others). The United States' ongoing greatness, if there is such a thing, still relies on a large pool of illegal immigrant labour, zones where others are expelled or destroyed (Guantanamo, extraordinary renditions), and stringent border controls. The apparent organic body politic of the United States achieves its unity only by displacing and drawing energy from migratory and dispersed others; it would not be controversial to note that the security measures that ostensibly operate to achieve safety for the United States have been crucial in controlling the homeland. In a slightly different manner, and to look beyond the United States, Australia not only displaces those who seek refuge outside the secure borders that were achieved at the expense of those self-same others; it also transforms its indigenous population into a seeker of refuge, captured by discourses of sovereignty, nationhood, rights, property and citizenship.

Put more concretely: rather than see nations as blessed spaces that accept refugees, one should see the nation as the outcome of a violent expulsion of the migratory movements that are its original *and* ongoing condition. The condition of life *is* migration and refuge, the searching out of hospitable conditions after metabolic processes exhaust or transform milieus. That process of ongoing migration can be halted only with an odd or exceptional distribution of stasis: the stable first world of 'nature' increasingly requires an inert pool of labour, along with energy and waste disposal elsewhere. Global nomadism gives way to stable flourishing states and dead zones (of labour, waste disposal and energy extraction, all of which generate a century of refugees). If, today, we are beginning to imagine all of humanity as being in the condition of seeking refuge because of an increasingly volatile planet, it might be better to think of this not so much as a loss of what we are properly entitled to, but rather as the resurgence of an ongoing displacement and migration that had been warded off by modern 'man' (but always at the expense of others). I would like to pause here to consider an increasingly common imagined scene: the planet has become inhospitable and 'we' have sought refuge elsewhere (*Elysium, Interstellar*) or somewhere else has suffered depletion and is now colonizing us (*Colony, Oblivion*). If we can imagine an entire species suffering from refugee status, this is perhaps an indication of some awareness of the fragility of all life and its necessary migratory condition, with affluent modern humans now exposed to a volatility that had been managed and exported to other lives. The 'species as climate refugee' figure is also, however, an intensification of the ongoing sense of species privilege. There is a presupposed 'we' of species privilege, the point of view that views and manages (but never seeks) refuge. The 'humanity' that is now (supposedly) newly exposed to vulnerability and a loss of world is a 'humanity' that regards itself as always necessarily having its own world, a world that it will regain, sustain or re-establish elsewhere.

Even if – as the claims for the Anthropocene seem to demand – the only path to survival is to abandon all traditionally political modes and shift to the register of the earth as a living system, with geoengineering being our only realistic or actual path forward, should 'we' assume that the path forward (of sustaining the world as it actually is) is an incontestable good? Even if other modes of humanity – the value of which are only discernible now with the triumph and decay of the Anthropocene – are no longer possible, are such other humanities not yet worthy at the level of potentiality? The Anthropocene might be the occasion for seemingly fruitless counter-factuals: *if* other histories had unfolded, 'we' might not be in this mess, and there might not have been an inescapably global 'we'. Thinking about such counter-factual statements now might not save us, but is 'our' survival the only possible value for the future?

THE COUNTER-ANTHROPOCENE

In order to think this counter-history, I want to hold on to the deconstruction of the relation between sovereign nation and refugee. As I have already suggested, migration is not a chance occurrence within history, but *is* history. The specific historical trajectory that generated the Anthropocene might be considered exceptional in its halting of migration by way of the ongoing creation of city-states, industry and empires, allowing some populations to experience nationhood while relying on the energy of other populations (of humans and non-humans) to be harnessed. To think about a counter-history would be to imagine migration *not* as the unfortunate exception in an otherwise stable world of nations, but to ask the question: What if there were no nation? I would suggest that the conditions 'we' are experiencing and imagining now – both climate refugees within the current system of globalism, and the possibility of humans as a whole becoming climate refugees – should prompt the thought *not* of how 'we' will migrate elsewhere in order to survive, but how we might think migration such that there is no 'we', no place like home. Rather than say that the Anthropocene imposes the global human imperative upon 'us', such that we have to think at species level, by either thinking about migrating elsewhere or acting as one species for the sake of one common future, we might think migration and refuge differently. Instead of scaling up to the level of humans as a species and adopting global, planetary and even geological timelines, one might scale down to think about multiple, dispersed populations and movements of migration that do not allow for the borders of nations, the forced migration that generates the seeking of refuge, and the insistence on stability, sustainability and survival (which is always a survival at the expense of migration and displacement elsewhere).

One might object: perhaps there was a time when non-Western modes of dwelling offered another path for humanity, but those days are over and now the only refuge open to us seems to be to accept the scale of the Anthropocene and to acknowledge that we are now looking at the earth as having shifted in terms of its equilibrium as a living system. It may be true that, *if* we want humanity to survive as it is, then our only option is geoengineering – such is the scale of the problem. Alternatively, one might argue that climate change and the Anthropocene are opportunities for 'us' to achieve the global human justice that 'we' deserve. Both of these global acceptances of 'a' new human condition allow the 'we' of stable humanity to survive, even though that same humanity that talks about its sustainability was established in a mode of existence that was never sustainable and that erased other modes of life. Both Klein's socialist utopia that sees the climate winning out over capitalism, or the geoengineering dream of capitalism conquering what was produced as climate presuppose humanity as a whole, and assert the supposedly proper and overriding scale of the globe. Or, to use Bruno Latour's succinct opposition: one would act for the globe against globalism (his choice) *or* globalism against the globe. There is another possibility.

What I want to suggest in what follows is that we think beyond the possible and the actual towards the virtual: we do not need to be poised between the Hobson's choice of believing either in a promised land where humanity continues in a better and more just form, or a catastrophe so great that only geoengineering (or planetary migration) will save us. Perhaps lost and impossible forms of humanity still have something to say to us. If one were to contemplate the transcendental migration of life – the migration that *is life* from which the human emerges, and from which the nation is generated as a fleeting and parasitic stability – one would not be abandoning 'the human' in a moment of resigned mourning, but would be allowing the thought that what is known as the human depends upon a certain scale of thinking and that other scales are not only possible but are imposing themselves upon life and thinking in ways that may not be catastrophic.

In 1972, in response to a refusal by the Australian government to grant Indigenous Australians land rights – awarding mining rights instead to a corporation – Australian Aborigines erected a tent embassy outside the

Australian house of parliament (Foley et al. 2013). By constructing an embassy the Aboriginal peoples performatively declared themselves to be aliens in their own land, but also implicitly took part in discourses of sovereignty and nationhood. They were, therefore, in the very gesture of declaring themselves aliens in their own land *also* becoming discursive hostages. By occupying an embassy Indigenous Australians deployed the very concepts of nation, sovereignty, ownership, land rights and legitimate usage that were the hallmarks of the very legal system that had allowed Australia to be declared *terra nullius*.

In 1971, in the case of *Milirrpum v Nabalco Pty Ltd*, the Supreme Court of the Northern Territory deemed the land in question to have *not* been occupied at the time of invasion because it was not being used in a manner deemed to be legitimately productive. At this point in history one can see already a war between a conception of migration between and among nations – where sovereign peoples can take over land that is supposedly bereft of sovereignty – and another concept of migration where it is movement that defines a people, and where the land that is traversed *is itself defined by movement* rather than being property to be owned. I do not have time here to go into Indigenous Australian culture, or the violently exceptional nature of modern concepts of nationhood. I will mention briefly that Indigenous Australians hearken from a tradition of thought that does not place a strict distinction between human and non-human persons, and have a relation to land that is defined by a history of movement and change. Land is not property to be owned and persons are not defined by nation but by groupings across a space of mobile and dynamic relations. One might contrast imperialism and state forms (that have drawn a halt to movement and that immobilize and 'striate' space) with Indigenous forms that encounter space and persons in an ongoing 'war'. I am not suggesting that contemporary Aboriginal Australians are, or ought to be, still defined by traditional indigenous thought. I am not implying that Indigenous Australian thought has somehow remained stable and pristine while a history of colonialism has attacked its territories. Nor would I want to encourage a sense of nostalgia where there was a golden pre-imperialist age of movement and migration that was rendered inert and lifeless by state forms. What I do want to do, as I mentioned earlier, is deconstruct the relations among the concepts of climate, change, migration and refuge. Instead of being attached to the eighteenth-century image of a stable nature, with seasons in accord with the European cultural calendar, and *then* seeing this 'nature' destroyed by an unfortunately overproductive capitalism, it would be better to see unchanging climate as *produced* by capitalism's demands for production and consumption. There is no such thing as climate that is not the effect of practices of stabilization; the climate change that was once intrinsic to thought – in a world experienced as volatile, improper and dynamic – is now seen as an unfortunate effect of hyper-consumption rather than that which was temporarily displaced in the history of empire. Second, rather than see migration and refuge as unfortunate events that befall the proper condition of citizens of nations, it would be better to see the liberal subject of global humanism as a temporary and unsustainable effect of a fetish for stability that has always required the brutal capture of other bodies (human and non-human).

THE ABORIGINAL TENT EMBASSY: 1972

By assembling as an embassy and occupying land in front of the Australian House of Parliament, the Aboriginal people were forced to seek refuge, having been deprived of their homeland, while also having nowhere else to flee. What would it mean to look back on this moment, now, when we might see the path of another Australia, or when we might now feel more empathy for an entire people who have not only been physically displaced but whose space has become hostile?

By the time Indigenous Australians established a tent embassy in response to a refusal of land rights, anthropogenic climate change had already intensified the new unity of the human species, which was reinforced or mirrored by geopolitical conditions. The world of migration and peoples had long since given way to a world of immigration, refugees and the fiction of humanity as a whole. One might say that in order to be a refugee or in order to seek the protections and representation an embassy might afford, certain theoretical assumptions must be in play, most notably those of personhood, sovereignty and nation. These concepts, which in 1972 would appear to be inescapable, are now reaching their limit. The tent embassy of 1972 was already part of a political field that placed mining interests ahead of all others; the response of Aboriginal sovereignty was in part discordant with the legal system of the day (by declaring another sovereign nation) and in part evidence that there was still only one geopolitical game in town (sovereignty).

That is to say, when Indigenous peoples become refugees in their own land, and have to seek nationhood by setting up as an external sovereign people (as they did in the 1972 tent embassy), they have already bought into – and *must buy into* – discourses of sovereignty that become compulsory at the moment that they also become impossible and exhausted (Franke 2009). If the declaration of sovereignty was a refusal of Australia's legal system, it nevertheless fell into the geopolitical system that would increasingly see national sovereignty become less and less possible in a world of global finance, climate change and a series of other inescapable humanisms. If humanism began as an indulgent strategy – the positing of a universal 'we' that would enable blindness to untranslatable modes of existence – it has increasingly become a violent predicament. The hunter-gatherer societies who had nothing to do with the dream of global capital and global humanism will nevertheless be part of the species that will once again become nomadic. What we know as the complex system of immigration – persons moving from nation to nation, persons seeking refuge, illegal immigrant labour, offshore sweatshops, imported skilled labour, anti-immigrant fear-mongering around elections – is the outcome of centuries of some peoples achieving exceptional and unsustainable stability.

In the 2016 US election campaign Donald Trump declared that, if only we could build a wall, we might make America great again, and Australia has also experienced the use of figures of hordes of migrants and refugees as a way of shoring up political bravado: such sentiments are not as simple as scapegoating, or blaming others for our own ills. They sustain the confused temporality of the sovereign nation as primary, with the migrant and refugee as secondary, unfortunate and avoidable events. Sovereignty does not only scapegoat the migrant to displace its internal ills, but emerges from a field of migration that it at once negates while also harnessing its energies. When the Australian Aboriginal peoples declared sovereignty and erected an embassy they at once took part in the games and assumptions of nationhood, while also creating the possibility of counter-sovereignty: a declaration of an assemblage defined by movement rather than ownership. If the Australian Aborigines declared themselves *ex post facto* to be a sovereign people prior to European invasion, and constituted another mode of sovereignty (a sovereignty of movement that did not rely on the stabilization of nature), they were at once captured by a global system that could only recognize peoples as sovereign nations, while nevertheless disturbing the relationship between sovereignty and land as potential property. If sovereignty were to be defined by time and movement, by what has taken place and by past trajectories, then migration would not be between sovereign states but would be constitutive of a mode of political assemblage in which bodies (human and non-human) and place would be equi-primordial.

It is possible to say, distorting the work of Giorgio Agamben (1998), that all humans are now *homo sacer*, no longer protected by the rights and justices of personhood but have become mere life to be exposed to the sheer difficulty of living on. The condition of Western sovereignty that defined an interior of stability with an exterior of placeless movement has now shifted in scale such that the species in general is increasingly exposed in a fragile and unstable space. But rather than consider this human exposure within the frame of Agamben's conception of biopolitics (where the exposure to fragility and placelessness is a lamentable effect of sovereignty's increasing abandonment of more and more humans), I would like to argue that what has seemed to be an exceptional and contentious category – that of the climate refugee – is now an appropriate way of beginning to think about humans in general. Further: the condition of exiting one milieu after a transformation of a living system to a condition of non-viability has always marked the historicity of life. Where the present differs is that some happy few humans have *not* known that condition and have maintained a sovereign existence at the expense of intensifying the exposure of others. And yet, for all its exception and privilege it is this hyper-consuming portion of humanity that congratulates itself for exercising compassion towards the refugees and migrants who are conditional for its ongoing enjoyment, and it is now this *same* humanity that is imagining itself as a species facing the condition of being an exile in its own once-sovereign space.

One might say that there is no refuge from what has become the scale of the Anthropocene, and that this is so even as that scale casts every other potential humanity into the shadows and operates at such an intensity that its very specificity is discernible only in the moment of its decline. The mode of hyper-consumption and hyper-production that generated a species capable of altering the dynamic of the earth as a living system – the same humanity of globalism, universalism and personhood – can only be seen as the limited condition of a portion of humanity precisely at the point at which it sweeps all humanity into its moment of decline. That is, one should accept that this is indeed the Anthropocene – that there is now, effectively, a single 'humanity' (Hamilton 2013) – and that this manufactured universal humanity is the effect of capitalism and white supremacy (Moore 2016). Today, in the light of the scale of the Anthropocene, it seems that we are compelled to shift away from the ecological justice among humans, to the predicament of the earth as a whole: the possible value of other modes of humanity, discernible in the light of the Anthropocene, can now only appear as a path not travelled, and now closed off forever (at least in human actual time).

Why did the Aboriginal people of 1972 feel compelled to occupy a space and claim a certain type of sovereignty, and what was sacrificed in so doing? One might make two observations regarding the refuge taken within the Australian legal political system. First, in terms of geopolitics, for the Aboriginal people and because of colonization and its long reach, there was nowhere else to go. The Aboriginal peoples needed to form a sovereign unity and then insist upon the existence of this sovereign body prior to invasion and dispossession. This was so both discursively, where the opportunity to occupy a space required submitting to discourses of sovereignty and nationhood, and geopolitically, where the colonization of Australia as a single land mass precluded any possibility of dispersed, nomadic and differing peoples. But it is the second interconnection – beyond global colonization and global legal discourse – of scale and refuge that takes us forward to questions of climate. Existing nomadically, and relying on distinct modes of survival and temporality that were attuned to the land, would become increasingly impossible as corporate mining interests and anthropogenic climate change would sweep all humans into a unity. The scale of global humanity would become increasingly unavoidable, even if (from one point of view) Indigenous Australians had the one defining capacity of thinking time and space beyond the scale of human history. Aboriginal Australians sought refuge in an embassy not because they were suddenly not occupying their own land mass, but because 1972 saw a clash of scales. From the point of view of capitalism, colonialism and human survival, mining and resources would need to override traditional claims of occupation. For the Aboriginal peoples invasion was an event *within* their history; all the subsequent temporal markers of Australia's democratic history needed to be understood within the broader time and space of a quite different mode of sovereignty. From an indigenous point of view land is one's own *not* because of use and production but because of memory, including the memory of events beyond human history and beyond humans.

Let us imagine that there was a possibility, perhaps in 1972, that the Australian government had – even within the discourse of sovereignty – granted Aboriginal peoples something like native title, or had weakened the extensiveness and intensity of colonial globalism in the manner of the later 1982 high court decision of *Mabo v Queensland* that overruled *Milirrpum v Nabalco Pty Ltd* (1971). Would the Aboriginal peoples have been able to sustain their own scale of reference and history? By 1972 all the anthropogenic earth system changes that would (supposedly) demand global action were already in play. By 1982 when the notion of *terra nullius* was overturned and native title was recognized – but from within a system of white Australian sovereignty and legality – the granting of native title took place *within* a geopolitical order of intensive industry that already imposed a single scale of human capture. There was already no way – in 1972 – that Aboriginal peoples might have continued with their own temporality and their own geotemporality. Existing alongside late twentieth-century industrialism there were not only encroaching economic and cultural imperatives that swept everything into the same scale, there was also intensified awareness of climate change that would draw everything into a new global unity. Not only were Indigenous modes of existing with the earth being displaced by mining and industrialized agriculture, the colonizing reach of Western capitalism and the intensive hyper-consumption that led to deforestation, ocean acidification and global warming had already generated the single ecological, economic and conceptual scale that is now explicitly named in the Anthropocene. Once one considers earth as a single living system, something like 'humanity' as a species seems to be an inevitable category.

In 1972 Australian Aborigines – like all refugees – were already climate refugees. Their displacement was the result of an increasing demand for mineral resources by a Western world that had already exhausted its own domain. Indigenous peoples were displaced as a consequence of global capitalism's continued need for further space and resources, and were further displaced by a white invasion that took the form of a penal colony. Here, too, one can see the early white convicts and settlers in Australia as effects of the Western fetish for stable sovereign states that, in turn, relied upon mobile labour and the continual seizure of other nomadic peoples' resources. When, in 1972 and into the twenty-first century, mining interests supplanted all other ways of thinking about the earth, the relation between Indigenous Australian erasure and climate change became more explicit. Those forms of life that might *not* have generated geological impact, at least if we are thinking about the scale of stratigraphy, were always the victims of a mode of humanity that can now – in the waning light of hyper-industrialism – be referred to as Anthropocene man.

I would suggest, then, that we accept Clive Hamilton's criticism of those whom he claims do not understand the science of earth as a living system: we should not be defining the Anthropocene at a *political level* (to do with how humans behave among each other in terms of an ecosystem), and should instead shift the scale to think of the earth as a whole and its shift into a post-Holocene volatility. However, and at the same time, rather than accept this actual brute fact of the Anthropocene and its scale that trumps all interhuman relations, one might say that the scale of thinking and acting that precipitated the intensity of consumption responsible for the Anthropocene was a global political humanism that colonized the earth and other humans to the point that no refuge or other space was possible, and that this subsumption of all other modes of thinking and acting occurred before the geological subsumption of the Anthropocene. Rather, then, than scaling up from global humanism (in its liberal and Marxist forms) towards the earth system science of the Anthropocene, I would suggest that we open – virtually – other scales.

The Anthropocene does not label anthropogenic climate change in its narrow sense, or the impact of humans on their environment; it refers to the ways certain forms of impact have shifted the planet away from the Holocene's characteristic calm and stability to a high degree of volatility. When *this* occurs what happens is a shift of scale such that geology – a discipline that did once not really connect with humans – now becomes a legitimate scale for considering human life. Further, this shift in scale from smaller to *geological* considerations (where humans now transform the planet and not just ecosystems) necessitates a shift in political scale. It is (supposedly) not possible now to argue for the redemption or refuge that might be achieved by turning towards eco-feminist, indigenous or nomadic forms of human dwelling.

Even if, at the level of brute fact and actuality there can be no retrieval of a pre-Anthropocene world where one might have lived without reaching the intensity of planetary destruction, one might think – in these closing days, in the light of what we know – of living *as if* other temporalities and planes were possible. Rather, then, than say that the twenty-first century is marked by knowing what we need to do in order to survive and yet acting otherwise, we might think of knowing full well that the game of survival and extension is no longer possible, and that this thought generates a virtual and fully real counter-Anthropocene. There is no other planet, and there is no other history; there is – now – no other possible humanity, and yet the potentiality of the history that is not actualized might open another world *in the present.* A potentiality or virtual humanity that might have been other than the hyper-consuming industrialized humanity that generated the Anthropocene was once imaginable, if not possible, at the time of the formation of the Aboriginal tent embassy, and later at the time of the Mabo decision. Even at that point, which was also the beginning of a sense of the destructiveness of globalizing techno-science, those displaced by colonization and its ravages could only seek refuge within (and thereby confirm) the pernicious system of nation-hood, sovereignty and land ownership. The humanity of high industrialism is recognizing that its global reach and inescapability is precisely that which will make any sort of actual refuge impossible. It is nevertheless possible to recognize – by way of the all-encompassing and non-negotiable scale of the Anthropocene, where all parts of the earth are now caught up in the predica-ment generated by one mode of colonizing humanity – that the single-scale or single-system thinking that allowed for the historical success of one mode of humanity at the expense of others, *and* that enables all the technological expertise capable of theorizing the Anthropocene, is also one from which we now have no refuge. In conclusion, I do not want to confuse the geological conception of scale that marks the Anthropocene with the global human scale that marks the history of colonization; but what I do want to do is question the notion of *proper scale*, or the idea that survival is tied to a single scale that thought should follow in allowing one register or strata to subsume all others.

To conclude, one might say both that all refugees are climate refugees (dis-placed by forms of war and colonization that are tied to overconsumption and overproduction), and that humanity in general is now approaching the condi-tion of being a climate refugee. All humans – even, and especially, those who have suffered from Western colonizing globalism – are now finding the space of the earth to be inhospitable, and yet also finding that the seeking of refuge keeps them within the very system that caused displacement. The response so far has been one of maintaining sovereignty, but perhaps one might retrieve – even if it is too late – a post-sovereign conception of movement.

NOTES

1. http://www.theguardian.com/us-news/2015/nov/20/carson-trump-refugee-rhetoric-dog-whistle-politics, http://www.theguardian.com/us-news/2015/nov/20/ben-carson-screen-syrian-refugees-like-they-might-be-rabid-dogs.

REFERENCES

Agamben, Giorgio. 1998. *Homo Sacer: Sovereign Power and Bare Life.* Trans. Daniel Heller-Roazen. Stanford: Stanford University Press.

Agamben, Giorgio. 2000. 'Beyond Human Rights'. In *Means Without Ends.* Trans. Cesare Casarino and Vincenzo Binetti. Minneapolis: University of Minnesota Press.

Allen, Amy. 2016. *The End of Progress: Decolonizing the Normative Foundations of Critical Theory.* New York: Columbia University Press.

Deleuze, Gilles and Felix Guattari. 1987. *A Thousand Plateaus: Capitalism and Schizophrenia.* Trans. Brian Massumi. Minneapolis: University of Minnesota Press.

Foley, Gary, Andrew Schaap and Edwina Howell (eds.). 2013. *The Aboriginal Tent Embassy: Sovereignty, Black Power, Land Rights and the State.* London: Routledge.

Franke, M. 2009. 'The Political Stakes of Indigenous Diplomacies: Questions of difference'. In J. Beier (ed.), *Indigenous Diplomacies.* Basingstoke: Palgrave Macmillan, pp. 47–60.

Hamilton, Clive. 2013. *Earthmasters: The Dawn of the Age of Climate Engineering.* New Haven: Yale University Press.

Lister, Matthew. 2014. 'Climate Change Refugees'. *Critical Review of International Social and Political Philosophy,* 17, no. 5, pp. 618–634.

Moore, Jason. 2016. *Anthropocene or Capitalocene?: Nature, History, and the Crisis of Capitalism.* Oakland: PM Press.

Chapter 8

Strangers on a Strange Planet

On Hospitality and Holocene Climate Change

Nigel Clark

'Jakob, try to be buried in a ground that will remember you', commends the Greek geologist Athos to the young Polish Jew who has lost his family, his people, and his homeland to the Holocaust (Michaels 1997: 76). The ground that might come to serve the boy well is not a land where blood or filiation is rooted in soil, for it is such imaginings of an earth and a people that have shattered Jakob's world. What it might better be, if I have any handle on the story, is a place that is willing to take him in and give him support. Somewhere that will accept the child in his damaged and grievous state and not just because of what he has to offer or the solid citizen he might become. A place and a people, that is, that will nurture his stories and keep watch over his memories as well as providing the resources for a viable future.

A story of trauma, refuge and recovery, Anne Michaels' novel *Fugitive Pieces* (1997) might also be one of the first great literary expressions of the Anthropocene, though the book arrived just in advance of the concept. For the *Fugitive Pieces* of the title refers not only to the fracturing and rootlessness of diasporic lives but also to the disjuncture and mobility of the earth itself. It matters profoundly that the one who rescues Jakob and shelters him on the Ionian island of Zakynthos is a geologist. Athos becomes not only the boy's guardian but also his guide to another ground, another earth. In Jakob's voice: 'Even as a child, even as my blood-past was drained from me, I understood that if I were strong enough to accept it, I was being offered a second history. . . . I sat near him while he wrote at his desk, contemplating forces that turn seas to stone, stone to liquid' (Michaels 1997: 20).

Athos' accounts of deep geological time and the transformations of the earth – 'the great heaving terra mobilis' – help open the boy's drastically reduced horizons, offering imaginary resources to draw Jakob away from his lost past and precarious future (Michaels 1997: 21). This is not an earth that is expected to provide the stability that the social world has so fearfully failed to deliver. The lesson of Athos' geology is that the earth shudders and wrenches itself apart, time and time again, and yet it endures: 'The landscape of the Peloponnesus had been injured and healed so many times, sorrow darkened the sunlit ground' (Michaels, 1997: 60). Rather than pandering to the illusion of solidity and untroubled belonging, this is a geological imagination that encourages us to see that upheaval, dislocation, starting over is the way of the world. As Jakob recounts: 'I could temporarily shrug off my strangeness because, the way Athos saw the world, every human was a newcomer' (Michaels, 1997: 103).

Today, we hardly need reminding, traumatized and uprooted people are again finding their way to Greek Islands and the surrounding littoral. Once more, as in Hannah Arendt's diagnosis of the interwar and wartime upheavals of Europe, the refugee appears as 'the most symptomatic group in contemporary politics' (1973: 277). Like the boy Jakob, the refugees Arendt spoke of were deprived of rights and exposed to persecution by the same logic through which states operated and legitimated themselves. And in this way, beyond the immediacy of their predicament or the immensity of their numbers, the very existence of exiled, stateless people revealed deep cracks in the continuum of nation-territory-state.

But are today's refugees symptomatic in the same way? For those fleeing the Syrian conflict, a case has been made that long years of drought – partially attributable to climate change – have decimated rural livelihoods, accelerated rural–urban migration and exacerbated political dissatisfaction (Gleick, 2014, cf Selby and Hulme, 2015, see also Selby 2014). Others have argued that climate-related global grain shortages and resultant food price hikes served as a 'threat multiplier' in the Arab Spring uprisings (Johnstone and Mazo 2011: 15). Reports estimate that 70% of slum dwellers in Dhaka, Bangladesh, have previously experienced some kind of environmental shock that bears the mark of climate change (Cities Alliance, 2016). And so on across the world's agrarian regions: poor harvests, rainfall deficit, intensified cyclone seasons – one more reason to move, temporarily or permanently, to the nearest city or the distant labour market.

Commentators on the question of climate-induced mobility have long noted the lack of a clear political-legal definition of the climate refugee or migrant (Lazarus, 1990; White, 2011). Most add that a big part of this equivocation lies in the difficulty of distinguishing the impact of climatic or environmental change from a tangle of other motivations to move. These challenges may well prove intractable, for the problem of identifying a distinctive climate signature sooner or later opens up to the question of what exactly the earth is doing at any moment. Or, as I put it some time ago: 'The inherent dynamism of earth processes – the "geo" in the geopolitical – raises the possibility of displaced populations whose cause of unsettling defies final determination' (Clark, 2003: 7).

These are issues that are not necessarily becoming easier to resolve as the scientific study of the earth advances. Over the last half-century or so, geoscience orthodoxy has been developing a new appreciation of the complexity, dynamism and indeterminacy of earth processes. As palaeontologist Richard Fortey sums up: 'The story of our understanding of the face of the earth has been one of increased freedom of movement' (2005: 237). This story is far from over. Still reverberating through the natural sciences, *terra mobilis* is beginning to rumble beneath the social sciences and humanities, raising questions not only about what it means for humans themselves to mobilise, but also – as Anne Michaels' Athos would surely add – what it means to try and make oneself at home.

It does not take a restive planet to trouble the idea of home. As Arendt noted, it is the conviction that political order ought to be premised on a unitary or self-consistent identity that has made so many people into strangers in their own homes (1973: 299–232, ch 9; Dillon 1999: 109–110; Larking, 2014: 31–2). The link between nation and natality – the idea that birth out of a shared soil imposes a bond between peoples, Arendt and many subsequent political thinkers have insisted, systematically excludes those who appear to have sprung from a different earth or those for whom the common substrate has somehow failed to do its filial bidding (Arendt, ch 9; Agamben 2000: 21). As Michael Hardt and Antonio Negri put it: '"The nation-state" is a machine that produces Others' (2001: 114). The prevailing critical response to this predicament has been to show that human identity is inherently complex, multiple, heteronomous – a discursive complication of self-sameness that disavows any sense that social beings are 'somehow rooted in the land, as if they needed the soil' (Kieserling, cited in Beck, 2000: 80–1).

But as a critical gesture, extirpating social or cultural identity from the earth is no longer as convincing as it once was. For today, the earth itself is beginning to appear every bit as divisible, heterogeneous and non-self-identical as the social beings jostling on its surface. While the Anthropocene thesis has drawn attention to the capacity of collective human agency to impact upon earth processes, perhaps the more profound message of the science behind the idea is that such changes are possible only because of the multiplicity that inheres in the earth system – at every temporal and spatial scale. In the words of palaeobiologist and Anthropocene working group chair Jan Zalasiewicz: 'The Earth seems to be less one planet, rather a number of different Earths that have succeeded each other in time, each with very different chemical, physical and biological states' (cited in Hamilton, 2014: 6). And it is in this regard that – just as the borders between nation states have long been scenes of drama and conflict – the thresholds between one operating state of the earth system and another are emerging as sites of significance and contention (Clark, 2013; 2016).

As geologists tell us, discernible differences between the strata that make up the earth's crust provide evidence to tell a story of successive transformations in the earth system. But if the nation state is indeed 'a machine that produces Others', what might it mean, politically or ethically, to inhabit an earth that is 'a gigantic machine for producing strata'? (Zalasiewicz, 2008: 17). Or, to put it another way, if the symptomatic figures of twentieth-century politics were the ones who found themselves straddling cultural-political fault lines and borderlands – What are we to make of those who are caught on the threshold between states in the earth system? How do we begin to make sense of and respond to those who are pressed between a machine for producing Others and a machine for generating the very structure of the earth itself?

One of most promising aspects of the Anthropocene debate is the way that it is bringing social thought into an encounter with other geological epochs and eras. At very least, a more informed sense of the Holocene – an imagination encompassing millennia rather than mere centuries and decades – may be one of the gifts of Anthropocene geoscience. Though already such a span is anticipated by Gilles Deleuze and Felix Guattari, who, with Fernand Braudel as their guide, showed that the genealogy of any social phenomenon merges into geology if we pursue it far enough (1987: ch. 3). Rather than seeking to disentangle climate from other variables at play in human migration, I want to push back well into the Holocene and explore the possibility that climate and its incitements to mobility *are even more deeply implicated* with politics, ethics and culture than we usually imagine.

Most of all what interests me here is the experience of being 'unworlded' by environmental change and the question of how we encounter those who have been 'othered' by their very world becoming strange. How does the predicament of being, in the words of the ancient Middle Eastern Book of Exodus, 'a stranger in a strange land' (2: 22) – relate to the emergent scientific idea of an earth that is volatile, multiple and discontinuous – or indeed to older and enduring understandings of the variability of earth and cosmos? To put it another way, in what sense is exposure to changing climate – now and in the past – a scene of responsibility or of hospitality? The poignancy and power of Michaels' *Fugitive Pieces* lies not only in the way that it brings estrangement wrought by the pathologies of political ordering into conversation with the ongoing strangeness of the earth, but that in the midst of these vast machinations of state and planet the value of single human life is affirmed. If 'the face of the earth' has indeed become 'one of increased freedom of movement', what might this mean for the way we perceive the face of the one whose movement or immobility has become anything but free? There is, of course, no answer to this. But it opens new questions, and it keeps the questions coming.

SOCIAL THOUGHT AND *TERRA MOBILIS*

Coming of age in the 1990s, claims that global climate change would at some point in the foreseeable future trigger vast waves of refugees helped put climate-induced dislocation on the political agenda (see Myers, 1993, 2002). These so-called 'alarmist' approaches have subsequently been subjected to displacement of their own (see Piguet, 2013: 154–6). Taking issue with the monocausality of climatic drivers and wary of the resurgence of discredited environmental determinisms in such work, critical climate migration research has turned to closer-grained studies of the motivating, enabling and constraining factors behind human mobility (Piguet, 2010, 2013; Bettini, 2013). In the more 'pragmatist', multivariate accounts that come out of this turn, environmental variables tend to be carefully contextualized within an encompassing framework of mutually entangled socio-material processes. As Etienne Piguet characteristically concludes: 'Except in extreme cases, population displacements are always the result of a multicausal relationship between environmental, political, economic, social, and cultural dimensions' (2013: 517). Or, in the words of Warner, Hamza, Oliver-Smith, Renaud and Julca, more pointedly resisting any implication climatic determinism: 'Human agency is at the center of environmental change and the potential to respond to it' (Warner et al., 2010: 692).

Along with other work in the genre, Warner and her colleagues' disavowal of climate as an independent or exogenous force in social life can itself be seen as an expression of a prevailing ontological position as much as it is a summation of available empirical evidence. Piguet (2013), in his insightful survey of the vacillating fortunes of environmental variables in migration studies over the last century, observes that the weighting afforded to climatic-environmental factors at any moment tends to reflect broader disciplinary trends. That is, the ebb and flow of the explanatory role attributed to the natural environment as a trigger to migration is itself conditioned by longer-wave shifts in the relative significance given to physical and social variables in human geography and cognate social sciences (Piguet, 2013: 156–8). The importance of Piguet's point should not be underestimated, given that the relationship between the human and the non-human in critical social thought is by no means settled. For it raises the possibility that the ontological and epistemological commitment to more multivariate or 'climate minimalist' positions in recent critical migration studies themselves belong to a historical – we might say geohistorical – moment that may well turn out to be provisional.

For more than two decades, social scientists and humanities scholars across a range of disciplines have shown increasing willingness to account for the agency of non-human or 'more-than human' actors in the composition of social life. Over this time, the idea that no single type or category of agency – whether physical or social – ought to be privileged in the construction of the social has gravitated towards the mainstream – as has the insistence that the domains formerly referred to as 'society and nature' should be seen as mutually implicated and co-constitutive (see Clark, 2011: 30–6). Such a 'settlement' of the society–nature question provides a broad ontological–epistemological framework for the study of climate migration, as it does for the critical social study of a host of environmental and technological changes. It is notable, however, that until very recently geological or geophysical factors have rarely received sustained theoretical consideration in the refiguring of society–nature relations. The reasons for this are complicated, although – at risk of simplification – it would seem that the pronounced ways in which earth processes exceed the span and scope of human existence makes them difficult to fully subsume into conceptual frameworks centred on interimplication and co-enactment (Clark, 2011 7–11; 36–40).

But social thought's evasion of close encounters with earth science – in contrast to the inspiration it has taken from biology, linguistics, psychoanalysis, complexity studies and even mathematics – is remarkable when we consider the dramatic transformations that have occurred in scientific thought about the earth over the last half-century or so. As historian John Brooke recounts, the years 1966–1973 alone saw the emergence of four major new perspectives on the dynamics of the earth and the trajectories of terrestrial life: the confirmation of the theory of plate tectonics, a new appreciation of role of extra-terrestrial impacts in shaping in the planet's history, the thesis that evolution was 'punctuated' by catastrophic bursts linked to major geophysical events, and the beginnings of the idea that the different components of the earth functioned as an integrated system – as expressed in the Gaia hypothesis and earth systems theory (2014: 25–28, see also Davis, 1996).

What these increasingly convergent paradigms succeeded in doing, Brooke and others have argued, was both to shake up the idea of gradual, incremental change that had reigned since the mid-nineteenth century and to overcome the separation of different disciplinary fields (2014: 25–28; see also Davis, 1996). In retrospect, this perhaps overdue burst of scientific innovation provided the basis for the coming together of an older stratigraphic geology and a burgeoning earth systems science that is now at the core of the Anthropocene hypothesis (Clark, 2016). Those of us in the climatic change slow lane that social sciences have occupied should keep in mind too that from the 1960s onwards scientific research into human-induced global warming has been playing a significant role in the evolving understanding of complex, dynamic and integrated earth processes.

In the light of these revolutionary changes in earth or planetary science, we would do well to dwell on Piguet's 'except in extreme cases' proviso – in his demurring from an independent or dominating role for environmental change. Whether we look forwards or backwards, the idea of extremity as an exception may need to be reviewed – a possibility that some climate–migration researchers have begun to take on board in their more speculative explorations about the contours of climate-induced displacement in 4 degrees C warmer world. As paleo-environmental researcher Nick Brooks points out, the 'minimalist orthodoxy' – with its definitive reluctance to identify climate as the major driver of migration, 'is most heavily informed by studies of livelihoods and migration undertaken within the context of development studies, since the 1950s' (2012: 94). But as Brooks reminds us, if we want to find an analogue of global mean surface warming of the 3 degrees C or so now predicted for the latter twenty-first century, we need to go at least as far back as the mid-Pliocene – a journey of some 3.3 million years that takes us to a time well prior to the emergence of the genus *Homo* (2012: 94; see also Hayward et al., 2013).

If social thinkers are to give due consideration to the meanings of 'extreme', so too do we need to be mindful of the evidence of abrupt climate change that has been mounting since the 1980s (Broecker, 1987; Alley et al., 2003). An heir to the convergent revolutions of which Brooke was speaking, the discovery of abrupt or runaway climate change has been one of the most significant scientific surprises of recent decades. As climatologist Richard Alley puts it: 'For most of the last 100,000 years a crazily jumping climate has been the rule, not the exception' – a discovery that has 'revolutionized our view of Earth' (2000: 120; 13). It is this understanding that the global climate system has a propensity to rapidly tip from one state to another that is the crux of the more encompassing notion of a complex, dynamic earth system with multiple possible operating states – expressed earlier in Zalasiewicz's point about successive earths with very different physical conditions.

Over recent decades critical thought has generally held modernity's grand nature–society ontological divide to blame for the social science and humanities' conventional reluctance to account for non-human agency. What ought to be added to this diagnosis is that the long-reigning gradualism of the earth sciences had planetary processes lumbering slowly enough not to perturb social thought's assumption that the dynamics of social life were played out on an stable platform. Today, with the Anthropocene thesis gaining wide publicity and the concept of climate tipping points well ensconced in the vernacular, the notion of earth system change is making inroads into social thought (Clark, 2014; 2016). Though there is still a tendency to envision earth system change as a one-off 'apocalyptic' event in some quarters, the sense that episodic state-switching or regime change is an *ordinary* aspect of physical systems at many scales is beginning to insinuate itself in social and cultural thinking. And in this context, relational ontologies hinging on society–nature co-constitution are being nudged in the direction of more asymmetrical imaginaries in which the earth and cosmos are viewed as an unstable ground of social existence rather than as mutually present co-actors (Clark, 2016; 2011: 40–50).

A useful gauge for this shift is the 'Gaian turn' in the work of Bruno Latour. Latour, who has often been a touchstone for ontologies and epistemologies that position human and non-human actors in mutually generated networks, is increasingly speaking in terms of a 'geo' that is the antecedent and subtending condition of what we have tended to call the natural and the social. 'The prefix "geo " in geostory does not stand for the return to nature, but for the return of object and subject back to the ground – the "metamorphic zone "', as he recently put it (2014: 16). More broadly, commentators are now detecting a 'geologic turn' or 'fold' in the social sciences and humanities – a new appreciation of the dynamism of the earth that both recognizes the geologic agency of (certain) human populations and acknowledges that such social forces emerge late on an always already volatile planet (Chakrabarty, 2008; Cohen, 2010; Turpin, 2011; Yusoff, 2013).

This sense that the earth and its constitutive systems are the condition of possibility of human social life has important implications for conceptualizing climate migration. With the unsettling of ontologies that privilege human-non-human interimplication, climate change is permitted to be something other than one variable or factor amongst many. An exorbitant earth (Clark, 2016) – a planet that is never quite at one with itself – while it may not be able to shake off the totality of life that is part of its systemic functioning, most certainly has the potential to withdraw its support from specific populations of living beings. But such avowals of unmitigated inhuman force can easily encourage grandiose and melodramatic thinking: the kind of sweeping gestures that leave little space for the valuing of a single life. A planet that can become strange to itself, an astronomical body capable of unworlding its own inhabitants, I want to suggest, is also one that throws strangers into each other's paths. And just as the earth can stray from its orbit, so too can strangers draw each other out of their usual orbits. Turning now to a deeper history of climate-induced displacement, I will also be attempting to make room not only for human agency but for a passivity or receptiveness that might be seen as exceeding the very capacity for action.

HOLOCENE GEOPOLITICS

'Athos – Athanasios Roussos – was a geologist dedicated to a private trinity of peat, limestone, and archaeological wood' as Michaels describes her protagonist. 'But like most Greeks, he rose from the sea' (1997: 19). And she precedes to tell the story of Athos' mariner ancestors who passed down to him an understandings of the globes' watery interconnectivity (see also Goldberg, this volume) – setting the scene for his own enthralment with the slower flow of stone, continents and ocean basins.

Jakob is not the only one who is offered refuge on Zakynthos. When the Germans invade, the island's Jewish population is spirited away by their Christian townsfolk to lofts, cellars and caves. Michaels' tale has a factual heart. History tells us that when the island's civic authorities were ordered by the Nazis to produce a full register of the Jewish population, the bishop handed over a list comprising just two names, his own and the mayor's. Safely hidden, every one of the island's 275 Jews survived the Holocaust (Goldberg, 2009). Just as real is the quake that in the story eventually demolishes the house in which Athos shelters Jakob during the war: the great Ionian Earthquake that struck the island in August 1953 destroyed infrastructure and state archives, and left only three buildings standing in the city of Zakynthos.

Long before the Greek Islands found themselves playing host to the refugees from the Syrian conflict, well before the events of the Second World War, Zakynthos had a reputation for welcoming strangers. 'Venetian soldiers, refugees from Constantinople, the Peloponnese, Athens and Crete settle in Zante (Zakynthos) and turn it into a melting pot', accounts tell us, its communal life, cultural forms and built space taking shape as a compendium of elements brought by strangers who came to stay (zante-paradise.com). And earlier still, Greece itself – its peninsulas and islands reaching like gnarled fingers into the eastern Mediterranean – had long been a destination for strangers from over the sea. Even on the mountainous mainland of Greece, the sea is never more than 100 km from land, philosopher Rudolph Gasché reminds us, adding that right across the Aegean Sea, land or islands never fully slip out of sight. 'Each point of the topological space of Greece is pulled inside out, as it were, by its openness to the sea, that is, to the fluid medium, in which encounters with the other, the stranger, can occur', observes Gasché (2014: 85). In the ancient world, he continues, 'These factual conditions attracted the landless strangers from the Orient' (2014: 87). It is the presence of these 'others' in the ancient polis, writes Gasché, that makes the stranger such an important theme in Greek philosophy. Indeed, as Nietzsche pointed out, these foreigners made up a significant number of the very first philosophers of the Greek tradition (Gasché 2014: 86).

In Gasché's book-length exegesis of Deleuze and Guattari's (1994) difficult text on geophilosophy, the question of why there might be 'landless strangers from the Orient' is not pursued. Neither is the stranger a prominent theme in Deleuze and Guattari's own work, aside from their framing of the nomad as 'Other' to sedentary state-dominated peoples (1987: 413). What Deleuze and Guattari *have* explored in some detail is the emergence of state-level social formations in the alluvial valleys of the ancient Middle East – where the first states form or 'territorialize' around the capture of the matter-flow of the soil (1987: 412, 427–8). Michel Serres (1995) provides a simpler and rather more accessible version of the idea that territory is a process, an ordering device that cuts into and stabilises an earth that is in motion. Speculating about the origin of both law and politics – at least in the Western tradition – Serres goes back to the ancient 'geometers' whose task was to measure out the alluvial soils laid down by the annual flooding in the river valleys. In response to 'the great primal or recursive rising of the waters, the chaos that mixes the things of the world' comes the process of ordering: the demarcating and reapportioning of freshly sedimented soil 'out of which politics and laws were born' (1995: 53).

Like Deleuze and Guattari, Serres is beginning to engage with the idea of complex, self-organizing physical systems. While Deleuze and Guattari seek to ground thought in the openness and dynamism of the earth – proposing that all philosophy sets out as *geo*philosophy (1994: 95), for Serres all politics is ultimately *geo*politics – not in the old manner of great games played out across the global space but 'in the sense of the real Earth' (1995: 44). While both these interventions look prescient in the light of the contemporary geological turn in social and philosophical thought, there is also a sense in which the continued development of the geosciences over the intervening decades now offer empirical detail to thematics that Serres along with Deleuze and Guattari broached in more speculative ways. Taking advantage of a novel ability to reconstruct the rhythms of past climate, archaeologist and paleoclimatologists are now in sustained conversation – making it possible to establish close correlations between significant societal transformations and specific climatic events (Brooke, 2014: 134; Kennett and Kennett, 2006: 69).

Equipped with new understandings of the seesawing climate fluctuations of Pleistocene and their extended aftermath, climate scientists remind us that the exit from the last glacial maximum was anything but smooth. Between 15,000 and 6000 BP (before present), sea levels rose by 120–130 metres, resulting in extensive submergence of coastal land (Nunn, 2012). The Middle Holocene – especially the period around 6400 BP and 5000 BP – was a time of relatively rapid climate and environmental change associated with a global shift from the warmer, more humid conditions of the early Holocene to a regime characterized by cooler temperatures in the higher latitudes and enhanced aridity in the lower or tropical latitudes (Brooks, 2012: 94). In terms of contemporary climatology, what takes place is a decline in solar radiation caused by cyclical changes in the earth's axis of rotation – which is processed through the non-linear dynamics of the global climate system, eventually resulting in an abrupt reorganization of the planet's climatic regime. Sometime around 5200 BP, after a series of smaller stepwise changes, climate goes over a threshold or tipping point. Although it has different effects in different places, the signature of this 'Mid Holocene Climatic Transition' shows up more or less synchronously in environmental records from across the Middle East, Africa, China, South America and Europe (Brooks, 2012: 95).

There is now substantial evidence linking the Mid-Holocene Climatic Transition to the shift from small, relatively egalitarian villages based on subsistence agriculture to large fortified urban centres with intensified social stratification and administrative hierarchies. This correlation between abrupt climate change – manifest as enhanced aridity – and the emergence of the first 'state societies' has been most fully documented in the case of southern Mesopotamia, but similar patterns have been observed in the Nile Valley, central Sahara, north-central China, the Indus region in South Asia and coastal Peru. (Brooks, 2012: 96–99; Kennett and Kennett, 2006: 79). The evidence from Mesopotamia points to the drought-induced abandonment of many smaller villages and the rapid growth of settlements in the southern riverine floodplains – with the population in and around the city of Uruk-Warka growing an estimated tenfold over the course of the climatic transition (Brooks, 2012: 98).

While it is the development of intensive irrigated agriculture – closely tied to the rise of state administration of labour, land and produce – that enables larger populations to be supported, the expansion of the floodplains themselves is dependent on the deceleration of sea-level rise (Kennett and Kennett, 2006: 90). But this process of post-glacial sea-level rise – or 'marine transgression' – adds another whole level of chaos and dynamism to Serres' mythopoeic account of the annual redistribution of alluvial land, for the very deltas and floodplains in question are likely to have still been undergoing formation during their nascent marking out. There is a vital precursor to the aridity-driven urban growth on the Southern Mesopotamian alluvium, Kennett and Kennett (2006) argue, which is the earlier consolidation of settlements driven by the final surge of sea-level rise. Prior to the Mid-Holocene Climatic Transition, coastal land in the Arabo-Persian Gulf – whose attraction lay in its rich marine resources – was still retreating at a rate of around 100 metres a year: 'Optimal freshwater and estuarine environments continued to shift inland, displacing human populations', observe Kennett and Kennett. 'This dynamic mosaic would have stimulated increased competition for localized and circumscribed resources and the need to constantly redefine territorial boundaries and village locations as rapidly as within a single generation' (2006: 88). Over time, it also had the effect of concentrating populations in those urban centres such as Eridu or Ur that were on higher, more stable ground.

Mesopotamia is of course just one example, albeit the most intensely studied of ancient regions – and explanations for the rise and fall of its urban-centred empires remain highly contested. As is the tendency in contemporary critical climate–migration studies, most paleo-environmental researchers now prefer multivariate approaches over monocausal accounts. Climate change, scholars acknowledge, had markedly different effects at different times and places. It may even have incited near-opposite responses: urban consolidation in one location, more pastoral mobility in another (Brooks, 2012: 100). And yet, when all the variation is taken into account, there is a pronounced willingness in the telling of these paleo-stories to conceive of environmental change as an endogenous and context-setting force (Kennett and Kennett 2006: 68; Brooke, 2014: 267).

Many archaic societies appear to have been resilient in the face of changing climate, at times achieving remarkable durability (Brooke, 2014: 266–7). But there are decisive moments – discernible thresholds – at which climate and environmental change arrives with a speed or intensity that exceeds coping strategies. In the last 4 millennia BC, Brooke concludes, 'The trajectory and pulse of climate change provided one of the fundamental variables in the human condition, establishing the boundaries within which life was conducted' (2014: 317). When these boundaries were crossed, especially during the abrupt climate change episode just over 5000 years ago, the impacts were momentous and widespread. On an earth that was itself carrying out 'a movement of deterritorialization on the spot', in the words of Deleuze and Guattari, (1994: 85), the option for many populations seems to have been either abandon their existing settlements or perish. And what mobilization most often implied was an encounter with others.

HOSPITALITY AND THE CLIMATE MIGRANT

There are three points I want to draw from this all-too-brief engagement with the ancient world – more in the manner of provocations than conclusions. The first is that there is strong evidence linking climate change and its environmental effects to the emergence of state-level societies. As Brooke sums up: 'Boundaries and gradients in geography and climate, in space and time, form the essential root condition of circumscription that shape the timing of the pristine emergence of the state' (2014: 210). If this is the case, then climate is not simply a supplement to politics – as we imply today when we speak of 'climate politics' or 'climate governance'. It would be, rather, an originary complication of the political as we have come to understand it in Western discourses – and perhaps much further afield. In this sense, the very idea of a specialized system of rule and administration with jurisdiction over a population and a section of the earth's surface cannot be understood in isolation from climatic-environmental variability in the earth system. In a word, politics from the outset is always already climate politics or geopolitics

The second point is closely related. Gasché's passing comment about 'landless strangers from the Orient' (86) speaks of the ancient Greek milieu but arguably opens out into a much more generalized predicament. What paleo-environmental evidence suggests is that when climatic change – gradual or abrupt – exceeds a threshold, people attempt to relocate: there is 'out migration, in migration, population agglomeration in refugia', as Brooks sums up (2012: 101). While some of the growth of settlements in fertile, well-resourced locations would have been endogenous, a large proportion seems to have resulted from migration from unviable areas. That is: 'The southern alluvium attracted huge numbers of migrant peoples over the course of these millennia, either as refugees, or as transhumant peoples looking for better land' (Brooke, 2014: 210; see also Johnson, 1988). Climate migration, then, is not just a problem that polities have had to confront. It is intrinsic to the emergence of urban centres and their governance systems.

Which brings us to the third point: If those who have been estranged by climate change have a significant presence in the earliest cities, then we might also view the question of who or what is a stranger, and of how to treat the stranger, as taking on a constitutive role in urban social and political life. The stranger is present, and troubling in their presence, not only in Athens or Zykanthos, but in Uruk, Eridu or Ur – wherever there is a rural hinterland, which is to say in every premodern city. Or as Jacques Derrida liked to put it: 'Hospitality is culture itself and not simply one ethic among others' (2001: 16). Hospitality is at the heart of culture for Derrida, because it concerns 'one's home, the familiar place of dwelling': because it involves not only how we relate to others but how we relate to the otherness within ourselves – the strangeness within or the possibility of any of us of becoming estranged.

There are many ways that any one of us might lose our sense of dwelling, of being at home amongst family, friends and neighbours or being at one with ourselves. But what the paleo-story of climate change and displacement reminds us is that the experience of the physical world withdrawing its support is a primordial form of estrangement and thus likely to be an originary incitement to hospitality. As we have seen, Serres speculates that it is the swirling chaos of the flood and its deposits that prompt the decisions or demarcations 'out of which politics and laws were born'. But so too from the encounter with this worldly chaos – a chaos capable of unworlding as much as it renews the world – comes the appeal to suspend those boundary markers, to open the gate or the door, to be admitted to what is – at least for now – a more secure world. Alphonso Lingis, one of few thinkers to acknowledge the instability of the earth as a primary incitement to ethical relating, put it like this: 'You ask of my hands the diagram of the operations your hands are trying to perform, and ask the assistance of my forces lest yours be wanting. But you ask first for terrestrial support. The fatigue, the vertigo, the homelessness in your body appeal for support from my earthbound body, which has the sense of this terrain to give' (1994: 128–9; see also Dikeç et al., 2009: 12).

Whether or not this terrain is offered, how and with whom it is shared, I am suggesting, may well be one of the inaugural questions in the cultural, politico-juridical and perhaps economic formations of the ancient settlements of the alluvium. For these were the centres that functioned, in biological terminology, as 'environmental refugia': sites of relative stability during episodes of climatic change that attracted environmentally stressed people. Hospitality – the question of the stranger – arises in many, if not all cultures. But it is approached with particular ardour in the Middle East – where it has been described as 'a burning in the skin' inherited 'from the father and the grandfathers' (Shryock 2009: 34). If as an inheritance, hospitality seems to recede into an irretrievable past, it is certainly prominent in the books of the Old Testament, which counsel: 'the stranger that dwelleth with you shall be unto you as one born among you, and thou shalt love him as thyself' (Leviticus 19 34). And again, hinting that famine or hunger may be at issue: 'And when ye reap the harvest of your land, thou shalt not wholly reap the corners of thy field, neither shalt thou gather the gleanings of thy harvest . . . neither shalt thou gather *every* grape of thy vineyard; thou shalt leave them for the poor and stranger' (Leviticus, 19: 9–10; see also Deuteronomy 24: 19–21).

Noting the speed at which the waters advanced in the Arabo-Persian Gulf prior to the sea-level stabilization of the mid-Holocene, Kennett and Kennett ponder if biblical flood mythology may have originated in southern Mesopotamia (2006: 83), though as Peter Sloterdijk conjectures, the tale of the unworlding flood and the subsequent refounding of social life 'probably constitutes the most important shared memory trace in world cultures' (2014: 238). It is after the chaos of the flood and its related environmental upheavals, 'after the annihilation of nature by nature', as Sloterdijk puts it, that human agents fully take upon themselves the responsibility of shoring up, framing, shaping their own worlds – of rendering the inhospitable environment livable (2014: 240). This is why, for him, city building is originally as much a symbolic as a material process. Though paleo-climatic change is not Sloterdijk's primary concern, his argument that the stark verticality of the walls of the ancient Mesopotamian city – far in excess of merely defensive needs – are pre-eminently a gesture of permanence or durability resonates with the idea that cities rise and consolidate in the very face of environmental instability (on Sloterdijk, see Saldanha, this volume). And, for the one who has been estranged by the transience of the cosmos, we might further speculate, the iconic obduracy of the city wall may well serve as an attractor as much as an impediment.

While the architectonic appeal of the urban to the agrarian precariat may itself be proving remarkably enduring, we might also look to the emergent concern with identifying thresholds in earth systems and protecting them with non-transgressible 'planetary boundaries' as our own era's grandiose gesture in defiance of a once-more-upheaving cosmos (see Rockström et al., 2009). What the figure of the planetary boundary seems to be seeking to materialize is the understanding that the earth itself is something more and other than a unified, undivided, self-consistent planetary body. Henceforth it is no longer the community, the city, or even the nation state that stands as the scene of openness, permeability and transgression, but the very state of the earth. In this sense, it is worth recalling that the notion of hospitality for Derrida refers not simply to an ideal or a directive, but to an 'essential structure' of exposure to the arrival of the other or otherness – which is to say, the spatio-temporal modality of *non-contemporaneity with itself of the living present* (2005: 143, 1994: xix authors italics). And that disjuncture, that state of being temporally out of joint, poised always between an irretrievable past and a future-to-come, seems now to extend to the very earth.

But how might we be hospitable to the coming of a novel state of the earth system, to the passage over a threshold into what is now shorthanded as the Anthropocene? This is also a question, I have been suggesting, of how we inherit and rework ethico-political-juridical conventions for which the radical unworlding of climatic extremity may be an originary complication. As Derrida has often insisted, the unconditional side of welcoming the future necessarily involves openness, receptivity, a kind of passivity, even as it calls for the conditionality, the action of decision-making, an informed and calculated response (2005: 145; see Dikeç et al., 2009). Already, in the ancient cities of the Middle East we see the often draconian measures of the emergent state: 'Policies intended to ensure social stability and secure access to resources' in the face of uncertainty (Brooks, 2012: 96) that are perhaps the very inauguration of centralized economic policymaking. But so too do we catch a glimpse of an encouragement to welcome and provide for the stranger – a call to reap or harvest *uneconomically* that may be as primordial as the very idea of acting economically.

There is nothing to prevent fear of climate change – and fear of those mobilized by climate change – functioning as an impetus for reinforced spatial closure, for more tightly securitized boundaries, for bigger retaining walls (see Brown, 2010). At the same time, for those who aspire to be good hosts when environments turn inhospitable, the ancient conundrum of hospitality points to the need to keep one's own house in order, literally and metaphorically (Shryock, 2012: S24). Wall building may not be the most appropriate option, but as the more nuanced analyses of state power in times of environmental extremity remind us, looming uncertainty calls for measures to protect critical infrastructure – at every scale (see Collier and Lakoff, 2015). And it ought to encourage experimentation with and construction of whole new infrastructures. Trickier still are the innovations in governance that are summoned by the appeal of unsettled and bereft strangers, multiple others who will compete for our attention, who may ask for fair and equal treatment while deserving to be treated as singular and special, paradoxes that are at once ancient and novel.

Climate migrants, I am proposing, might be viewed as symptomatic of contemporary politics not just because their provocation is new but because they invite us to rethink the very idea of political – all the way back to its murky origins. And because once the idea of being unworlded by the mobility of the earth gets under our skin, there is no stopping it. As a trigger for migration, climate is difficult to tease apart from other variables (cultural, political, economic), I have been suggesting, not simply because these factors are entangled, but because all these aspects of collective life always already bear the trace of climatic and environmental change. Ebbing, shifting, tipping climate has been unsettling life, pushing and pulling it into 'refugia' since long before we were 'civilised', and indeed long before 'we' were human. If, for better and worse, the state is a machine for producing and processing strangers, this in part because the earth is a machine that in its own strangeness manufactures strangers. This means that in the face of every stranger – that is to say all of us – there is always the trace of the earth, the signature of changing climate, the memory of storms weathered and paths that changed course.

The thematic of hospitality, which may be at least as ancient as the polis, suggests that estrangement is more than a technical problem to be solved, but also more than a matter of inevitable or interminable conflict. Looking particularly at its Middle Eastern manifestations, anthropologist Andrew Shryock reminds us that 'hospitality is a test that can be failed; the stakes include life and death' (2012: S21). And even death is not the end of it. To try and be buried in a ground that will remember you, as Athos advises, is not just to be admitted or tolerated, but to be welcomed as one shaken and shaped by the strangeness of the world. And the ground that may offer this embrace will only do so because it too has been injured and healed a great many times.

REFERENCES

Agamben, G. 2000. *Means Without Ends: Notes on Politics*. Minneapolis, MN and London: University of Minnesota Press.

Alley, R. B. 2000. *The Two-Mile Time Machine: Ice Cores, Abrupt Climate Change, and Our Future*. Princeton: Princeton University Press.

Alley, R. B., Marotzke, J., Nordhaus, W. D., Overpeck, J. T., Peteet, D. M., Pielke, R. A., Pierrehumbert, R. T., Rhines, P. B., Stocker, T. F., Talley, L. D., and Wallace, J. M. 2003. 'Abrupt Climate Change'. *Science,* 299 (28 March): 2005–2010.

Arendt, H. 1973. *The Origins of Totalitarianism*. San Diego: Harvest.

Beck, U. 2000. 'The Cosmopolitan Perspective: Sociology of the Second Age of Modernity'. *British Journal of Sociology*, 51(1): 79–105.

Bettini, G. 2013. 'Climates Barbarians at the Gate? A Critique of Apocalyptic Narratives on Climate Refugees'. *Geoforum*, 45: 63–72.

Broecker, W. S. 1987. 'Unpleasant Surprises in the Greenhouse'. *Nature,* 328 (9 July): 123–126.

Brooke, J. 2014. *Climate Change and the Course of Global History: A Rough Journey*. New York: Cambridge University Press.

Brooks, N. 2012. 'Beyond Collapse: Climate Change and Causality during the Middle Holocene Climatic Transition, 6400–5000 Years Before Present'. *GeografiskTidsskrift-Danish Journal of Geography*, 112(2): 93–104.

Brown, W. 2010. *Walled States, Waning Sovereignty*. New York: Zone Books.

Chakrabarty, D. 2008. 'The Climate of History: Four Theses'. *Critical Inquiry,* 35: 197–222.

Cities Alliance. 2016. 'Climate Migration Drives Slum Growth in Dhaka'. Available at: http://www.citiesalliance.org/node/420 (accessed 26 June 2016).

Clark, N. 2003. 'The Drowning Fields: Environmental Disaster, Displacement and Hospitality'. Paper presented at the British Sociological Association Conference: *Social Futures: Desire, Excess and Waste*, April 11–13. New York: University of New York.

———. 2011. *Inhuman Nature: Sociable Life on a Dynamic Planet*. London: Sage.

———. 2013. 'Geopolitics at the Threshold'. *Political Geography,* 37: 48–50.

———. 2014. 'Geo-politics and the Disaster of the Anthropocene'. *The Sociological Review*, 62(S1): 19–37.

———. 2016. 'Anthropocene Incitements: Toward a Politics and Ethics of Ex-orbitant Planetarity'. In *The Politics of Globality Since 1945: Assembling the Planet,* (eds.). van Munster R., and Sylvest C., Abingdon, Oxon: Routledge, 126–144.

Cohen, T. 2010. 'The Geomorphic Fold: Anapocalyptics, Changing Climes and "Late" Deconstruction'. *The Oxford Literary Review*, 32(1): 71–89.

Collier, S. and Lakoff A. 2015. 'Vital Systems Security: Reflexive Biopolitics and the Government of Emergency'. *Theory, Culture & Society*, 32(2): 19–51.

Davis, M. 1996. 'Cosmic Dancers on History's Stage? The Permanent Revolution in the Earth Sciences'. *New Left Review*, 217: 48–84.

Deleuze, G. and Guattari, F. 1987. *A Thousand Plateaus: Capitalism and Schizophrenia*. Minneapolis: University of Minnesota Press.

Deleuze, G. and Guattari, F. 1994. *What is Philosophy?* London: Verso Books.
Derrida J. 1994. *Spectres of Marx: The State of the Debt, the Work of Mourning, and the New International.* New York: Routledge.
————. 2001. *On Cosmopolitanism and Forgiveness.* London: Routledge.
————. 2005. *Rogues: Two Essays on Reason.* Stanford, CA: Stanford University Press.
Dikeç, M., Clark, N. and Barnett, C. 2009. 'Extending Hospitality: Giving Space, Taking Time'. *Paragraph*, 32(1): 1–14.
Dillon, M. 1999. 'The Scandal of the Refugee: Some Reflections on the "Inter" of International Relations and Continental Thought'. In *Moral Spaces: Rethinking Ethics and World Politics*, (eds.). Campbell, D. and Shapiro, M. J., Minneapolis, MN: University of Minnesota Press.
Fortey, R. 2005. *The Earth: An Intimate History.* London: Harper Perennial.
Gemenne, F. 2011. 'Climate-Induced Population Displacements in a 4°C+ World'. *Philosophical Transactions of the Royal Society A*, 369: 182–195.
Gasché, R. 2014. *Geophilosophy: On Deleuze and Guattari's What is Philosophy?* Evanston, IL: Northwestern University Press.
Gleick, P. H. 2014. 'Water, Drought, Climate Change, and Conflict in Syria'. *Weather, Climate and Society*, 6: 331–40.
Goldberg, L. 2009. 'The Miraculous Story of the Jews of Zakynthos'. *The Jerusalem Post* (13 December). Available at: http://www.jpost.com/Jewish-World/The-miraculous-story-of-the-Jews-of-Zakynthos(accessed 26 June 2016).
Hamilton, C. 2014. Can Humans Survive the Anthropocene? Available at: http://clivehamilton.com/can-humans-survive-the-anthropocene/ (accessed 4 October, 2015).
Hardt, M. and Negri, A. 2001. *Empire.* Cambridge, MA: Harvard University Press.
Hayward A., Dowsett H., Valdes P. et al. 2009. 'Introduction: Pliocene Climate, Processes and Problems'. *Philosophical Transactions of the Royal Society A*, 367 (2009): 3–17.
Holy Bible: King James Version. Available at: http://www.kingjamesbibleonline.org (accessed 26 June 2016).
Johnson, G. 1988. 'Late Uruk in Greater Mesopotamia: Expansion or Collapse'? *Origini: Preistoria e Protostoria delle Civiltà Antiche*, 14: 595–613.
Johnstone, S. and Mazo, J. 2011. 'Global Warming and the Arab Spring'. *Survival*, 53(2): 11–17.
Kennett, D. J. and Kennett, J. P. 2006. 'Early State Formation in Southern Mesopotamia: Sea Levels, Shorelines, and Climate Change'. *The Journal of Island and Coastal Archaeology*, 1(1): 67–99.
Larking, E. 2014. *Refugees and the Myth of Human Rights: Life Outside the Pale of the Law.* Farnham and Burlington, VT: Ashgate.
Latour, B. 2014. 'Agency at the Time of the Anthropocene'. *New Literary History*, 45(1): 1–18.
Lazarus, D. S. 1990. 'Environmental Refugees: New Strangers at the Door'. *Our Planet*, 2(3): 12–14.
Lingis, A. 1994. *The Community of Those Who Have Nothing in Common.* Bloomington and Indianapolis: Indiana University Press.

Michaels, A. 1997. *Fugitive Pieces*. London: Bloomsbury.

Myers, N. 1993. *Ultimate Security: The Environment Basis of Political Security*. New York and London: WW Norton.

Myers, N. 2002. 'Environmental Refugees: A Growing Phenomenon of the 21st Century'. *Philosophical Transactions of the Royal Society of London*, 357: 609–613.

Nunn, P. 2012. 'Understanding and Adapting to Sea Level Rise'. In *Global Environmental Issues* (2nd edition), (ed.). Harris, F. Chichester: John Wiley & Sons, 87–107.

Piguet, E. 2010. 'Linking Climate Change, Environmental Degradation, and Migration: A Methodological Overview'. *Wiley Interdisciplinary Reviews: Climate Change*, 1(4): 517–524.

Piguet, E. 2013: 'From "Primitive Migration" to "Climate Refugees": The Curious Fate of the Natural Environment in Migration Studies'. *Annals of the Association of American Geographers*, 103(1): 148–162.

Rockström, J., Steffen, W., Noone, K., Chapin, F. S. III., Lambin, E., Lenton, T., Scheffer, M., Folke, C., Schellnhuber, H., Nykvist, B., De Wit, C., Hughes, T., van der Leeuw, S., Rodhe, H., Sörlin, S., Snyder, P., Costanza, R., Svedin, U., Falkenmark, M., Karlberg, L., Corell, R., Fabry, V., Hansen, J., Walker, B., Liverman, D., Richardson, K., Crutzen, P. and Foley, J., 2009, 'Planetary Boundaries: Exploring the Safe Operating Space for Humanity'. *Ecology and Society*, 14(2): 32. Available at: www.ecologyandsociety.org/vol14/iss2/art32/ (accessed 16 March 2013).

Selby, J. and Hulme, M. 2015. 'Is Climate Change really to Blame for Syria's Civil War?' *The Guardian* (November 29). Available at: http://www.theguardian.com/commentisfree/2015/nov/29/climate-change-syria-civil-war-prince-charles (accessed 26 June 2016).

Selby, J. 2014. 'Positivist Climate Conflict Research: A Critique'. *Geopolitics* 19(4): 829–856.

Shryock, A. 2009. Hospitality Lessons: Learning the Shared Language of Derrida and the Balga Bedouin, *Paragraph*, 32(1): 32–50.

Shryock, A. 2012. 'Breaking Hospitality Apart: Bad Hosts, Bad Guests, and the Problem of Sovereignty'. *Journal of the Royal Anthropological Institute* 18: S20–S33.

Sloterdijk P. 2014. *Spheres 2: Globes – Macrospherolog*. South Pasadena, CA: Semiotext(e).

Turpin, E. 2011. 'Reflections on Stainlessness'. *Fuse*, 35(1): 11–15;

Warner K., Hamza, M., Oliver-Smith, A., Renaud, F., and Julca, A. 2010. 'Climate Change, Environmental Degradation and Migration'. *Natural Hazards*, 55: 689–715.

White, G. 2011. *Climate Change and Migration: Security and Borders in a Warming World*. New York: Oxford University Press.

Yusoff, K. 2013. 'Geologic Life: Prehistory, Climate, Futures in the Anthropocene'. *Environment and Planning D: Society and Space*, 31: 779–795.

Zalasiewicz, J. 2008. *The Earth After Us*. Oxford: Oxford University Press.

Zante-paradise.com. 'Zante history Zakynthos'. Available at: http://www.zante-paradise.com/history.htm (accessed 26 June 2016).

Chapter 9

Globalization as a Crisis of Mobility

A Critique of Spherology

Arun Saldanha

INTRODUCTION: WHAT IS GLOBAL?

The Anthropocene is both a geological epoch and an unspeakably complex mixture of human and nonhuman movements, barely covered by the term 'globalization'. Politics and ethical philosophy have yet to confront these overwhelming biophysical flows, in relation to which they become both puny and necessary. If Hannah Arendt (1976) and Giorgio Agamben (1993) have been correct in seeing the refugee camp as a central place indexing the built-in exclusions of the geopolitical order supposedly built on human rights, there are flows of money, germs, crops, cement, heat, data and weapons that need to be analysed for appreciating how people become displaced in the first place. A more materialist understanding of the Anthropocene sees it as not just a historical or evolutionary rupture but a capitalist ecology of distributions and migrations in crisis. This book chapter will argue in a generally Marxist vein, but revamped with Doreen Massey, that just like scarcity, waste or environmental disaster, refugees are inevitable products of the violent territorializations of capitalism itself. Since the political-economic system inherently pushes certain populations across borders to flee from compound disasters which are already worsening because of climate change and rising racism, the refugee camp can be called emblematic of the twenty-first century. I will contrast Massey's topology of differential mobilities and interconnection, which she calls power-geometry, with that of Peter Sloterdijk, which he calls spherology, a grand philosophical project of thinking the spatiality of human existence. Reading Sloterdijk through a critical lens, the distinction between the conservative and the progressive positions on refugees becomes abundantly clear. To make of climate change and increased migration a political opportunity instead of generating more militarized biopolitics, a precise understanding of the interplay of place and movement is indispensable.

Sloterdijk's spherological continuation of Heideggerian phenomenology corresponds to a mythico-historical theorization of more or less what geographers call *place*. Also influenced by phenomenology, the so-called humanistic geographers of the 1970s contrasted place as the realm of embodied meaning and experience to space as the realm of disembodied maps, movement, quantification, comparison and planning (Tuan 1977). 'Sense of place' is understood to be basic to human life and society, though it has come under threat in modernity from the homogenizing impact of what we now call globalization: endless strip malls, electricity masts and cul-de-sacs. Massey (1994: chapter 6) famously criticized this humanistic defence of place for its intrinsic tendency to a reactive Romantic poetics which could only operate by drawing boundaries around a location and presuming a timeless essence presiding within it, tangible only to the gentle and tranquil observer, usually a bourgeois man at leisure to appreciate landscape and heritage. The sense of place concept has to bracket the flows which constitute every place in order to maintain the fantasy of its sameness over time. Even a village economy does not subsist without itinerant traders and goods from elsewhere, often from very far away. In what Massey calls a *global* sense of place, therefore, space constitutes place. The concept of globalization is intrinsic to the concept of place and vice versa. Humanism is wrong to oppose the familiarity of place against the alienating fluidity of globalization and thereby pretend both are homogeneous and without conflict. Without the differences in space there can be no globalization, no change.

POWER-GEOMETRY AND UNEVEN MOBILITY

It is essential to have a deeply geographical understanding of globalization to avoid essentializing both the local (place as bounded and static) and the global (development as homogenous). The most accomplished and influential theorization of globalization as a multiplicity of uneven, heterogeneous, unpredictable and non-converging flows can be found in Doreen Massey's notion of power-geometry. Power-geometry is a topological 'mapping' or schematization of the power relations which constitute the interconnectedness of humans under modernity. Globalization is about movements – movements of money, people, commodities, ideas, data, food, crops, germs, storms and a thousand other human and nonhuman things – but Massey insists that power relations do not exist without controlling those movements. She departs from Marxism by theorizing power as relatively autonomous from class and monetary processes, so there is no one flow, capital, which would determine the others. If for Foucault power is a contingent social multiplicity created and changed through institutions and 'discursive practices', Massey adds a much more layered and dynamic appreciation of what the exercise of power concretely consists of.

The power of the business and diplomatic elite, for example, consists not just in its access to money and particular information (which are themselves flows), but in its physical mobility and access to particular spaces. The powerlessness of refugees consists not just in the lack of a work visa and legal protection, but in the particular journey they are trying to make. The distribution of vulnerability and control is highly unequal between countries, but also within the same city, even within the same household. Following a strong feminist strand in her thinking Massey (1994: chapter 8) recasts the power relation between men and women as one which is necessarily materialized in differential mobility and imaginations of space and place. In most societies men define the public sphere and are more mobile while women become identified with domesticity. It is crucial to understand that the mobility of one group can be structurally implicated in the (im)mobility of another. Men can travel only if their wives take care of the house and children. Charter tourism to Israel goes hand in hand with severe restrictions on movement for Palestinians. The profuse travel of EU functionaries is crucial for sustaining the megamachine of Fortress Europe. The causality is usually complex enough for responsibility to be shirked, but the power-geometry of capitalist globalization brings almost all human flows and homes into one huge splintered system. In short, the concept of power-geometry holds that it is impossible to think human difference (gender, class, race, health) without movement; impossible to think globalization, as the mass of flows, without the enormous disparities and physical constraints it brings to humans along the intersecting 'axes' of difference; and impossible to think place without the ongoing struggles about its past and future.

Freedom of movement is central to liberal democracy and equality under the law. What gets left out in the (neo)liberal narrative of human interconnectivity, however, are some very obvious facts whose omission effectively maintains the inequality between the haves and have-nots, the movers and the moved. We will mention four. First, interconnection is always stratifying. While the explosions of tourism and shopping malls are presented as horizontal exchanges in a flattening world, they could also make inequalities more pronounced and entwined. Stratification does not mean that everywhere the rich get richer and the poor poorer, but that 'global' linkages create new social differences all the time, which reorganize the geographies of wealth and destitution. The 'emerging economies' (a deeply ideological way of saying everyone must follow the same capitalist path the United States has stipulated) prove that stratification is an uneven process. Homogenization, convergence, equalization do happen. Marx himself never denied that capitalism lifts people out of poverty and spreads good things like science and education. But elsewhere, capitalism exacerbates poverty and violence. At some point, too, there will be an economic crisis. On Massey's interpretation, the class, gender and racial inequalities in mobility and wealth should be analysed before any horizontality or cosmopolitanism is claimed.

Second, globalization is about immobilization as much as it is about flows and networks. If power relations are nothing but the differential control over mobilities, the erecting of boundaries with particular selection mechanisms become crucial. To introduce a Foucauldian term Massey did not use much, globalization is directly *biopolitical* in that it requires the governing of entire populations. Biopolitics occurs when the life and vitality of the people of a territory is maintained not only by promoting its welfare and productivity, but by making sure anyone who is deemed to stand in the way of that vitality is incapacitated. Wendy Brown (2010), Slavoj Žižek (2014, interestingly following Sloterdijk) and many others have observed that globalization entails an increase in border control, surveillance cameras, security industry, 'rogue nations' and apartheid-like segregations (gated communities and five-star resorts next to slums). The incarceration of 2.2 million Americans, the checkpoint system of the Occupied Territories of Palestine and the militarization of the borders of the European Union are just some of the more egregious instances of a global trend to inscribing biopolitical inequality on space. Barbed wire can be said to define our present as much as satellites do. While we would like to think modernity elevates curiosity and adventurousness amongst the middle classes, modernity's affects also include the fear of losing the enjoyment of one's property.

The third dimension of globalization I will mention here is its nonhuman dimension, today comprehensively brought under the term Anthropocene. The Anthropocene is a concept that is often criticized for hiding power relations behind a vague ideological notion of humanity or man (*anthropos*). This obscuring of difference continues the imagination of unicity in the dominant discourse of globalization, which itself continued the ideology of humanism dating back centuries. It is not 'man' but particular populations, the upper classes of Western Europe and the United States, and a particular mode of production, capitalism, which have been at the centre of exploiting earth systems. In her later work Massey (2005) also took issue with the anthropocentrism of traditional definitions of place. What a place *is* includes layers of inscrutable nonhuman flows: What is Los Angeles without the San Andreas fault line? Power-geometries are superimposed on cycles of earth systems that are becoming unhinged. Critical conditions leading to the displacement or exclusion of whole populations must be understood through both physical and human geographies.

The fourth element of the power-geometrical analysis of global capitalism that pulls the carpet from underneath techno-optimistic globality is politics. Following the post-Marxist theory of hegemony of Ernesto Laclau and Chantal Mouffe, Massey (2005: 42ff) argues that no geographical imagination succeeds in imposing itself completely, just like no flow is actually worldwide. An ideology like neoliberalism is a temporary articulation of stories and arguments only tenuously linked to the interests of particular classes, hence bound to be equivocal and full of contradictions. If different people are implicated in globalization in vastly different ways, their grasp of social systems and their feelings and aspirations about their place in those systems are literally *part of* that implication. On Massey's Spinozist conceptualization (2005: 188ff), it is not that one's perspective on the capitalist system is a straightforward 'reflection' of one's positionality in it, but that one's embodied perspective and experience make that positionality possible. What the politics of globalization does, then, is deny there is any inevitability to globalization. However relentless the drive to compete and accumulate, it can be and is resisted. Politics is the active engagement with one's relation to the others one is irrevocably interconnected with, both in one's own city and 'on the other side of the world'. Understanding globalization's uneven geography prepares the way for the assumption of a *responsibility* to create a collective movement demanding more just forms of globalization (Massey 2005: 191–95). One cannot pretend one lives in a bubble separate from the rest of the world.

THE PRODUCTION OF REFUGEES

Marx understood the nefarious and unsustainable aspects of capitalism to be systemic. Twentieth-century social democracy and multiculturalism were projects of creating a capitalism which was to champion human rights and an economy with maximum employment, adequate housing, education and right of asylum and without famine, epidemics and war. Elites saw their power curtailed through the welfare state and further questioned through new social movements. Neoliberalism was from the beginning an incremental project of reintroducing the conditions for capital flow – especially through financialization, technology and real estate – so as to restore class privileges (Harvey 2005). The result has been, predictably, the return of steep inequality. Ultimately, no benign pastoral, social-democratic or liberal biopower can contain the powerful inhuman logic of capital. Moreover, the multiple crises that the world now faces – climate change, refugees, terrorism, 'failed' states, resistant viruses, mass depression and anxiety, nationalism and fundamentalism – are *built into* capital's crazy machinic logic.

Climate refugees form one particularly pertinent phenomenon to analyse the disaster-prone nature of the our mode of production. It is a phenomenon that completely undermines capitalism's ideological self-presentation as rational and moral. Climate change proves capital has been far more destructive and self-destructive than even Marx and Engels (and even the utopian socialists and anarchists of their time) could imagine. The refugee and migrant flows it will trigger are going to put enormous pressure on the supposed closeness of free trade, freedom of movement, democracy and human rights. In fact, climate refugees could be the most lucid and tragic indication of a capitalist world order becoming ever more desperate and unstable. There might be hundreds of millions seeking refuge from environmental stress by mid-century (see e.g. Parenti 2011). Will they be refugees of climate change or capitalism? Obviously the construct 'climate refugee' itself plays an ideological role in making displacement seem to be a result of 'natural' factors beyond political control, while raising the alarm about a white civilization in terminal crisis because of immigration. I would argue it is precisely this strong affective force emanating from the figure of the climate refugee which makes it a central symptom of the disaster-prone power-geometry of the Anthropocene (Baldwin, 2016).

Few have explicitly theorized the production of refugees under capitalism even if violence and displacement are old topics in Marxism. The enclosure laws in early-modern Britain consolidated land holdings and dislodged thousands of bankrupted farmers, many of whom became vagabonds and petty criminals when no work could be found. Marx (1999: chapter 26) was clear that capital undertakes coercive methods, especially in colonial situations, to dispossess and displace entire populations in order to secure revenue streams towards the propertied classes locally and in the metropole. Industrialization intrinsically tends to cause sectors of populations to abandon their rural or pastoral lives for the city or other countries and to introduce various forms of violence, including addiction and crime. Marx (1999: chapter 25, section 3) famously warned that a Lumpenproletariat, a 'reserve army' or 'surplus population' of poor unemployed people, beggars, smugglers and so on, is a permanent feature of the system.

All these forms of dislocation were coerced only gradually by markets. While the distinction is notoriously fuzzy, the phenomenon of refugees is different: the events which turn people into 'refugees' and 'asylum-seekers' are more acute, localized and sudden than is the case with 'migrants' or 'the homeless'. It is the catastrophic nature of the displacement that generates the moral or legal obligation on the part of the host society to grant asylum. Refugees flee not just economic hardship but bombs, torture, persecution, famine, epidemics and environmental disasters. They are per definition 'illegals' and 'undocumented' because they lack the right to be where they are. This fundamental legal conundrum about their situation made Hannah Arendt (1976) theorize, just after the Second World War, that refugees lie at the heart of international relations and political theory. The situation where millions of people find themselves in need of basic necessities is a phenomenon defining of the twentieth century. It is the flip side of state borders, population density, a global food system and warfare with industrial means.

Mass refugee movements did not yet exist as a major political concern in Marx's day. But just like migration and homelessness, with which it interacts to the point of being in many cases indistinguishable, the refugee phenomenon is endemic to capitalism. One needs Marx's basic understandings of crisis, expansionism and urbanization to explain how the dislocation of populations comes about. Where Marx and Engels proved too wedded to Enlightenment notions of progress is in their disparagement of the 'backwardness' of agrarian sectors and nomads and their oblivion, overall, to the environmentally destructive forces of technology. A cause of displacement almost unimaginable until the late twentieth century is that the entire atmosphere of the earth is warming up due to the massive emission of carbon dioxide as part and parcel of the energy needs of industrialization. 'Global' warming means that the *average* temperatures of the atmosphere, conceived as one system interacting with oceans, life, volcanoes, the sun and so on, are climbing. Regional weather systems are changing everywhere. Severe storms, heat waves, droughts, flooding and wildfire become more frequent and exacerbate the melting of the planet's icecaps, which cause oceans and seas to encroach on coastal cities. Severe weather means local economies and institutions, always on the verge of crisis anyway, are more vulnerable. This increased vulnerability means more people have to move and find work or safety elsewhere. Importantly, local crisis conditions are usually managed (or mismanaged) by political and financial decisions far away.

The concept of climate refugee is even more difficult to define and legally dubious than that of refugee. Precisely thanks to that vagueness it is more often than not mobilized to create a subtly racialized fear in the West of hordes of desperate and dangerous masses fleeing the Global South. There is no doubt a chain of causality between industrialization, global warming and displacement, but seldom is the causality direct. For example, disasters like the one in the wake of Hurricane Katrina in the Mexican Gulf in 2005 are becoming more frequent, but it is nonsensical to say they are 'caused by' climate change. What caused the flooding of New Orleans and the neglect and injustices in its aftermath were political and economic conditions. Indeed, if there ever was a time critics affirmed 'there is no such thing as a natural disaster', it was then. The storm simply exposed the neglect. As infrastructures are disaster-prone across the world, increasing climate instabilities, rising sea levels and all kinds of pollution and shortages are definitely making disasters like Hurricane Katrina and Typhoon Haiyan more probable.

It would seem the Anthropocene is nothing but a planetwide megamachine which continually manufactures disasters. There was disaster in ancient Mesopotamia and China, of course, and extreme inequality in ancient Egypt. The collapse of the Mayas is a textbook example of how moribund inequality and unsustainable resource management spell the end of empire. But only capitalism *thrives* from crises which it manufactures itself, so much so that Naomi Klein (2007) calls its neoliberal stage 'disaster capitalism'. Christian Parenti (2011) meanwhile alerts us to the increase of warfare, crime, corruption, insurrections, xenophobia and securitization under conditions of climate change. A systemic analysis shows that Western governments and capital are often complicit with the refugee and migrant flows which disasters instigate. Disaster does not have to be of the size of the Fukushima meltdown or the Syrian refugee crisis. Shops go bankrupt, factories close, forests are cleared and farmers commit suicide. Only capitalism engages in disasters at all levels and all the time, including what mainstream economists enthusiastically call creative destruction.[1]

As some would respond at this point, one cannot blame something as monolithic as 'capitalism' for everything. Patriarchy and various kinds of discrimination must play a role too. It is indeed important to deepen Marx's analytics to take such psychocultural dimensions into account, but his strength lies in understanding what *connects* the multifarious phenomena into a self-enhancing system. This connection operates through the most volatile, almost gaseous, element in the system: capital, or rather debt. Another response is, does the Marxist not herself rely on the fruits of capitalism? Few deny the material comforts this mode of production has created, from jeans and fridges to mp3. The point is that it simultaneously produces violence, famine and displacement. What even the mainstream concept of the Anthropocene offers, against (neo)liberal optimism, is that in the twenty-first century disaster is set to override comfort or even liveability for a large section of the species – as well as for many other species. Moreover, one person's luxury is predicated on the denial of the basic conditions of life for someone else. The Anthropocene is in itself structural injustice. To conclude, the displacement of populations, as extreme weather conditions make their safety under capitalism *even more* tenuous, makes manifest the disastrous nature of global interconnectedness.

SPHERES OF IMMUNIZATION

We turn now to Peter Sloterdijk's philosophical anthropology of globalization. His take on human dwelling and society might be the best example of

how capitalist society obfuscates the power-geometry of the planetary predicament and actively closes off possibilities for challenging it. It is important
to single out Sloterdijk as *preventing* a clear framework for understanding
globalization. First, already a fashionable intellectual in Germany and the
Netherlands, his work is becoming important to the European public sphere.
Second, more than anyone in the tradition of philosophical anthropology and
more than most in today's cultural theory, Sloterdijk offers a remarkably
spatial understanding of globalization. The problem is that it is exactly the
approach to space which I have critiqued with Massey. Hence, third, Sloterdijk
exemplifies the phenomenological theorization of place which critical geography has argued with and about. Fourth, Sloterdijk's direct influence has
been growing in Anglophone theoretical circles, including geography (see
Elden 2012). And fifth, he is far from an apologist for capital, and ostensibly
poses questions about liberal democracy's celebration of fluidity. Altogether,
it behoves critical geographers to carefully unpack Sloterdijk's work because
it might be the most seductive and complex expression of the conservative
reaction to globalization's crises of mobilities.

Introducing Spherology

For the purposes of this book chapter I will focus on Sloterdijk's magisterial
trilogy *Spheres*, a richly illustrated overview of the human lifeworld num-
bering 2600 pages in English. With unparalleled erudition Sloterdijk details
what we could call the territorialization of human life from a (European)
historical perspective, at the bodily, architectural, continental and planetary
scales. The history of civilization has revolved around the organization and
the imagination of fragile structures that Sloterdijk calls 'spheres', material-
semiotic contraptions with a definite centre, an inside and borders which keep
the hostile outside at bay. Spheres are necessary for humans to feel safe. In
fact there is no such thing as an individual subject without a life-long history
of various kinds of being-together preceding and shaping it. No one can live
in a bubble by himself or herself. The American English term 'comfort zone'
is a nice synonym for what Sloterdijk is getting at, but the zones extend from
bodily organs to empires, and comfort can also be imprisonment. Hence
Sloterdijk theorizes the way that institutional powers like the Roman Catholic
Church subject populations to hierarchical structures in the same movement
as they create a world and sense of community. He calls his spherological
approach a kind of *immunology* because it asks how humans, by living in
spatial and affective proximity to each other, protect themselves against the
dangers of contamination and aggression from without, whether perceived
or real. Ultimately, the spherological approach anchors what Sloterdijk calls
the 'macrospheres' of city, civilization and world upon the eminently fragile
'microsphere' of preindividual life, that is, pregnancy and infancy.

In seeking to rethink the highly unstable and even catastrophic modern predicament in historical light, Sloterdijk explicitly follows in the footsteps of an earlier post-Nietzschean conservative thinker, Oswald Spengler. Spengler's famous tome *The Decline of the West* (1991), first published at the end of the First World War, is a classic of pessimistic world history. Spenler argued that the European nations were experiencing a civilizational dead-end just like the Egyptian, Indian, Persian or Roman had before. His authoritarian nationalism had some influence on Nazi ideologues even if he distanced himself from racialism. Like Spengler, Sloterdijk is staunchly anti-Marxist and anti-individualistic, but like liberals he fully accepts the inevitability of the decline of the nation. Sloterdijkian methodology is joyfully eclectic and iconoclastic and he owes much to Foucault and Derrida. There is nothing of the heavy-handedness of philosophy of history; instead there is the lightness of postmodernism, which paradoxically offers a new metanarrative which Sloterdijk for more than a decade propagated through his own talk show on German television. Though he seldom addresses politics directly, the upshot of Sloterdijk's position is optimistic. What the project of writing the final crisis of European civilization calls for is nothing more than an affirmation of the redeeming functions of artistic and knowledge practices.

Sloterdijk is known in Germany for creating controversies. The most acute controversy arose when he suggested, picking up Nietzsche's most misunderstood argument, that there needs to be a new kind of 'breeding' (*Selektion*), a cultural eugenics in an age of digital technoscience and generalized mobility (Sloterdijk 2009: 21ff). He first gained notoriety when his debut treatise (Sloterdijk 1987) dared question the position of the country's then-primary public philosopher, Jürgen Habermas, who continues the Kantian and Marxian tradition of critique and is one of the main spokespeople of the European liberal left (see e.g. Habermas 2012). Having usurped Habermas' position as Germany's best-selling living philosopher, Sloterdijk provokes intelligentsia to abandon critical theory for his own sprawling philosophy of culture (*Kulturphilosophie*) in the very German, and generally conservative, tradition of philosophical anthropology. His Heideggerian background brings in a frequent focus on technology. In attempting to recreate a certain aristocratic tradition of learning and to annul the influence of the Frankfurt School, the Sloterdijkian position (or better, quasi-position) depends on an *infidelity* to the left both old and new, supposedly in the name of progressive engagement. Unfortunately, but tellingly, this mischievous conservatism is mostly left unanalysed in the reception of Sloterdijk's work outside Germany (see e.g. Elden 2012).

In the *Spheres* project Sloterdijk claims to provide nothing less than a *Being and Space* in which the concrete processes of being part of a geographical world come to circumscribe the platform for human and civilizational cohesiveness. Heidegger's *Being and Time* philosophized the ways human existence plays out through a temporal unfolding in relation to its milieu. Heidegger's theory of place has been central in humanistic geography, and Massey (2005: 183) critiques its pretension to redeem the authenticity which is supposed to have been obliterated by technological modernity. While *Spheres* engages few details of Heidegger's formidable philosophy, it nonetheless has some basic (and unproblematized) Heideggerian presuppositions. First, being is always being-with (*Mit-sein*), and there is no such thing as an individual person existing by itself (Heidegger 1996: 110ff). Secondly, in an age after the death of God, finitude is the definitive characteristic of being, and human life is being-towards-death without the guarantee of an afterlife. Thirdly, being-in-the-world is always a dwelling, a delineating of a bit *of* that world as a space to live *in*, through the recursive use of speech and the routine-bound nature of specific things. Human life is the ceaseless attempt to feel and *be* at home, construing a safety bubble that countervails the fact of being 'thrown into' the world (Heidegger 1996: 176–80). Even if one's home is never quite one's own and (self-)alienation is ultimately inescapable, a Heideggerian makes room for the poetics of somewhat melancholy authenticity which withstands the meaninglessness Newtonians call space. And the fourth inheritance of Heidegger in Sloterdijk is that language and myth 'unveil' Being. It is especially art that tells us how spherical life concretely happens. All cultural products from European civilization of the last two thousand years (and a few from elsewhere) can fit into and illuminate Sloterdijk's voracious hyper-framework. Relying heavily on Christian theology, instead of the pre-Socratics in Heidegger, the *Spheres* trilogy is a secular re-enchantment of the world through the creative qualities of erudition itself. Sloterdijk makes philosophical literature out of art history, somewhat like Nietzsche but rather without the revolutionary impulse to a 'reevaluation of all values'.

As probably the most encyclopaedic venture ever in writing a phenomenology of place qua comfort zone, it should come as no surprise that Sloterdijk's spherology could be called the discourse for which Massey's critique of the ideology of place was *a fortiori* written.[2] That is, even if it draws on poststructuralist philosophies, spherology is fundamentally engaged in an old-fashioned humanist essentialization of place which does not grasp its own constitution by internal heterogeneities and changing outsides. This will also mean Sloterdijk is structurally incapable of understanding displacement and environmental destruction as central to modernity: To what place, what sphere, would climate refugees belong?

Socialization In Utero

Spherology is meant to debunk liberal individualism through a new valorization of intimacy. In the first volume *Spheres*, subtitled *Bubbles*, Sloterdijk

(2011a) develops an ontology of the relationality at the basis of human society. This 'microspherology' goes further than Heidegger's conceptualization of intersubjectivity by recovering a 'forgotten' (in the Heideggerian sense, 1996: 311–12) *pre*-subjective and fully corporeal condition of togetherness which our navels bear witness to: our intimate dependence on the placenta, the 'primal companion' (Sloterdijk 2011a: chapter 5). What Sloterdijk calls a 'symbiosis' of the mother's body and that of the foetus and infant consists in the exchange of nutrients and affects. The resulting 'negative gynecology' (2011a: chapter 4) sees the entire world-making capacity of humans as the continuation in obverse of this uterine experience of being umbilically connected, which all humans start with and forever try to emulate. In a whirlwind tour through mythological and theological layers of meaning surrounding such themes as the heart, the face, mesmerism, the womb, twins, sirens, angels, the Holy Trinity and so on, Sloterdijk unearths an original twoness without which human individuality would never be possible. At its most basic, the non-individuality of prenatal space prefigures what adult social space will consist of. What makes twins or a doppelgänger so uncanny is that humans unconsciously remember they are not corporeal 'individuals' at all.

Why bubbles (*Blasen*)? This is more than a metaphor, as there is a topological organization that is shared by bubbles in the narrow sense (of soap, for example) and the volumes of intimacy that the foetus–placenta dyad, and then full-grown humans, construct around themselves. Both have a clear inside and outside, yet both also have membranous openness to their surroundings; both exist in a dynamic tension; both are mobile; and both are from their inception on the verge of vanishing or metamorphosis. Just like being is being-towards-death in Heidegger (1996: 231ff), there is a catastrophe haunting and awaiting the warm interior of a microsphere, or 'little world' (Sloterdijk 2011a: 438). This fragility of proximity is carried over into the macrospheres of home, city and globe.[3] While Sloterdijk cannot be accused of taking human togetherness for granted, he refrains from developing a theory of the existential threats to the human bubble. He says *that* spheres are threatened from outside but not *by what*. Through his literary meanderings it becomes clear that art and religion have over the ages registered the fact (or facticity) of a fundamental vulnerability that accompanies human individuality from birth, an anxiety of being invaded by the outside. But it seems the fragility is entwined with the structure of bubble itself instead of deriving from *particular* forces impinging on it from outside. The fragility is admitted but not problematized.

Ultimately, then, Sloterdijk presents human being-together as a self-sustaining, largely homeostatic and self-unfolding space constructed only from its internal intensities and not by any external prompts. From a feminist perspective this is disturbing. By making the amniotic sac the ground of the social itself, Sloterdijk walks a fine line between a widespread conservative sentimental celebration of motherhood and a more disturbing blurring of a celebration of breeding and the vitality of the nation (derived, of course, from *nascere*, be born). Who is a woman pregnant *for*? Who is saying her womb has a higher meaning? While Sloterdijk is no fascist, he chooses to leave unexplained how his beatifying 'requiem' for the placenta would *not* be biopolitically imbricated in the body politic of a nation or community. If social formations are to be reconceptualized in analogy to the foetus-placenta, should we also presume them healthy and pure as long as their delicate boundaries remain intact?

Pregnancy can and often does result from various kinds of violence and coercion. Sloterdijk takes what he sees as a stable transhistorical condition to be the bedrock for what is human, making of pregnancy an ontological substratum for all larger social formations. This makes microspherology difficult to align not only with feminism but also with the basic discoveries of psychoanalysis. Following Freud, Melanie Klein (1949) theorized the complicated combinations of love, aggression and frustration which childhood consists of for both children and mother. The infant manipulates the mother into caring as much as the mother manipulates the infant into becoming a member of society. Hence the 'original' dyad represented paradigmatically in the Madonna is not original at all. Obviously an affective bubble is essential for the first years of a human's life, but Sloterdijk's anti-psychoanalytical position deliberately omits the traumas of weaning, bodily discipline and the intrusion of a male figure which, psychoanalysis shows, echo throughout later life. Furthermore, as Massey would remind Klein, these 'microsocial' events and life chances are structured by wider power-geometries. Pregnancy and breastfeeding occur within geographies of contraception, food, religion, health care, housing and population policy. One is reminded of the Nestlé scandal in which the multinational actively discouraged breastfeeding in poor countries. Mother–baby symbiosis is an *achievement* within flows which make it difficult. It is not a quasi-metaphysical given.

More generally, to suppose harmony in utero makes it impossible to think the increasingly problematic nature of sexuality under the Anthropocene. Now that the reality of climate change appears to be vindicating at least some of the Malthusian fears over an overconsumed planet, some women in the rich world decide against pregnancy on environmental grounds (Ostrander 2016). Even if we can assume Sloterdijk is not glorifying motherhood for the sake of a nation, a religion, or life as such, there is very little standing between him and the right-wing discourses which look at abortion, homosexuality, sex work, orphanage, teenage runaways, drug addiction, sex change and other complications in patriarchy's reproduction as aberrations from the norm.[4] And all these phenomena are connected to differential mobilities. As Marx and Engels (2000: section II) pointed out in the 1840s, prostitution and the breakup of families happen because of the displacement and impoverishment that is part of industrialization. The defence of 'family values' in Christian and bourgeois discourse (and conservative feminism) is based on a refusal to take into account the economic pressures which cause phenomena like alcoholism and domestic violence. What could be called the 'placental turn' which Sloterdijk advocates in the field of body studies continues this senti- mental ideology of primordial harmony. In starting with intrauterine space as if untouched by patriarchy and the will of the mother herself, microspherol- ogy embarks on a decidedly conservative ontological trajectory.

Culture as Endospheres

We turn now to macrospherology, the phenomenology of cities, civilizations, nations and worlds as laid out in the second volume of *Spheres*, subtitled *Globes*. For Sloterdijk civilization is an immunological effort, an inoculation of a collective that can keep out evil, foreign armies and natural catastrophes through its boundary drawing and chauvinism (see Mutsaerts 2016). But, just as with the microcosm, it isn't clear in *Globes* why there needs to be inocula- tion at all. What are humans afraid of that makes them unconsciously yearn for the uterus? The chapter 'Arks, City Walls, World Boundaries, Immune Systems: The Ontology of the Walled Space' starts with the ark myth because it is the primordial story showing the requirement for separateness in the reproduction of civilization. When Noah saves humanity and animals from the planetwide deluge, his ark is like an incubator for saving the select few from creation to restart the true civilization once the earth has been destroyed. Sloterdijk writes:

> The ark concept – from the Latin *area*, 'box' (compare to *arcanus*, 'closed, secret') – exposes the most spherologically radical spatial idea which humans on the threshold of advanced civilization were able to conceive: that of the artificial, sealed inner world can, under certain circumstances, become the only possible environment for its inhabitants. This gives rise to a new kind of project: the notion of a group's self-harboring and self-surrounding in the face of an outside world that has become impossible. (2014: 237)

The spatiality of the ark captures what might be the most extreme story of divine selectness, of patriarchal progeny, of killing in order to let live, in short, of biopolitics. 'In all ark phantasms, the selection of the few is affirmed as a sacred necessity; many are called, but few embark' (Sloterdijk 2014: 246). Obviously, in an age of rising sea levels and populations on the move, the ark phantasm starts to have particular resonance. At this point in

Sloterdijk's volume a surprising photo appears without explicit connection to the text: the 'boat people' fleeing communist Vietnam over the South China Sea. The only reference to refugees in *Spheres* (and one of the very few to human mobility other than heroic colonialism), the inclusion of the photo raises intriguing questions. Are these boat people somehow special? Is the destruction that causes refugee streams necessary for a new civilization to arise? (That of Vietnamese America?) In any case, the comparison between boat people and the ark myth is inconsiderate or even obscene if Sloterdijk is implying they are taking world history in their own God-guided hands like Noah did.

The uneven interconnectivity that we saw is coextensive with globalization disappears in macrospherology, for which 'civilizations' seem to exist by virtue of blocking exchange and promoting xenophobia. Furthermore, on Sloterdijk's perspective, Noah's ark or the Christian world community is immune not only to outside threats but also to internal strife. He does discuss heresy and anti-Semitism (Sloterdijk 2014: 728ff), and military technologies and terrorism are recurrent themes (on gas warfare, for example, see Sloterdijk 2004: 89ff). In Nietzschean and anthropological vein, macrospherology presumes social cohesion as predicated on sacrifice and shared ecstasies and fears. Thus most of Sloterdijk's examples allow for developing the biopolitical dimensions intrinsic to maintaining community around a sacred centre. In one excursus he analyses the 'immune paradox' that sedentary society faces (or smells): the more people live together, the more shit must be somehow ejected (Sloterdijk 2014: excursus 2). But Sloterdijk never elaborates on dissension and power relations as topics in their own right. His civilizations and cities are self-contained, self-propelling, ultimately harmonious and eager to grow just like the placenta-foetus *as long as* they are securitized against the deadly outside. In his own words:

'The human being is the animal that, together with its significant others, produces endospheres in almost every situation because it remains shaped by the memory of a different having-been-inside, and by the anticipation of a final being-enclosed. It is the natal and the mortal creature that has an interior because it changes its interior. Relocation tensions are in effect in every place where humans exist; that is why their entire history is the history of walls and their metamorphoses'. (Sloterdijk 2014: 198)

If social formations are 'endospheres', there will be a tendency to essentialize them in both practice and theory. As he moves from prehistoric villages to Joseph Beuys to torture instruments to copious Christian imagery, Sloterdijk provides only *snapshots* of cultures, which he very much enjoys arranging but has no conceptual basis to interrelate. Even less does he have an apparatus for discussing why exactly some social formations and ecosystems became imperialistic at all. Take this passage:

> If we observe the countless small cultures that arose from the primordial world up until historical times, watching this swarm of shimmering bubbles filled with languages, rites and projects spouting out and bursting, and if we can, in select cases, watch as they float further, grow and rule, one wonders how it can be that everything was not born away by the wind. The vast majority of older clans, tribes and peoples disappeared almost without a trace into a sort of nothingness, in some cases leaving behind at least a name and some obscure cult objects; of the millions of tiny ethnospheres that have drifted over the earth, only a fraction survived through metamorphoses based on enlarging, self-securing, and positing power symbols. (Sloterdijk, 2014: 149)

Two classic ideological moves are evident here. First, all societies or 'ethnospheres' start tiny and fragile. Presumably all want to become global. That some grew into 'civilizations' and that only one, the Christian-European-American sphere, became world dominant is thanks to its own desire to irradiate outwards (Sloterdijk makes a case especially for the telecommunicative work of the apostles and missionaries, 2014: chapter 7). Second, humanity is a collection of mutually unintelligible cultures floating aimlessly over the earth rather like separate animal species. They don't experience ruptures, they don't interact. Change is gradual and it occurs in only societies with history, with symbols, which thereby grow bigger and dominant. In contrast to this essentialism of a 'mosaic of cultures', contemporary anthropologists take movement and exchange as ontologically prior to cultural identity (e.g. Clifford 1997). Historians too now conceive humanity as a web, not a collection of bubbles (e.g. McNeill & McNeill 2003). When large societies go extinct, that is mostly because of conflict with others. Power does not primarily emanate from symbols endogenously, but it is a system of controlling the flows passing through it.

The fundamental problem in Sloterdijk's spatial ontology is that for him there is a 'repetition' of micro in macro: 'We shall make it clear how the basic phenomenon of the microspheric world – the mutual evocation of the two, unified in a strong relationship – repeats itself in the macrosphere, the orb-shaped universe' (2014: 91). Cities and world cultures (*urbi et orbi*, as the Pope says about Rome) are symbiotic communities referring back to the womb. While we have seen that the concept of microsphere was already dubious, this concept of scale bears no relation to reality at all. Scale does not work concentrically as it does in political myth: the Christian civilization as family, the father as ruler, the world centred on Rome, the symbolism of the crown and so on. In such a scalar picture there is no movement, and nothing jumps scales. For geographers like Massey, the global (macro) simply cannot be an enlargement by repetition of the local (micro), since it is precisely the differentiality specific to the global that constitutes places. Pilgrimage, trade, colonialism, migration, mass tourism and climate change cannot be situated within this Russian-doll image of scale. Expelled from one body politic by its position in global processes, then refused entry into another, refugees can in the sphero-immunological model only be conceived of as unbelonging. Sloterdijk is not so reactionary as to endorse a *Blut und Boden* ideology in which nation (or race) and territory are coterminous. But by not theorizing the inevitable cultural and political heterogeneity of macrospheres (they are modelled on placental symbiosis after all), we are left to wonder.

From Globes to Foams

In *Globes* Sloterdijk discusses the universalizing tendencies of European cultures and philosophies in absorbing detail, especially Neoplatonic Christianity and early-modern cosmology. And yet he describes an earth devoid of motion. As a kind of postmodernist he has, of course, discussed space travel and auto-mobility. But Sloterdijk cannot think spheres as constituted by flows. When he mentions a vector like missionaries, Columbus, the Crusades or Internet, it is always going from middle to margin, an irradiation. Hence the title of the key chapter in *Globes*, 'How the Spheric Center has Long-Distance Effects through the Pure Medium' (2014: chapter 7). Globalization is simply the centralizing of the cosmos, first around Rome, then Jerusalem, then the dollar.[5]

For Sloterdijk globality is a struggle between man and cosmos instead of struggles between social formations, classes and companies. As God comes to inhabit an increasingly worldly empire of wealth, man takes His place. 'The world-navigators, cartographers, conquistadors, world traders, even the Christian missionaries and their following of aid workers who exported goodwill and tourists who spent money on experiences at remote locations – they all generally behaved as if they had understood that, after the destruction of heaven, it was the earth itself that had to be take [sic] over its function as the last large-scale curvature' (Sloterdijk 2014: 773–74). Globalization is today mostly profane, but the switch occurred already in the Renaissance when world maps started to become practical, that is, aimed at European colonization. A species coming to understand itself as a unified *anthropos* which has pushed the planet into a new age is exactly what comes after the death of God. For Sloterdijk (2014: 935ff) the premodern generative fantasy of a transcendent everlasting life in the City of God becomes replaced with the shrinking, oversaturated, synchronous, polyglot, *ecumenical* world of instant telecommunications. Sloterdijk's separate book *In the World Interior of Capital* (2013a) delves into this interiority at the level of the planet, this re-creation of the globe in the image and interest of Western civilization through the vector of capital.

In practice, Western Europe was of course never immune from the influences of its outside. On the contrary: was the Renaissance not deeply indebted to Muslim traders, scientists, philosophers? Was capitalism not kick-started thanks to the investments generated from transatlantic slavery? Sloterdijk's ruminations formulate the *ideologies* of globality, not the real social relations as such which, as we saw, have nothing to do with globes in the morphological sense, but a lot with displacement and disparity. In a tremendous irony Sloterdijk's obsessive writing on circles, globes, bubbles, domes, capsules and so on embodies the very immunization he is by many readers supposed to critique. It seems the idea of an exterior gushing in, while fundamentally presumed in the immunological argument, is too scary to theorize as an actuality. Yet it is exactly such a collapse and desperate reinstatement of state immunity that the humanitarian and political crisis around the Syrian refugees of 2015 consists of. Sphericality is a real biopolitical project, but it is a response to more fundamental mobility which Sloterdijk leaves unanalysed.

Foams is the final volume of the *Spheres* trilogy and presents a 'plural spherology' in which micro and macro are fused. Continuing his critique of individualism and coming close to the left-wing analysis of atomization but with opposite sentiments, Sloterdijk (2004) imagines planetary techno-capitalist society as generalized insulation and insularity. Individuals are trapped in self-animated spheres without overarching transcendences or universalities left to protect them. Greenhouses and air conditioning are some of Sloterdijk's favourite examples showing how 'atmospheres' are the stuff of postmodernity. Apartment blocks with families glued to the television, cars in traffic jams, people immersed in their smartphones: the compartmentalization and homogenization of postmodernity proliferates with every new gadget. All these 'cells' are wrapped in their own world, so to speak. And yet their membranes are in constant contact, and this makes them 'co-fragile' and 'co-isolated' as they compete for space (Sloterdijk 2004: 250–57). With the demolition of the welfare state (that is, of national immunization), each neoliberal individual becomes responsible for its own little cell. If this sounds gloomy, Sloterdijk insists moderns are in fact quite pampered with all their indoor oceans and Hummers (2004: 815–19). His point is that cells are isolated together within networks which provide a fleeting sense of belonging.

The foam space of postmodernity is a multiplicity of centreless, amorphous, directionless artificial volumes. Many of these volumes are fun. At the Love Parade, when up to 1.5 million bodies danced to techno in the streets of Berlin, or at a foam party, there is a concerted effort to create a bubble of ecstatic togetherness (Sloterdijk 2004: 604 and 810). Even if such events don't overcome the fundamental isolation after the disappearance of modernity's grand narratives, they provide what Sloterdijk calls 'luxuries' which should be cherished (787ff). But, is luxuriousness the most important thing to note about foam space, about air conditioning? As with the ambiguous reference to boat people in *Globes*, when *Foams* includes undiscussed photographs of homeless men sleeping in boxes and Mongolian nomad tents (544 and 547), the question of whether encapsulation is coerced or chosen and the question of environmental and long-term impacts are entirely elided. Perhaps the most telling symptom of the *Spheres* trilogy's anti-critical conservatism is that it never discusses those cells or spheres increasingly crucial to militarized biopolitics: incarceration.

Again, therefore, we see Sloterdijk unwilling to provide a framework for explaining and analysing the uneven geographies of fragmentation, mobility and comfort. All his mobility seems to be voluntary. There is an infinite plurality of worlds and no capitalist logic lies underneath it. His discussion of space stations complete with vegetable garden (2004: 317–21) is fascinating, but how can their encapsulation be thought without the geopolitical (or exo-geopolitical) constellations they stitch? While *Foams* exaggerates the disappearance of metaphysical unifications (the nation state, religion, universality), it denies any possibility of cells resisting the fragmentation and fighting in the name of a solidarity. At the same time Sloterdijk wants nothing to do with nihilism and pessimism (2004: chapter 3). In fact he sharply accuses the left of a fundamental melancholy, continuing to moan, for example, about global inequalities (the conclusion to the book on globalization is actually called 'In Praise of Asymmetry', 2013a: 258–64). If there is any politics here, it is definitely a jolly one. Capitalism for Sloterdijk is defined not by labour, resource depletion and the resurgence of nationalism, but by leisure, innovation and pluralism. When he comes to write an ethical manifesto with the title *You Must Change Your Life*, Sloterdijk (2013b) proposes that humanity should come to grips with its constitutive 'eccentricity' through a new kind of ascesis, a Nietzschean working-on-oneself. The book does not say anything about getting rid of the immuno-spherical or biopolitical partitionings which exclude and attempt to homogenize. A Marxist politics would instead come closer to what Žižek (2016) proposes a propos the refugee crisis: an international anticapitalist front which aims at removing the structural conditions for inequality and displacement. Disappointingly, however, Žižek often quotes Sloterdijk to point out the glaring contradiction between the neoliberal dogma of hypermobility and the erection of new physical and psychic borders.

In a recent controversy Sloterdijk says about Angela Merkel's (brief) open-door refugee policy that 'this cannot go well' (Kissler and Schenicke 2016). He consistently avoids Islamophobia and says an incident like the mass sexual harassment of local white women in Cologne by North African asylum seekers on New Year's Eve 2015 fits into intercultural misapprehension as much as a culture of fear about terrorism, a situation he calls phobocracy.

Unlike the authoritarian conservatives and right-wing populists shaking Western democracies, Sloterdijk does not (as far as I know) call for further militarization in the face of refugees and terrorism. Instead, he says Germans should remain 'serene', continue learning from art and literature, avoid mass media, and think calmly through such difficult topics as religion, war, and anger. But he does remind his public that state sovereignty is defined by the capacity to block entry to migrants and refugees, and that Merkel's 'culture of welcoming' (*Willkommenskultur*) has been naïve. He mocks the strained German 'integration' policy, as he thinks intercultural gaps cannot simply be bridged: 'We have not learned the praise of the border'.

Sloterdijk chooses not to offer any long-term solutions to end the conditions that will displace millions more in the future, nor to extend his post-Nietzschean concept of generosity to demand an openness to strangers and radical change. Interestingly, he admits that 'the twenty-first century has one mega-theme: migration'. But for a philosophy of spheres actual mobility can only be an afterthought. The reality of refugees this century will demonstrate that human life does not start out from spheres at all.

CONCLUDING REMARKS

While geographers such as Massey have worked hard to reconceptualize space and place against neoliberal dogma-turned-common sense, the conservative spatiality of Sloterdijk takes exactly the wrong starting point in understanding globalization. This makes it intriguing and an important foil for a politics of mobility, provided it is understood *why* spherology can have no adequate concept of movement. An immunological framework implies that there is a potentiality of contaminants, but remaining silent on what these impurities are is tantamount to admitting that *any* in-flow is a threat. If conservative is that thinking which takes the endogeneity of place as its starting point, and progressive are those who know that place emerges only within structural inequality and friction, Sloterdijk's position is conservative, even if *Foams* seems to accept and partially even welcome techno-mediated fragmentation. His history of globalization (2013a) is quite deliberately the opposite of the Marxian schema in which the wealth of Europe arose through the pillaging of the rest of the world. In a manner typical of the more jovial tendencies of postmodernism, Sloterdijk in fact ultimately shuts down the possibility of geography as such. If globality is an ecumenical world interior, there can be no analysis of differences and conflicts between places and populations. Hyperbole has its place, as in some other prodigious theorists of globalization like Félix Guattari or Paul Virilio, but in Sloterdijk hyperbole serves mostly to aestheticize, not to critique.

There is no place without flow, no globalization without unevenness. Sloterdijk attempts to dismantle the Marxist tradition indirectly by simply directing attention to the material-semiotic construction of supposedly separate and horizontal spheres. While the reality of refugees, extreme weather and financial meltdown compels us to theorize capitalism qua system, this diversion tactic should be seen for what it is, a plunge in brilliant conservative erudition. More than Massey, I would emphasize that most volatile, ephemeral and deterministic of all flows, capital. If there is something (some 'thing') that spherology cannot think – like most phenomenology – it is capital. Despite the 'bubbles' it creates sectorially and regionally, and despite the simulacra of foamy cosiness it fabricates as a matter of course (new urbanism, Facebook, Tamagotchi), capital itself has absolutely nothing of the unity, immunity or homogeneity conjured by the image of a sphere. When Sloterdijk (2013a) mentions capital at all, it seems a largely benevolent force dedicated to bringing ever more people into the fold, into the comfortable interior.

I have compared Massey and Sloterdijk for understanding the matrix in which climate refugees emerge. Like all conservatives Sloterdijk is well worth reading as counterweight to the liberal exuberance about globalization. He provides plenty of inspiration for thinking through the deeper affects and narrations which buttress Fortress Europe. Globally, new versions of illiberal apartheid are appearing whose phobic immune systems are nurturing new fascisms. The resurgence of archaic race, religion, and nation motifs pose a grave threat to the future of open and democratic borders, whether in the United States, the EU, South Africa, Russia or India. Against globalization and its endemic crises, demagogues on the right would have us return to endospheres supposedly untouched by migration. Sloterdijk cannot, and does not want to, explain why environmental stress and armed conflicts over dwindling resources are going to increase, hence why more people will be on the move. Refugees are a systematic outcome of the multilayered Anthropocene and spring from a larger constellation of interlinked mobilities. To meet the challenge of the new fascist immunologies, what is required is scrutinizing this megamachine which produces war, disaster, refugees and border control as part of its normal functioning.

NOTES

1. A neatly ideological explanation of the Schumpeterian notion of creative destruction can be found in a short YouTube clip disseminated by Competitive Enterprise Institute, a libertarian think-tank: www.youtube.com/watch?v=8N08Kkjq9gA.

2. I do not think Massey had read Sloterdijk but it is plausible, as she read most of the key theorists of space. As a former student I am certain she would have criticized

the place-essentialism running through Sloterdijk's encyclopaedic exuberance, the division of labour yielding his sources, the masculinist adoption of maternalism and his posturing as the television-friendly *enfant terrible* of philosophy.

3. For a more sympathetic reading of Sloterdijk that makes of his notion of the catastrophic intimate a more critical possibility by linking it to Žižek, see van Tuinen (2009).

4. One wonders what Sloterdijk felt about the disturbing photograph of the lifeless Turkish boy on a Mediterranean beach, which turned Western European public opinion briefly in favour of hospitality towards the refugee streams from the Middle East in 2015.

5. While not entirely ignorant of Islam, Sloterdijk misses the opportunity to theorize Mecca as sphero-affective geometrical centralization of world community.

REFERENCES

Baldwin, Andrew. 2016. "Premediation and White Affect: Climate Change and Migration in Critical Perspective". *Transactions of the Institute of British Geographers*, 41, 78–90.

Brown, Wendy. 2014. *Walled States, Waning Sovereignty.* New York: Zone Books.

Clifford, James. 1997. *Routes: Travel and Translation in the Twentieth Century.* Cambridge, MA: Harvard University Press.

Elden, Stuart, (ed.). 2012. *Sloterdijk Now.* Cambridge, UK: Polity.

Habermas, Jürgen. 2012. *The Crisis of the European Union: A Response.* Cambridge: Polity.

Harvey, David. 2005. *A Brief History of Neoliberalism.* Oxford: Oxford University Press.

Kissler, Alexander and Christoph Schwechater. 2016. "Das kann nicht gut gehen". interview with Peter Sloterdijk, *Cicero*, January 27.

Klein, Naomi. 2007. *The Shock Doctrine: The Rise of Disaster Capitalism.* New York: Knopf.

Klein, Melanie. 1949. *The Psycho-Analysis of Children.* London: Hogarth.

Marx, Karl 1999. *Capital, Volume 1*, https://www.marxists.org/archive/marx/works/1867-c1/index.htm.

Marx, Karl and Friedrich Engels. 2000. *Manifesto of the Communist Party*, https://www.marxists.org/archive/marx/works/1848/communist-manifesto.

Massey, Doreen. 1994. *Space, Place and Gender.* Cambridge, UK: Polity.

———. 2005. *For Space.* London: Sage.

McNeill, J.R. and William McNeill. 2003. *The Human Web: A Bird's-Eye View of World History.* New York: Norton.

Mustaerts, Inge. 2016. *Immunological Discourse in Political Philosophy: Immunisation and Its Discontents.* London: Routledge.

Ostrander, Madelin. 2016. "How Do You Decide to Have a Baby When Climate Change is Remaking Life On Earth?" *The Nation*, April 11–18.

Parenti, Christian. 2011. *Tropic of Chaos: Climate Change and the New Geography of Violence.* New York: Nation Books.

Sloterdijk, Peter. 1987. *Critique of Cynical Reason*, translated by Michael Eldred. Minneapolis: University of Minnesota Press.

———. 2004. *Sphären, Band III. Schäume. Plurale Sphärologie*. Frankfurt am Main: Suhrkamp.

———. 2009. "Rules for the Human Zoo: A Response to the *Letter on Humanism*", no translator, *Environment and Planning D: Society and Space*, 27(1): 12–28.

———. 2011a. *Spheres, Volume 1: Bubbles. Microspherology*, translated by Wieland Hoban. New York: Semiotext(e).

Sloterdijk, Peter. 2013. *You Must Change Your Life*, translated by Wieland Hoban. Cambridge, UK: Polity.

Sloterdijk, Peter. 2014. *Spheres, Volume 2: Globes. Macrospherology*, translated by Wieland Hoban. New York: Semiotext(e).

Sloterdijk. 2016. "Gespräch Peter Sloterdijk zur Flüchtlingsproblematik", with report and interview, "Lebens Art", on German television station 3sat, https://www.youtube.com/watch?v=rev7x9jBGLI.

Spengler, Oswald. 1991. *The Decline of the West: An Abridged Edition*, (ed.) Helmut Werner, Arthur Helps, translated by Charles Francis Atkinson. New York: Oxford University Press.

Tuan, Yi-Fu. 1977. *Space and Place: The Perspective from Experience*. Minneapolis: University of Minnesota Press.

van Tuinen, Sjoerd. 2009. 'Breath of Relief: Peter Sloterdijk and the Politics of the Intimate'. In *The Catastrophic Imperative: Subjectivity, Time and Memory in Contemporary Thought*, (eds.) Dominiek Hoens, Sigi Jöttkandt and Gert Buelens. Houndmills, UK: Palgrave Macmillan, 53–82.

Žižek, Slavoj. 2014. "Disposable life", talk, Histories of Violence Project, www.historiesofviolence.com.

Žižek, Slavoj. 2016. *Against the Double Blackmail: Refugees, Terror and Other Troubles with the Neighbours*. London: Allen Lane.

Part III

ALTERITY: CLIMATE, MIGRATION AND THE (RE)PRODUCTION OF PAST AND FUTURE DIFFERENCE

Chapter 10

The Ecological Migrant in Postcolonial Time

Ranabir Samaddar

I

This chapter enquires into the process of the postcolonial production of what can be called surplus populations as a consequence of ecological marginality. The first section briefly discusses the colonial history of resource exploitation, agrarian crisis and displacement in India. Against this background the chapter moves on to the second section, which undertakes an analysis of the dynamics of the political economy of environmental displacement today. The third section shows how a particular model of development is linked to environmental displacement. The final section concludes the chapter with some reflections on the implications of the environmental and developmental displacement in terms of accumulation of capital and the production of mobile labour.

In such an enquiry, one cannot but refer to the seminal work of Mike Davis on the relation between markets, states and climate in the late nineteenth century, *Late Victorian Holocausts: El Nino Famines and the Making of the Third World*. Davis argued that in the late nineteenth-century climate change, social factors, abrupt economic transitions and particular political command structures combined with devastating effect to cause massive population shifts and millions of deaths across large parts of the world (Davis, 2002). Davis drew on the works of several historians including David Arnold, who showed how the colonial organization of power in India was crucial in accentuating environmental impact on peasantry and the ruinous effect it had on the customary ways of providing relief to the victims (Arnold, 1993). To take another instance, Jean Dreze's writings on the origin of the Famine Code in India in the late nineteenth century are of enormous help to us in having a historical understanding of the relation between ecology, politics and survival that was structured by colonialism (Dreze, 1990, ch.1).[1] Similarly,

James Vernon's work on hunger in Great Britain shows the intimate link between hunger, migration and the combined effects of environmental changes and a catastrophic political economy (Vernon, 2007). The interesting point about Vernon's work is that it shows how the British governmental attitude to hunger and the forced marches including hunger marches was shaped in the last 100 years by the attitude it had towards hunger and famines in the colonies, and the dilemma of a budget exercise, as to whether coping with calamities in the colony was to be regarded as an exceptional event of drawing on available resources or whether this should be part of a normal budgeting exercise – all these had their origin in the colonial age. Thanks to these studies we have now a better historical understanding of the issues and the origins of some of the policy dilemmas on the ecological management of our time.

In India, colonial rule had intervened with several legislations in the critical situations of drought, flood, famine and hunger – the best instance of which was the Famine Code (1883).[2] The Famine Code came into being at a time when peasant communities were crashing out of the market and becoming victims of hunger. Blood ties were destroyed as children and wives were sold in numbers. In addition to famines, colonial legislations on property, particularly land, and common property resource exacerbated the impact of the switch from custom to contract. The histories of famines, say from 1770 to 1873, and then the massive Bengal famine of 1943 give us accounts of the devastating impact of the colonial management of the subjugated population groups and massive migrations in search of security of life.

The point is, is the situation any different today? The questions that should be asked are: How do various factors combine today to produce hunger marches of our time, new resource crises, new migrants and the new refugees? If hunger, famines and floods played a crucial part in the making of the colonial economy, what are the postcolonial realities of political economy, particularly in terms of primitive accumulation that globalization requires as its fuel? How are the structures of inequalities reproduced through these environmental catastrophes? How are fringe economies produced?

An inquiry into these questions will help us to understand how environmental change, resource crisis and migration even today act as the locomotive of accumulation and development. Colonial history is crucial, because an understanding of the colonial time can help us to see how the postcolonial destiny awaits the entire world. It will (a) help bring back the issue of the colonial dynamics, which continues, of course with changes; (b) point out in this context how a new science of governance tries to make sense of the phenomenon; and (c) understand how the migrant, through the act of crossing borders and boundaries (borders of hunger, starvation, death and life; of places and countries; of stations in life and occupations; finally, of positions in the discrete map of division of labour), copes with a system that teams up with nature's calamities to turn millions into perishable lives.

Two recent important papers have explored the long duration colonial history of migration, and have brought to light the environmental factors underpinning the migration process. Subhas Ranjan Chakraborty's (2011) study on the figures on emigration drawing on various sources concludes in this way:

> The observations of a number of district collectors suggest that many 'disbanded sepoys', weavers, agricultural labourers and others engaged in low-caste service occupations . . . were from rural areas and from 'overcrowded agricultural districts', where 'crop failure could plunge sections of the village community into near-starvation'. In fact, there was a strong correlation between emigration and harvest conditions. Acute scarcity during 1873–75 in Bihar, Oudh and NW Provinces provoked large-scale emigration through the port of Calcutta. The famine in south India during 1874–8 also resulted in heavy emigration. Conversely, in good agricultural years recruits were not easily available. It has been reported that road blocks were hastily established to stem the flood of 'stick-thin country people' into Bombay and Pune, while in Madras the police forcibly expelled some 25,000 famine escapees. There is little doubt about the correlation between scarcity and forced migration. Most of the emigrants probably left their villages for the first time in their lives, and they were not fully aware of the hardships involved in long voyages and in living abroad. Diseases – cholera, typhoid, dysentery – were often rampant in the depots. Mortality among the emigrants was consequently high. Mortality at sea was alarmingly high. Before 1870, about 17 to twenty per cent of the labourers deported from the port of Calcutta died before they reached their destination. . . . During what constituted, in the imagination of the likes of Kipling and Curzon, the 'the glorious imperial half century' (1872–1921) life expectancy of ordinary Indians fell by a staggering twenty per cent. Pax Britannica, it would appear, had more victims than long centuries of war.[3]

In the other study focused on one century of migration from one single district, dry and repeatedly drought prone, Purulia (in West Bengal), the researcher Nirmal Kumar Mahato brings out the interface of scarcity, starvation and migration. In his words:

> Due to ecological degradation, the *adivasi* (indigenous) society plunged into repeated crises. With the dislocation of their ecological economy it was difficult to survive. There was nutritional crisis also. In the postcolonial period the same trend continued. Sometime the Government took developmental initiatives but it did not try to recover the lost ecosystem so that the people could survive on their own. Traditional water management was also lost. In the district, scarcity and nutritional crisis came not as a phenomenon but as a process. Thus, people were forced to migrate for their survival. The migration had a significant gender dimension. Large number of women emigrated in the colonial period not only

for economic reasons but also due to their crumbling position in their own families. . . . This also occasioned sexual exploitation which continues till date. (Mahato, 2010)

Likewise, studies on labour migration in colonial India have brought out with varying emphasis structural factors like land relations, land utilization pattern and nature of resource extraction (Chottopadhaya, 1979; Chakraborty, 1978; Mohapatra, 1985). In the perspective of these researches, Nirmal Mahato's specific case study is important as it brings out the interrelations between climate, decline in household economy, land question, commercial crisis, institutional deadlocks and labour migration. Environmental crises in indigenous belts of habitation in India show why in place of a push and pull framework a relational framework may be more fruitful to understand colonial migration.

II

All in all, colonial history is crucial to make sense of how the postcolonial policy regimes intend to tackle increasing environmental insecurity, yet ensure and facilitate labour supply in a mad rush towards what it perceives as 'development'. Migration control policies and mechanisms appeared in India in the wake of policies and administrative measures of controlling hunger and mitigating the effects of environmental disasters. Both have now exacerbated the notion of food insecurity, and the two discourses of food insecurity and disaster feed into each other. Each calamity is followed by debates on soaring food grain prices, withdrawal by the state of food subsidies, role of government and market forces in food grain market as well as global food politics.

For instance, the Indian government almost a decade back (UPA I – the Indian National Congress led first United Progressive Alliance government) had offered 100-day job guarantee scheme as an improved measure in place of earlier food-for-work schemes. The UPA II regime then followed up the earlier measure by taking up the task of guaranteeing food security. In a vast country like India, the conceptualization and implementation of such a massive food scheme created debates: Could such a scheme be implemented properly? Would it not give rise to greater corruption? Would this be sustainable? And, was this the best way to ensure food security, for the main task was to guarantee a greater and easier supply of food grain to poor homes. While these were general concerns, the free market advocates further argued: Would this not dampen prices and thus harm the farmers and grain trade, and this block asset formation in the villages?

Environmental calamities exacerbated these debates, as agricultural and rural wages remained depressed in the wake of calamities. The government replied by saying that if the beneficiaries did not get supplies, as pledged in the Food Security Act, there were provisions to ensure financial assistance to them for buying the staple grains from the open market. It remained debatable if the prescribed amount of financial assistance would be enough to buy rice and wheat at open market rates. Markets run by their own rules, priorities and pressures. Agricultural economists have been often asked by common people as to what is this notion of food security, when India is supposedly surplus in rice, wheat and other food items of daily consumption, and yet food insecurity hovers over large tracts of the country accompanied by about 200,000 farmers' suicides in nearly last two decades?[4] Each calamity brings in its wake price rises, and while production over the long run has gone up manifold, prices including the cost of production have soared correspondingly. Besides this huge commercialization of food, each year a large chunk of farmland is being diverted to non-farm use. Thus, a study of a comparison between the years of implementation of the WTO agreements (1990–1991 to 1995–1996) and the next five years (1996–1997 to 2001–2002) shows that barring rice and onions the production of other farm produces has come down (Chand, 2003). In short, green revolution, reckless commercialization of land and farm produce, risk-based trade of agricultural commodities and diversion of land from farm production to non-farm use have combined to defeat the goal of food security. Natural calamity has acted as a catalyst of the entire process.

Even though we are living under democracy, which is concerned with freedom and promises us improved life conditions, natural calamities nonetheless force us to ask: Does democracy do away with basic challenges of living? What clearly comes out of studies of disasters is that in a democracy characterized by conditions of political equality, calamities make inequality durable by accentuating the structure of differential access of groups and classes to food and food market. What also comes out equally clearly is that democracy is becoming deeply biopolitical with issues of life, ecology and economy overdetermining each other.

It was not sheer coincidence that in the late eighteenth and nineteenth centuries when the idea of democracy was overwhelming the European continent, reports of famines from colonies started rocking the political establishments 'at home'. The Irish Famine (1845–1852) caused deaths of approximately 1 million people and emigration of another million. Ireland's population fell between 20 per cent and 25 per cent. The questioning of the idea of democracy in relation to its ability or inability to secure food and more broadly biological survival for common people began around that time. Breadlines appeared in due course in world's wealthiest country, the United States; probably breadlines had never vanished there, and they continue till today. They are, as journalist Sasha Abramsky puts it, the 'hidden scandal of American hunger' (Abramsky, 2009). Charles Tilly's accounts of collective actions in

seventeenth- and eighteenth-century Britain show how food riots were occa-
sions for the development of various tools of collective protest – marches,
night vigil, torchlight processions, collective petitions, sit-ins, barricading,
formation of committees and vigilante groups, drawing up and submissions
of memoranda, and setting up popular councils besides the time-honoured
modes such as burning and looting grain stores (Tilly, 1995). In short, democracy never did away with differential access to resources. Inequality proved
durable. Hunger accompanied the onward march of democracy and provoked
collective protests and violence. All these features have come to mark our
critical understanding of democracy thanks to disasters and the post-disaster
relief, rehabilitation and resettlement programmes.

Exactly as the colonial time, we can now find in India different categories of hungry people – categories created by government policies, such as
below poverty line (BPL) and above poverty line (APL). Thus, with the
governing principle of creating a hierarchy of eligibility for food provision
and assistance, the situation is like what it was after the New Poor Law of
1834, in Great Britain. Like then, new social policies are now being discussed and implemented in order to tackle hunger in the wake of the humanitarian discovery of hunger. The discovery of hunger has led to a discovery
of the 'social', on the basis of which new social legislations such as the
National Rural Employment Guarantee Act (NREGA) have been founded.
The social discovery of hunger has led to the issue of hunger as one of the
major questions in the public arena in order to oppose government policies.
The issue of hunger also played a crucial role in building the tradition of
hunger strike in the country, the message being: *It is better to die in starvation than to accept a wrong government.* And as in Britain, in India too, in
the wake of protests over scarcity of food, a new form of social government
emerged with the welfare of the hungry during famine and flood as its aim.

This has required expertise in form of science and calculation of hunger so
that government can devise policies and measures to assuage hunger. James
Vernon (2007) tells us how nutritionists became important in this form of
social governance. In India in the 1980s and 1990s, nutritionists debated the
quantum of calories required to assuage hunger, and specialists argued as to
who could be called full hungry and who partially so. On this depended a
quantum of assistance, the kind and form of assistance, the mode of supply,
the budgetary requirements and identification of most needy areas, and along
with all these emerged an entire panoply of graded vulnerabilities. Science
facilitated administration of food provisions. The discovery of vitamins and a
biochemical explanation of nutrition meant that social governance of hunger
became in time a reality. Yet, precisely because of this social governance, hunger
has become now politically relevant, forcing all sections of the political class
in the country to join the 'hungry India' debate. The public interest litigation

on universal access to food, the debate on the role of *panchayats* (organs of village self-governance) in mitigating hunger, legislation of NREGA and its efficacy, administrative inefficiency in the state, judicial activism on this, quarrel over the exact cause of a hunger death – starvation, or illness, or suicide – all these are dimensions of social governance. The accounts of hunger in the wake of famines, floods and droughts reveal other lessons as well.

For instance, governance of food access has to be both disciplinarian and welfarist. Market mechanisms dictate the nature of institutional efficacy, and welfare is dictated by market considerations. The rights bearing institutions, such as judiciary, trade unions, farmers' organizations and civil rights groups, and state bodies, such as the National/State Human Rights Commission, meant to guarantee the right to food, become adjuncts to this disciplinarian welfare regime, which cannot allow any illegal claim-making process. As part of the protection and welfare strategy, the federal state now asks communities and provinces to adopt insurance plans – thus a variety of insurance businesses have sprung up: drought insurance, flood insurance, earthquake insurance, insurance of houses, crops, vehicles, education, to name a few. Ecological calamity is now a matter of risk and insurance. Politics in such time of calamity becomes irrevocably biological, and migration has emerged as a policy of preoccupation in this context of food insecurity, environmental calamities and developmental disasters. If natural calamities and disasters heighten the notion of *politics of life*, the other side is the notion of *resilience*, equally brought to prominence in times of disasters. In this milieu of resilience, migration forms the core of economic common sense.

The colonial history of the interlinked themes of environment, precarious life, resilience and migration continues to have strong resonance, and it is in this context that neo-liberal capitalism aims at strengthening particular governmental mechanisms to deal with life on the margin – mostly life of the migrant who stands on the margin of society, economy, climate, security, market and reproduction.

Let us present briefly some of the findings on the emergence of the precarious migrant as the key figure in the Brahmaputra and Barak Basins in North East India and Deltaic West Bengal and Bihar in India. These findings presented only in select manner tell us of the way ecology, developmental politics, and survival migration link with each other in producing what can be called a 'moving region'.

III

On the recurrent flood of the Kosi River in the four districts in North Bihar in India, researches have demonstrated the intrinsic relation between ecology, politics and survival migration in the last decade. These researches have brought out new governmental modes of encouraging the exit option for the villagers of the flood-trapped hamlets, the regular train journeys of the (predominantly male) migrant labour from North Bihar to the northern part of India including Delhi, the entire political economy of flood, the public works on flood control and the developed modes of relief and rehabilitation that make a government successful (Kumar, 2015, 206–26; Jha, 2012, 109–53). Features of popular politics, resistance and the role of caste in the making of the migrant labour in today's India have been also brought out.[5]

A study on the delta region of West Bengal brought out the social impact of erosion of the Ganga and Jalangi riverbanks in the districts of, respectively, Malda and Murshidabad, and of Saltia riverbanks in Cooch Behar. In Malda, after a piece of land goes under water, a silt-bank or *char* (river islands or land emerging out of the riverbeds) often rises on the other side. At times, the displaced people settle on these *chars* admittedly with great difficulties and manage to till the land, though the yield is low. However, in the district of Cooch Behar the resurfaced land is often a sandbank. Hardly any crop except mustard can grow there (Bandopadhyay, 2006).

The gendered aspects of such displacement and migration came out in the study in clearer light. With shrinking agriculture and loss of land, the report spoke of men migrating with women left behind with the responsibility of feeding their children. Women roll *bidis* (rolling leaves with raw tobacco inside), some fry puffed rice (*muri*), make *badis* (small round cakes) with gram or *dal* paste or do pottery or other work. More and more women are trying to pick up other skills now under economic compulsions. However, women get less than the rates negotiated between the *bidi* workers' unions and the owners/contractors. Also, women beedi workers are unorganized. They also join work in the fields during the sowing season, digging and carrying the soil. Again, in this work the wage discrimination also exists. Add to that the fact that women from the low-caste Bagdi community, for instance in Murshidabad, go out for fishing and face perpetual harassment by border security men. Women also say candidly that besides fishing or participating in agricultural work they are engaged in smuggling. In Jalangi, one can see scores of women crossing the Bangladesh borders with sugar, electronic items, cloth and so on. In this case again, they must please the security men. Yet, amidst all these, women must send the girls to school because, as they say, a girl's value in the marriage market falls if she is not educated to some extent. Boys can be sent to work on embankment projects, such as handling the boulders. In any case, schools are also temporarily closed or shut down or shifted due to the changing course of river and riverbank erosion. But world is merciless. Even with little bit of education girls are not 'safe'. The marriage market includes rackets arranging 'marriage' of girls from displaced families to distant places.

However, the victims of displacement and forced migration have not remained passive in face of river erosion, violence of the borderlands and breakdown of agriculture. They have formed their own organizations with participation of people from diverse political affiliations and various communities and age groups. Women, though fewer in number, participate actively in these forums and show remarkable forwardness in narrating their conditions and voicing their needs and demands (Bandopadhyay, Ghosh and Dutta, 2006, pp. 16–20).

Flood and riverbank erosion are two of the major global environmental disasters the world has experienced recurrently, making the life and livelihood in flood-prone areas precarious. South Asian countries, especially, India, Bangladesh, Pakistan and Nepal, are open to such calamities. According to a report of the National Space Research Organisation, India is one of the worst flood-affected countries in the world. Roughly one-fifth of global deaths due to floods occur in India. The report adds that the most flood-prone areas in India carrying 60% of the nation's total river flow are the Brahmaputra, Ganga and Meghna River basins in the Indo-Gangetic-Brahmaputra plains in North and Northeast India.[6]

In this connection, we may also refer to a significant study by the Calcutta Research Group focused in West Bengal on the deltaic mangrove forests of the Sunderbans and the districts of Nadia, Murshidabad and Malda.[7] The study found the Sunderbans as a contested space caught in the quagmire of fragility, resource crisis, outmigration, but also new patterns of resource sharing. The study brought to the fore various coping mechanisms of people following the cyclone Aila (2008) there. It was marked by the migration of the able-bodied males of the region to other parts of the state and the country, and a decrease in agricultural activities as a result of an increase of salinity of the soil. Similar trend was observed in the study conducted on the district of Murshidabad. Loss of agricultural lands as a result of encroaching Padma, Bhagirati and Jalangi rivers had also forced many men to migrate to big cities. Vulnerabilities have led to a high rate of trafficking of young girls from the district of Murshidabad. In Nadia district, extreme pollution and continuous siltation in the river Churni have forced the local fishermen to search for an alternative source of living. A study on the district as part of the same programme revealed that more than 200,000 people residing besides the river are searching for alternative sources of life and living. Deltaic Bengal is also characterized because of the soil by mushrooming of brick kilns along the banks of the rivers like Ganga, Bhagirati and Padma. The brick industry attracts seasonal labourers from Bihar and Uttar Pradesh. So, while a considerable section migrates out of Bengal, a considerable section migrates into the state. Another study revealed that in Malda district, along with other problems, there was the issue of loss of identity for people residing in charlands. While they have access to certain amenities like drinking water or electricity, courtesy the state of Jharkhand, they are not accepted as residents by the state of West Bengal. In this light, the report 'Non-existing Population in the Char lands of Malda' highlights the point that with the amendment of The West Bengal Land Reform Act (1955) in 2000, the people of charlands got stripped off of their rights and became 'illegal residents'. Once again, caste and gender are found to be two major fault lines in the map of vulnerability.

The same study also looked into the impact of construction of several dams in the Northeast. Construction activities in and near a protected forest area began without necessary clearance. During the construction phase, these activities led, in the words of *The International Rivers Network*, 'to the disruption and destruction of habitats of endangered species'.[8] The project not only has affected the migratory route of the elephants but also threatens to affect the livelihoods of many people as Subansiri River, with her mineral resources alone, has supported the lives of about 20,000 people. Local people earn their livelihood either as salary or as daily wages by working under the *maholder*.[9] Two experts have noted that the quarrying business of sand and gravels is totally regulated by the free-flowing Subansiri without having any physical barrier in its course.[10] The timbers that come floating on the river facilitate timber business. The demand for housing material is met with the woods carried by the river, and parallel to it, a business network sprang up. But the construction of the dam signals a probable change in livelihood pattern, which might force people to other parts to look for jobs.

The state of Arunachal Pradesh has been identified as a potential hydroelectric power generation with 173 dams that has been sanctioned. The areas inhabited by the Monpa community also fall among these areas. Although dams account for a major cause of affecting these people, other projects like that of national highways undertaken by Ministry of Road Transport and Highways are also responsible for displacing people. The people belonging to tribal and ethnic minorities in particular are victims of dispossession of land and other resources, absence of or inadequate compensation and human rights abuse.[11] There is a gradual shift in the occupational pattern from agriculture and forestry to jobs offering daily wage.

The research on the Northeast is significant because it brings out the strong relation between development-induced displacement and environmental displacement. This makes the task of estimating the number of internally displaced persons (IDPs) caused by environmental degradation additionally difficult. However, as one report puts it, as a result of flood and riverbank erosion in the plains and landslide in the hills – exacerbated by developmental works – population displacements have become endemic. Intensity of flood, riverbank erosion and landslide has increased substantially over the years in terms of area and victims and has caused innumerable deaths and destruction of settlements (Hossain, 2006). Monirul Hossain, long-time observer of displacement in the Northeast, has observed:

It would be pertinent to point out that the plight of the riverbank erosion induced IDPs are much more severe than that of the victims of flood. The victims of flood . . . can go back to their original land once the flood water recedes. However, the riverbank erosion induced ID peasants cannot go back to their land. . . . It is not only the Brahmaputra but also the . . . small and medium . . . rivers that [cause] havoc in the plains of Assam. . . . According an official report, the river Brahmaputra eroded 429,657 hectares of prime agricultural land. Roughly, 7% of the land in the plains has been eroded between the years of 1951–2000. This has . . . displaced at least 3 million peasants . . . who constitute the most pauperised community in Assam's plains. In the absence of proper resettlement and rehabilitation policy, most of them have experienced multiple displacements. (Hossain, 2007)

In the study (to which we have already referred)[12] that covered the population groups living in the river islands of Assam, known as *chars*, it was found out that what was earlier small peasant migration from the northeastern parts of East Bengal in the early decades of twentieth century to these *chars* in Assam has now transformed, in the wake of floods and river erosion, into a second wave of migration – this time to petty urban jobs like rickshaw pulling, construction labour, janitors and service employees. The report also confirms the findings from North Bihar – namely, the crucial role of governmental politics in regulating flood, relief, rehabilitation and other aspects of life, particularly education and heath in the emergence of a specific migration regime. The report pointed out that while the nation state (and by implication citizenship) was inseparably anchored with territory and land, the question of land was based on the notion of ownership of land and his/her capacity to hold on to the land. Loss of land impinged on his/her citizenship.

Land, identity, claims and citizenship remain crucial aspects in India. Studying the struggles of the urban refugees and other displaced rural people looking for shelter in Kolkata, another researcher confirmed the issue of land in the making of citizenship. Writing on the lesson of her study, she wrote: "Land itself became a medium for people's claims to the State . . . and a breeding ground for resilience" (Prins, 2014).

River, land and forests still remain central to the accounts of mobility in large parts of the postcolonial world.

IV

We can make a greater sense of this incessant production of migrant labour that capitalism can neither digest nor do away with, by placing the interrelations between ecology, migration and political economy at the heart of our understanding of early twenty-first-century capitalism. On this, because of shortage of space, we can only by way of concluding this chapter make a few observations drawn from my own nearly two decades-long research and other studies mentioned in this paper.

First, we have to take note of the neo-liberal relief, rehabilitation and resettlement agenda in the wake of the ecological disasters. Already a decade back when the new century was taking off in studies of the dynamics of post-Tsunami relief, rehabilitation, and resettlement patterns, researchers found that not only earlier patterns of inequality were being reproduced through the governmental dynamics, but that the public–private partnership (PPP) policy on R&R facilitated by the State in India and Sri Lanka was crucial in this reproduction on an extended scale.[13] Markets were becoming crucial in the neo-liberal agenda of disaster management. Humanitarianism combined in this way with a neo-liberal developmental agenda. Policies assumed that markets could make resilient the population groups vulnerable to environmental disasters. Thus, various forms of insurance policies and programmes in the framework of PPP have emerged in the last two decades of policy explosion in India with the emergence on substantial scale policies such as agricultural insurance, disaster insurance, flood insurance, communal violence insurance, earthquake loss insurance and so on.

Second, the big question seems to be: How are disasters combined with making money and creating capital out of disasters? This cannot be explained without reference to the extractive methods by which capitalism operates today. Environment and ecology are double-edged concepts, for if they make us wise and conservationist, they also make us aware of the economic worth of what we call resources, that is to say worthy of producing surplus value. Thus, the issue of land has returned for unprecedented attention. Rent now occupies the core of profit; land, air, water, waste, forest – everything is now up for extraction. Thus, while in Arunachal Pradesh, in India's Northeast, river water is sought to be harnessed for power generation, downstream management of the same water ensures the destruction of the lives of thousands turning people into precarious labour. Likewise the expansion of mobile telephony and construction of towers on a stupendous scale tells the story of extraction of air. So is the story of mining expansion with the rise in demand of iron ore and so on. Development, we are told, will need extraction. Yet, at the same time, extraction, we are told, if unbridled will mean disasters and more displacement of people. All in all, it is the extractive nature of modern capitalism that makes resource, destruction of resource due to ecological disasters and consequent migration of people the primary question of our time.

Third, this situation directs our attention to a complex method of producing mobile labour in twenty-first-century capitalism. Two theorists have explored how contemporary globalization has proliferated borders and the implications of this proliferation for migratory movements and capitalist transformations.[14] They have written, 'What we call the multiplication of labour and the related proliferation of borders signal . . . the heterogenization that today characterizes the spectrum of labor positions' (Mezzadra and Neilson, 2013, p. 125). These writings have thrown up new perspectives on the relation between migration, labour management and capitalism. Disasters work as mediating mechanisms in the transition from the moment of production of labour (power) as commodity to the moment of its circulation. Not only natural disasters, wars – the greatest of disasters – have traditionally cleared the ground of labour force expansion and a consequent capitalist boom; likewise, floods and famines have been catalytic agents in the contraction and expansion of labour market.

Finally, disasters are a major piece in this complex web of migration, mobility, inequality and generation of profit, because they represent in a congealed form what Paulo Tavares calls 'the contest over government of nature'.[15] The relation between disaster and migration is also governed by the state of infrastructure, dynamics of relief, resettlement and rehabilitation and by the centre–periphery interface. This has been always evident in the destructive cyclones and earthquakes in colonial and postcolonial histories. The relation also influences the political consequences of the event known as disaster.

To conclude: the postcolonial production of precarious migrant labour is based on the interrelations of three marginal conditions: ecological marginality, economic marginality and political marginality. In fact, that is how postcolonial labour is reproduced.

NOTES

1. Also to be found as WIDER Working Paper, 45, May 1988 – http://www.wider.unu.edu/publications/working-papers/previous/en_GB/wp-45/ (accessed on June 1, 2015); also see Dreze and Sen (1989).

2. In the context of famines, floods and earthquakes, the lineage of the complementary discourses of precarity and resilience are long. In India, the imperial administration of Lord Lytton (1876–1880) was the time of the Great Famine of 1876–1878; his reign became the reason for the passage of the Indian Famine Code in 1883. In 1876, when the Lytton administration began, a famine broke out in South India claiming between 6.1 million and 10.3 million people. Apart from the colonial policies on landed property and water management system, two other factors, namely, extraction of wealth (known as wealth drain) and implementation of Britain's trading policy were also blamed for the severity of the famines. The Famine Code classified situations of food scarcity according to a scale of intensity, and suggested commensurate steps in the event of a famine. Ironically, the contemporary policies of the Indian government in creating two categories of poor (Below Poverty Line group, commonly called BPL and Above Poverty Line group commonly called APL) to ensure food access to people resembles the approach of the Famine Code of 1883.

3. Chakraborty, (2011, p. 13); the sources he drew from are: Hunter (2004, 497); Visaria and Visaria (1984, 515); Davis (2002, 26–27 & 311ff); Tinker (1974, 161–66); and Davis and Huttenback (1988, 110).

4. On farmers' suicides, Nagraj (2008); see also, Mishra (2008).

5. On the relation between migration, labour+ and primitive accumulation of capital, see Samaddar (2009).

6. http://www.nrsc.gov.in/Earth_Observation_Applications_Disaster_Management_Floods.html (accessed on May 15, 2015).

7. "Ecosystems for Life – A Bangladesh-India Initiative: Ecology, Politics and Survival in India's Northeast and Deltaic Bengal," A CRG-IUCN Report, 1915 –, http://www.mcrg.ac.in/IUCN/IUCN_Executive_Summary.pdf (accessed on October 5, 2016); for the full report, Ecosystem for Life- A Bangladesh-India Initiative- Ecology, Politics and Survival in the India Northeast and Deltaic Bengal, CRG archive, file no - CD/IUCN/MCRG/005.

8. *Financing Dams in India: Risks and Challenges*, report by International Rivers Network, February 2005 – https://www.internationalrivers.org/sites/default/files/attached-files/financingdams2005_text.pdf (accessed on September 1, 2015), 6.

9. *Maholders* are those who take lease in the queries.

10. Debojit Baruah and Lakhi Prasad Hazarika, "Hydroelectric Project and Livelihood Risk Assessment of Subansiri River in North East India," *Green Heritage* – https://sites.google.com/site/greenheritageassam/hydroelectric-project-and-livelyhoods-risk-assessment-of-subansiri-river-in-north-east-india (accessed on October 12, 2016).

11. http://www.culturalsurvival.org/publications/cultural-survival-quarterly/brazil/world-commission-dams-review-hydroelectric-projects-

12. See note 10; section on "Watery Zones of Refuge: State Practices and Popular Politics in the River Islands of Assam."

13. *Report on a Symposium on Tsunami and the Issues of Relief, Rehabilitation and Resettlement*, prepared by Paula Banerjee and Sabyasachi Basu Ray Chaudhury, 2005, Calcutta Research Group, www.mcrg.ac.in (accessed on June 20, 2015), a summary of the findings to be found also in *Forced Migration Review*, June 2005 – http://www.fmreview.org/tsunami (accessed on June 21, 2015); also De Silva, "Protecting the Rights of the Tsunami Victims: The Sri Lanka Experience," 28; Luke, "HIV and the Displaced: Deconstructing Policy Implementation in Tsunami Camps in Tamil Nadu," 38–63; Pathiraja, "Compare and Contrast the Situation of Conflict Related IDPs and Tsunami Related IDPs in Sri Lanka," October 2005 – http://www.mcrg.ac.in/DP.pdf (accessed on June 20, 2015); also see various entries in the special issue of *Refugee Watch*, 24–26, October 2005.

14. Mezzadra and Neilson (2013); other theorists of borders and borderlands also have noted the violence surrounding these borders and borderlands, and border struggles in the postcolonial world. See for instance, van Schendel (2004); Banerjee (2010); Samaddar (1999).

15. One of the best studies on this theme is by Tavares (2013, chapter 8, pp. 123–64).

REFERENCES

Abramsky, Sasha. 2009. *Breadline USA: The Hidden Scandal of American Hunger and How to Fix It*. Sausalito, CA: Polipoint Press.

Arnold, David. 1993. "Social Crisis and Epidemic Disease in the Famines of Nineteenth Century India." *Social History of Medicine* 6, no. 3: 385–404.

Bandopadhyay, Krishna, Soma Ghosh, Nilanjan Dutta. 2006. *Eroded Lives*. Kolkata: Calcutta Research Group. http://www.mcrg.ac.in/eroded_lives.pdf (accessed on October 2, 2016).

Banerjee, Paula. 2010. *Borders, Histories, Existences: Gender and Beyond*. New Delhi: Sage Publications.

Baruah, Debojit and Lakhi Prasad Hazarika, "Hydroelectric Project and Livelihood Risk Assessment of Subansiri River in North East India," Green Heritage – https://sites.google.com/site/greenheritageassam/hydroelectric-projectand-livelyhoods-risk-assessment-of-subansiri-river-in-north-east-india (accessed on October 12, 2016).

Chakraborty, Lalita. 1978. "Emergence of an Industrial Labour Force in a Dual Economy: British India, 1880–1920." *The Economic and Social History Review* 10: 249–328.

Chakraborty, Subhas Ranjan. 2011. "Colonialism, Resource Crisis, and Forced Migration." CRG Research Paper Series, *Policies and Practices*, 42. Kolkata: Calcutta Research Group.

Chand, Ramesh. 2003. Government's Intervention in the Food Grain Market in the New Context, Policy Paper 19, National Centre for Agricultural Economics and Policy Research, New Delhi.

Chottopadhaya, H. 1979. *Indians in Sri Lanka, A Historical Study*. Calcutta: O.P.S. Publishers.

Davis, Lance and Richard Huttenback. 1988. *Mammon and the Pursuit of Empire: The Economy of British Imperialism*. Cambridge: Cambridge University Press.

Davis, Mike. 2002. *El Nino Famines: Late Victorian Holocausts and the Making of the Third World*. London: Verso Books.

De Silva, Nirekha. 2010. "Protecting the Rights of the Tsunami Victims: The Sri Lanka Experience." CRG Research Paper Series, *Policies and Practices*, 28.

Dreze, Jean and Amartya Sen. 1989. *Hunger and Public Action*. Oxford: Oxford University Press.

Dreze, Jean. 1990. "Famine Prevention in India." In *The Political Economy of Hunger*, Volume II, *Famine Prevention*, edited by Jean Dreze and Amartya Sen. Oxford: Clarendon Press.

Hossain, Monirul. 2006. "Status Report on IDPs in the Northeast." Report of the Workshop on the IDPs in India's Northeast, August 24–26. http://www.mcrg.ac.in/idp1.asp (accessed on October 2, 2016).

———. 2007. "A Status Report on Displacement in Assam and Manipur." CRG Research Paper Series, *Policies and Practices*, p. 19. http://www.mcrg.ac.in/pp12.pdf (accessed on October 4, 2016).

Hunter, W. W. 2004. *India and the Indians*, Volume 1. Edited by Herbert Risley, 497. Reprint, New Delhi.

Jha, Manish K. 2012. "Disasters: Experiences of Development during the Embankment Years in Bihar." In *New Subjects and New Governance in India,* edited by R. Samaddar and Suhit K. Sen, Chapter 3, 109–53. London and Delhi: Routledge.

Kumar, Mithilesh. 2015. "Governing Flood, Migration, and Conflict in North Bihar." In *Government of Peace: Social Governance, Security, and the Problematic of Peace,* edited by R. Samaddar, Chapter 7, 206–226. Furnham, Surrey: Ashgate.

Luke, Ratna Mathai. 2008. "HIV and the Displaced: Deconstructing Policy Implementation in Tsunami Camps in Tamil Nadu." *Refugee Watch* 32: 38–63.

Mahato, Nirmal Kumar. 2010. "Environment and Migration: Purulia, West Bengal." CRG Research Paper Series, *Policies and Practices*, 30. Kolkata: Calcutta Research Group, p. 2.

Mezzadra, Sandro and Brett Neilson. 2013. *Border as Method, or, the Multiplication of Labour*. Durham, NC: Duke University Press.

Mishra, Srijit. 2007. "Risks, Farmers' Suicides, and Agrarian Crisis in India: Is There a Way Out"? Working Paper, Indira Gandhi Institute of Development Research. Available from: http://oii.igidr.ac.in:8080/jspui/bitstream/2275/60/1/WP-2007-014.pdf (accessed on June18, 2015).

Mohapatra, P. P. 1985. "Coolies and Colliers: A Study of the Agrarian Context of Labour Migration from Chotanagpur 1880–1920." *Studies in History* 1, no. 20: 297–298.

Nagraj, K. 2008. *Farmers' Suicides in India: Magnitude, Trends, and Spatial Patterns*. Chennai: Bharathi.

Pathiraja, Dinusha. 2005. "Compare and Contrast the Situation of Conflict Related IDPs and Tsunami Related IDPs in Sri Lanka." http://www.mcrg.ac.in/DP.pdf (accessed on June 20, 2015).

Prins, Annemiek. 2014. "The Plight of Dwelling: East-Bengali Refugees and the Struggle for Land in Kolkata." *Refugee Watch*, 43–44: 49. http://www.mcrg.ac.in/rw%20files/RW43_44/RW43_44.pdf (accessed on September 8, 2016).

Samaddar, R. 2009. "Primitive Accumulation and Some Aspects of Work and Life in India." *Economic and Political Weekly* 44, no. 18: 33–42.

Samaddar, Ranabir. 1999. *The Marginal Nation: Transborder Migration to Bangladesh to West Bengal*. New Delhi: Sage Publications.

Tavares, Paulo. 2013. "Lines of Siege: The Contested Government of Nature." In *The Biopolitics of Development: Reading Michel Foucault in the Post-Colonial Present*, edited by Sandro Mezzadra, Julian Reid, and Ranabir Samaddar, Chapter 8, 123–164. Heidelberg: Springer.

Tilly, Charles. 1995. *Popular Contention in Great Britain, 1758–1834*. Cambridge: Harvard University Press.

Tinker, Hugh. 1974. *A New System of Slavery: The Export of Indian Labour Overseas, 1830–1920*. London, Oxford: Oxford University Press.

van Schendel, Willem. 2004. *The Bengal Borderland: Beyond State and Nation in South Asia.* London: Anthem Press.

Vernon, James. 2007. *Hunger: A Modern History.* Cambridge: Harvard University Press.

Visaria, Leela and Pravin Visaria. 1984. "Population". In *Cambridge Economic History of India*, Volume II, edited by Dharma Kumar, 515. Indian Edition.

Chapter 11

Floating Signifiers, Transnational Affect Flows

Climate-induced Migrants in Australian News Discourse

Katherine E. Russo

On the fifth anniversary of the September 11 terrorist attacks, Al Gore was in Australia as part of a campaign to raise public awareness of climate change. On the occasion, Daniel Ziffer wrote a news report for the Australian daily newspaper, *The Age*:

> 'I don't think that we should see terrorism and the climate crisis as an either/ or choice', he said from Sydney yesterday. 'We need to be resolved to win the battle against terrorism, but at the same time we need to recognise and respond to the most serious threat human civilisation has ever faced . . . even if (warming) doesn't cause the same kind of immediate fear that a terrorist attack or an act of violence does'. But Australia would bear the brunt if we didn't, with the potential consequences of 'catastrophic' sea-level rises, parched land and the mobilisation of hundreds of millions of climate refugees. The effects on Australia would be more severe than elsewhere, and some were already with us, Mr Gore said. (12/09/2006)

The report is an apt example of the way in which Australian news reporters have 'framed' news about climate-induced migration during the last twenty years, foregrounding sensational elements, chaos and catastrophe and backgrounding planning (Goffman 1974). While the reporter distances himself from the comparison with terrorism through the use of quotations, he sides with Gore's alignment and hasty generalization of 'sea-level rises, parched land and the mobilisation of hundreds of millions of climate refugees' as equally fearful consequences of climate change. Moreover, as Ziffer's account shows, while the voices of affected actors are not heard, news reporters often recentre Australian interests and concerns, amplifying affects, such as fear and anxiety. While news reporting follows a well-established tradition, which claims to be 'objective', 'neutral' and 'impartial' and which often obscures the subjective role of the reporter in constructing the text, the article clearly activates a negative assessment of climate-induced migrants through affect and the exaggerated suggestion of 'hundreds of millions' of refugees as an impending threat (Thomson and White 2008, 3). Besides providing background and explanatory information on Gore's opinions, the reporter intervenes on morale (Anderson 2010; Baker 2006; Massumi 2009; Thomson and White 2008; Wodak 2008). News Discourse may be regarded as a central aspect of 'cosmopolitics', as it is a potential trigger of xenophobia and racism or encounter, connectivity and conviviality. Arguably, the culture of alarm which was found in the report has constituted a defining aspect of the Australian media coverage of (climate-induced) migrants from neighbouring South Asian countries, the Maldives and Pacific Islands, such as Tuvalu and Kiribati.

A number of reasons explain the recourse to alarmism. Climate change and the role of fossil fuels in the national economy have been at centre stage during the Australian election campaigns of the last twenty years. This has resulted in heated and contested accounts in media coverage. In response to climate change scepticism, environmentalists and journalists have often resorted to dramatized representations of severely affected countries as a sensationalist 'proof' to 'concretize climate science's statistical abstractions'; in this context the dimension of climate-induced migration has often been amplified (Farbotko 2010, 58). Climate-induced migrants have also been represented as helpless and powerless victims of climate change, or as climate 'refugees' requiring salvation. The latter representations have been particularly contested by the very groups who were identified as climate-induced migrants: they have often reclaimed their role as active agents of change (i.e. developing mitigation and adaptation strategies such as mangrove planting and solar power), and have stressed their concerns over the loss of sovereignty, agency and self-determination related to forced migration and refugee status (Dreher and Voyer 2014). The contestation is particularly important since, as Bridget Lewis notes, 'If migration is undertaken willingly it can be an effective strategy and can assist those who remain behind but where it is involuntary it can have significant harmful impacts. . . . It is essential that migration strategies are planned' (2015, 86–87). However, these contrasting perspectives have been largely filtered out of media accounts. The alarmist 'climate refugee' narrative has been relatively impermeable to alternative framings. Unfortunately, news reporters often rely on prior reports in the same sphere (i.e. with those who have previously taken a stand with respect to an issue) and draw upon familiar images and language patterns to construct a discursive framework of alignment and rapport through which readers may be 'affected' (Martin and White 2005). This repetitive character of media coverage should not be understood as an 'innocent' trait – it has important power effects. As Norman Fairclough (1995) put it in his seminal work on media language and power:

> The hidden power of media discourse and the capacity of power-holders to exercise this power depend on systematic tendencies in news reporting and other media activities. A single text on its own is quite insignificant: the effects of media power are cumulative, working though the repetition of particular ways of handling causality and agency, particular ways of positioning the reader and so forth. (54)

As Teun van Dijk argued in his popular work on news and social cognition, people rely heavily on media accounts for their knowledge, beliefs and opinions, which in turn form socially shared knowledge and limited interpretative repertoires (1988; 1996). Such limited 'repertoires' may condition the social apprehension and response to climate-induced migration, hindering the possibility of transnational solidarity (Blommaert 2012, 12). Based on the premise that the power of media discourse lies in the repetition and incremental effect of images and language patterns, which may be closely examined to reveal presuppositions, cultural stereotypes and ideological inferences in discourse (Stubbs 2001), this chapter closely enquires into the circulation of familiar and seemingly new discourses across transnational borders. The chapter draws on findings in Corpus and Critical Discourse Analysis in order to draw some conclusions on the representation of climate-induced migration in a corpus of Australian news reports.

DATA, METHOD AND CONTEXT

Media discourse has recently offered fertile ground for the combination of Critical Discourse Analysis and Corpus Linguistics. The use of quantitative techniques, such as keyword searches, concordance and collocational analysis using specialized corpus software, has been fruitfully combined with qualitative approaches to investigate concordances and collocations of the terms 'refugee(s)' and 'asylum seeker(s)' in large corpora (Baker 2006; Baker and McEnery 2005; Baker et al. 2008). Drawing upon these seminal studies, this chapter takes into account the following levels of analysis: frequency of language patterns, the level of the text, the relation between different texts and discourses, the context in which texts are produced and the wider historical and political context (Reisigl and Wodak 2001). It therefore situates the quantitative analysis of language patterns and the qualitative analysis of a wide range of linguistic discursive strategies within a wider analytical framework which includes extra-linguistic social/sociological variables and situational frames (Reisigl and Wodak 2001). The analysis was carried out using AntConc, a concordancer developed by Lawrence Anthony (2005) to explore the context and collocation of terms in order to identify consistent language patterns, collocations and the semantic prosody of lexical items, that is, 'the consistent aura of meaning with which a form is imbued by its collocates' (Louw1997, 157). The search was later narrowed from bulk data retrieval to identify discursive strategies such as referential or nomination strategies, predicational strategies, argumentation strategies and mitigation or intensification strategies of discursive patterns.

In order to carry out the analysis for the chapter, a specialized corpus was created covering the years 2004–2014. The corpus consists of a set of Australian newspaper articles from the broadsheet news and features sections of the Fairfax digital archive (*Illawarra Mercury, Sydney Morning Herald, The Age, The Sunday Age, The Sun Herald* and *Newcastle Herald*). The corpus was designed by selecting texts with the query terms climate-induced migra*, climate-induced refug*, climate migra*, climate refug*, 'climate change refug*', 'climate change migra*', 'environmental refug*'and, 'environmental migra'*. The query matched 201 documents amounting to 510,000 words, which are diversely distributed per year.

Climate change was one of the most contentious and divisive issues in Australian politics in the 2004–2014 decade. Australian governments have applied different sets of logics and priorities to climate change over time, ranging from the frontline of climate change supporters to active obstructionism (Beeson and McDonald 2013). The oscillation of public opinion and the frequent contestation of federal government policy were and still are determined by the paradox that while Australia is a major agricultural producer deeply affected by heat and drought, it also has an immediate economic interest in the maintenance of a global fossil fuel economy as the world's largest exporter of coal. Moreover, while the Australian Green political party is one of the oldest in the world, its citizens are among the largest per-capita greenhouse gas emitters.

Unsurprisingly, the concordance plot shows a greater use of the term 'climate-refugees' in the years 2007–2009. In 2007, after years of climate change denialism during John Howard's government, Prime Minister Kevin Rudd signed the Kyoto Protocol and called for a cut to greenhouse gas emissions by 60% before 2050 as his first official act after being sworn in. Yet both the Howard government and the Rudd opposition committed to some form of carbon pricing scheme in the lead up to the 2007 election, even while the former remained opposed to the ratification of the Kyoto Protocol. On 15 December 2008, Rudd released a White Paper on reducing Australia's greenhouse gas emissions, which included a plan to introduce an emissions trading scheme in 2010, which is known as the Carbon Pollution Reduction Scheme, and gave a target range for Australia's greenhouse gas emissions in

2020 of between 5% and 15% less than 2000 levels. The Rudd government pushed hard to secure an agreement at Copenhagen in 2009, with Rudd taking a large delegation and assuming the role of the 'friend of the Chair' at the conference (Beeson and McDonald 2013, 334). Hopes for establishing a post-Kyoto agreement at Copenhagen in late 2009 were dashed with the reticence of both China and the United States, a failure that undermined Prime Minister Rudd's case for strong climate action in Australia.

Climate change was central to political election campaigns and debates throughout the following years and in 2009, the future prime minister, Tony Abbott announced his opposition to the Rudd government's Emissions Trading Scheme proposal and eventually achieved Liberal Party leadership over this issue. The change in leadership of the Liberal Party (from proponent of climate action Malcolm Turnbull to climate-sceptic Tony Abbott) was decisive not only in driving policy priorities, but in undermining public consensus on the science of climate change and the need for action.

CLIMATE-INDUCED MIGRANTS IN AUSTRALIAN NEWS REPORTING DISCOURSE

News reporters have a pool of lexical items, terms and semiotic resources available to them from which they choose to represent individuals and groups of peoples. Quantitative analysis of the classification of social actors in the corpus reveals that, in Australian news reporting, climate-induced migration is not referred to as an abstract process, but is generally personified with reference to climate-induced migrants. On the other hand, climate-induced migrants are referred to collectively and are therefore an anonymous and generic category (Machin and Mayr 2012, 81), as shown by the number of occurring words or tokens: climate refugee (8 tokens), climate refugees (86 tokens), climate migrant (0 tokens), climate migrants (4), environmental refugee (8) and environmental refugees (33). Moreover, climate-induced migrants are mainly characterized by quantification and statistics. In fifty-five occurrences there is overlexicalization, that is, 'a surfeit of repetitious, quasi-synonymous references' (Machin and Mayr 2012, 37), and the use of exaggerating quantifiers to refer to the number of potential climate-induced migrants, as in the case of 'the millions of' or 'hundreds of millions, or even billions', or imprecise references such as 'swelling numbers'. As in previous findings on aggregation in the representation of migrants and refugees in media discourse (Baker 2006), numbers are utilized to give the impression of objective research and scientific credibility, where in fact no specific sources for the figures are mentioned. By way of example, the following headline and openings suggest that the number of climate-induced migrants is the newsworthy issue under consideration in numerous reports in the corpus, while the argumentation fallacy lies in the presupposition that climate-induced migration is an inevitable scenario:

> Ex 1. " Climate refugees: 20m and counting". (*Sun Herald*, 06/12/2009)

> Ex 2. 100 million people will be displaced by a meter rise in sea-levels, the expected rise this century even if the world could agree on drastic emission cuts. (*Sydney Morning Herald*, 19/04/2010)

> Ex 3. The combination of higher rainfall and higher sea-level rises in the Asia-Pacific region will create millions of climate refugees. (*Sydney Morning Herald*, 06/08/2007)

A first preliminary consideration regarding lexical and term choice is that the corpus reveals a high frequency of the terms 'climate refugees' and 'environmental refugees'. The popularization of these denominations is noteworthy as they have been heavily criticized by scholars (McAdam 2012), and do not have any legal grounds – they do not appear in and are not compatible with key legal texts such as the *United Nations Convention Relating to the Status of Refugees* (1951). The corpus also shows a high instability in term variation and co-occurrence of different terms (climate refugee, climate migrant, environmental refugee), which may be due to recent coinage and to the preferred use of compressed noun modification devices in texts with high information density. Thus, the related extensive use of the premodifying noun 'climate' used in place of 'climate change' or 'climate-induced' in noun + noun sequences may have been adopted to save space and convey complex meanings and relations between nouns in condensed form (in this case Noun2 is caused by Noun1, Biber 2003). In news reporting names serve the purpose of sorting people out into rigid social categories. Moreover, meaning must be compressed into a few words, as in the case of actionyms/praxonyms, such as migrants, refugees and asylum seekers. As Reisigl and Wodak note (2001), naming strategies focus on membership categorization devices and include references by tropes, biological, naturalizing and depersonalizing metaphors and metonymies, as well as by synecdoche in the form of a part standing for a whole and vice versa. A trait, specific feature or characteristic (e.g. the action of moving to a new country as a consequence of climate change) is selected as a representative depictor and the involved people often have no agency in the nomination process. This linguistic identification through synecdochization involves evaluation and in the case of the coinage 'climate refugees' it is based on terminological catachresis[1] since 'climate refugees' are not a category under the Refugee Convention. Even more so, as the International Law expert Jane McAdam notes in an article in the corpus, it is not based on a legal claim on behalf of the interested party:

As a matter of law, that terminology is completely wrong. And what was really fascinating was that the islanders said 'We don't want to be called refugees. We think of refugees as people who are victims, who are stuck in camps and reliant from handouts from the international community, people who really have lost their human dignity. We want to be seen as active members of any community we might move to. We do not want to be seen as victims who are passive'. (Sydney Morning Herald, 10/12/2011)

In van Dijk's words, 'The formation of news events, and the formation of news values is in fact a reciprocal, dialectical process in which stereotypes are the currency of negotiation' (1988, 17). Through personification and strategies of involvement, news reporters express inner states, attitudes and feelings or degrees of emotional interest and engagement, which aim to engage readers both emotionally and cognitively. These are opposed to strategies of detachment, which are realized to encode distance. In the following examples, the reports describe the different positions of the Howard and Rudd governments on climate-induced migration:

Ex 4. Bishop Browning also criticised the Federal Government for its 'utter obsession' with growth and warned that climate change refugees would be a bigger problem than terrorists in a century of desperate struggle. (*The Age*, 25/10/2007)

Ex 5. The Rudd Government is also looking at allowing climate refugees – people from countries hit by rising sea levels – to resettle in Australia, as well as a scheme to accept unskilled guest workers from Pacific islands. (*The Age*, 20/03/2008)

In both examples, 'impersonalisation' (i.e. the reference to a whole institution, political organization, etc., instead of a single person) grants extra weight to the governments' position and at the same time conceals the beliefs and responsibilities of the prime ministers (Machin and Mayr 2012, 79). On the other side, in example 4, the use of direct quotation and the use of the honorific 'Bishop' indicates the reporter's distance from a single person's opinion, while amplifying particles, such as 'utter' and 'bigger', and the adjectives 'desperate' and the nouns 'obsession' and 'terrorists' diminish the authority of the opinion. In example 5, the government's proposition is mitigated through the verb phrase 'looking at'. Yet most importantly, in both cases, the discursive strategy of typification (the creation of a type of person or group of people) is achieved through comparison with other categories such as unskilled workers and terrorists, which suggest that climate refugees cause problems. In this manner, the semantic merging of climate refugees, terrorists and unskilled workers may result in the demand for restrictions for all groups.

As Reisigl and Wodak note, social actors are linguistically inscribed with certain qualities through the use of predicational strategies. These may be realized as stereotypical, evaluative attributions of negative and positive traits in the linguistic form of implicit or explicit predicates (Reisigl and Wodak 2001, 47). In the corpus, climate-induced migrants are often depicted and associated with metaphors and topoi, which are consistent with previous findings on the representation of migrants and refugees in media discourse as natural disasters, dangers and threats. According to previous studies (Baldwin 2013; Baker 2006; van Dijk 1988, 1991, 1996; Wodak 2001, 2008), the most frequent and stereotypical metaphors employed in the predicational qualification of migrants, asylum seekers and refugees are:

Natural disasters	Dragging hauling	Water	Fire	Plants and fertile soil	Genetic material
Growth/ Growing	Pollution/ impurity	Melting	Body	Blood	Disease/ infection
Animals	War/fight/ military	Goods/ commodities	Food	Vehicle, boat, ship	House, building, door/bolt

Source: Reisigl and Wodak 2001, 59–60.

The analysis of the corpus reveals a high context-dependent preference for figurative expressions or metaphors related to natural disasters and water, as in the case of 'swamped by', 'a wave of', 'a mass wave', 'waves of', 'swelling numbers of' and 'washing up', which may be related to the context specific image of Australian migrants and refugees:

Ex 6. First wave of 'climate refugees' on the seas. (*The Age*, 09/04/2009)

Ex 7. Australia could be swamped by climate refugees if it developed a unilateral policy without worldwide backing. (*The Age*, 14/03/2007)

Ex 8. The President of what could be the first country in the world lost to climate change has urged Australia to prepare for a mass wave of climate refugees seeking a new place to live. (*Sydney Morning Herald*, 07/01/2012)

In other cases, climate-induced migrants are merged by way of cumulative associations with natural calamities of great magnitude and in need of urgent control and risk management by the nation:

Ex 9. The scenarios predicted failed states proliferating because governments couldn't feed their people; waves of climate refugees washing up against the borders of more fortunate countries; even wars between countries that shared the same rivers. (*Illawarra Mercury*, 06/12/2008)

The consistent occurrence and prominence of this limited set of topics confirms the implicit/explicit portrayal of climate-induced migrants in terms of previous analyses of migrants, refugees and asylum seekers: They have or cause problems' (van Dijk 1993, 179). Previous findings on migrants and refugees in news discourse are also confirmed by the fact that in the corpus climate-induced migrants are always in an object (affected/patient) position, as demonstrated also by the frequent case of verb phrases such as accepting, allowing, processing, rescuing, helping and fleeing and by attributes such as starving, fleeing and forgotten. On the other hand, powerful spokespeople such as prime ministers and politicians, or legal experts are always in a subject (agent/participant) position. Humanitarianism, burdening and weighting are common *topoi* in both discriminatory and anti-discriminatory discourses in the corpus. As in the following example, climate-induced migrants are backgrounded as the passive recipients of natural disasters and the beneficiaries of help:

> Ex 10. Despite influential former World Bank chief economist Nicholas Stern last year warning that millions of people in the Asia Pacific region could be displaced by global warming, the Howard Government has refused to acknowledge the prospect of climate refugees. (*The Age*, 14/03/2007)

In numerous examples, news reports align readers alongside or against climate-induced migrants through 'ideological squaring' (van Djik 1993). Ideological squaring is achieved through the use of referential choices which create opposites to make issues appear simplified in order to control their meaning. In example 10, the use of 'influential' to define the social actor Nicholas Stern may be regarded as a superfluous lexeme and may be defined as an overlexicalization, which indicates an area of ideological contention or uncertainty, confirmed by the use of the honorific 'former World Bank chief economist' and by the metapropositional verb 'warned'. On the other hand, the use of the discursive strategy of impersonalization, 'the Howard Government', gives extra weight to the statement and indicates a high level of authority, mirrored by the assertive verb 'refused'.

Similarly, in example 11, the call for 'global citizenship' is firstly distanced from the text's internal authorial voice, that is, 'leaders of developing nations' and 'A statesman would' attribute values to an external voice. Yet the use of the verb 'enraged' creates an opposition, which through the deictic pronoun 'we' re-establishes a collective national voice and borders. Moreover, the social actors of the proposition are the leaders, the statesman and John Howard, confirming previous examples in which climate refugees are not active social actors:

Ex 11. Leaders of developing nations are becoming enraged by our indifference to the impact of emissions on their citizens. A statesman would recognise that the fate of the earth is a shared responsibility, but we have turned our backs on potential climate refugees from waterlogged Tuvalu. Isn't it about time John Howard was asked to sign a pledge of global citizenship? (*The Age,* 23/09/2006)

As in previous cases, the three fundamental types of linguistic realization, which according to Martin and White, are fundamental to appraisal are exploited in the corpus: saturation (this type of realization is opportunistic, a modal verb may for instance be picked up in an adverb), intensification (this type of realization involves amplification, repetitions, exclamative structures, superlatives) and domination (relevant meanings may include a longer stretch of discourse by dominating meanings in their domain) (2005, 19–26). In the corpus, lexico-grammatical resources are employed explicitly to inscribe and/or implicitly to invoke affects such as worry and fear, not to prevent and restrain them, rather to intensify and diffuse them (Martin and White 2005). Likewise, in example 12, negative affects such as fear, anxiety and uncertainty are invoked: the appraisal of the number of climate-induced migrants is conditioned by the premodifier 'feared' which marks an emotional reaction and by the negative connotations of the lexeme 'horde':

Ex 12. Along the conventional border with Bangladesh, India is building a fence to keep out a feared horde of millions of Bangladeshi economic and climate refugees. (*Sydney Morning Herald* 23/04/2012)

As Andrew Baldwin (2016) notes, another important aspect of the discourse 'concerns its temporality. Almost without exception the migration effects of climate change are narrated in the future tense' (80). As in the following example, collectivization and the generic use of the category 'climate refugees' place their stories in a news frame where climate-induced migrants are a 'future', 'potential' or 'inevitable' problem, catastrophe or threat. The latter discourse contributes to framing 'climate refugees' in apocalyptic tones:

Ex. 13. You have to wonder how long it will be before the worst-affected developing nations start planning to foster the inevitable mass emigration of hundreds of millions of climate refugees. (*The Age,* 25/11/2009)

Thus, the apocalyptic representation of climate migrants is not just incidental but central to their subjectification (Bettini 2013). Quantitative and qualitative analysis confirms the correlation of climate-induced migrants and discourses of chaos and risk based on rhetorical refrains by journalists, politicians and pundits, that insistently reiterate the magnitude and catastrophic impact of the hazards (Friedman 2011). As this chapter hopes to have confirmed, contextual information is pivotal in the analysis of naming and representational strategies in media discourse since the meaning potential of any name is exploited in different ways.

The attested use of different names for climate-induced migrants in the corpus may be viewed as an example of how news reporters capitalize on the capacity of an existing lexical item to encompass new meaning, since the same referent is often referred to in texts from various perspectives if different characteristics of the concept are activated, or if different relations to other concepts are established due to the common ground and the shared representations that language users draw on to communicate with each other (Rogers 2004, 221; Calsamiglia and van Dijk 2004; vanDijk 2009). As has been shown in key studies on news discourse (Baker 2006; Baker and McEnery 2005; Baker et al. 2008; van Dijk 2009), lexical items such as migrants or climate migrants are not 'context-independent' units per se. On the contrary, they are heavily 'context- and cotext-dependent' and have to be described according to their function in discourse, to their reliance on previous scripts, shared meaning and beliefs (van Dijk 2009, 153).

Moreover, the choice of the term 'climate refugees' may be related to the capitalization of news reporters on the framing of new stories according to shared typifications and schemata. For entertainment purposes, news reporters place people in the social world and highlight certain aspects of identity through tacit mental categories, frames, schemata and general propositions (van Djik 1993). Therefore, the high instability in term choice in the corpus manifests the fluidity of such definitions and membership categories, providing further confirmation of the conflation of the semantic concepts of 'migrant' and 'refugee' in Anglophone news reporting to label 'all foreigners who are not welcome' (Wodak 2008, 57). As in most recent forms of 'neoliberal racism', the denomination is dereferentialized: it is removed from any direct relation to a specific subject, and it operates as a 'floating discourse' or 'empty signifier', in which covert xenophobic attitudes and racist stereotypes are combined (Delanty et al. 2008, 4). In other words, the denomination is not inherently racist, but its analysis as a context-dependent linguistic realization reveals that the racist discursive construction of climate-induced migrants starts with the 'labelling of social actors, proceeds through the generalization of negative attributions and then elaborates arguments to justify the exclusion of many and inclusion of some' (Delanty et al. 2008, 4). The creation of new knowledge in popularization discourse in the press is characterized by context, which may be defined as the mental model of participants in the communicative event and the beliefs that are shared by epistemic communities and certified by criteria that are historically and culturally variable (van Dijk 1999). Following this line of thought, the 'climate refugees' denomination may be regarded as an example of the ideological and creative power of representational strategies in popularization discourse, which 'needs to be formulated in such a way that non-specialized readers are able to construct lay versions of specialized knowledge and integrate these with their existing knowledge' (van Dijk and Calsamiglia 2004, 370). While terms must be recognized by the members of the scientific discourse community in order to be used, in news reporting they undergo processes of language variation and change in order to facilitate structured 'mediation' and 'communication' between expert and non-expert readers (Pecman 2014, 5). The role of knowledge production must be read against the entertainment function of media: in this case the debate among experts on the term 'climate refugees' may be regarded as the 'newsworthy' side of scientific discussions on climate change. In fact, analysis of the corpus reveals that climate-induced migration is never mentioned as a process and is therefore always related to the representation of people. This personification plays a vital rhetorical role in giving a human form and imagined 'collective subject', to an inanimate or abstract idea or phenomena. In this manner, it may engage readers through affect or rhetorical pathetic fallacy, appealing to prejudiced emotions, opinions and convictions instead of employing rational arguments (Wodak 2008, 65). Thus, the focus on climate-induced migration during the 2004–2014 decade pertains to the fondness of news reporters to focus on the social contexts and participant roles in science, such as conflicts, problems and developments, and the relevance of scientific knowledge in the everyday lives of citizens and politics rather than on scientific information.

MIGRATION AND TRANSNATIONAL AFFECT FLOWS

The analysis has found that news reporting on climate-induced migration may be conditioned by investment in the language of affect for entertainment purposes (Anderson 2010; Baldwin 2016). Through various discursive strategies, news reports were found to modulate the circulation and distribution of worry, anxiety and fear, intensifying, multiplying and saturating communication. Furthermore, the use of topoi related to natural disasters, chaos and catastrophe and intensification strategies were found to emphasize ideas of security and safety.

The analysis of the corpus confirmed previous findings on migration in British newspapers which have found that spectacular, unexpected events still have a much higher chance of becoming news than more structural processes of oppression and displacement of minority groups. Indeed, as van Dijk put it, 'Ordinary people usually fall outside the press picture of news actors and may only collectively be involved as the patients of political action or the victims of catastrophes, or individually, in negative terms, for instance, in crime news' (1993, 140).

In the last three decades, Australian newspaper reporting discourse has been affected by wide-ranging changes, including the growth of online services to accommodate demand, the continuing expansion of English as a global language and the ever-widening reach of media companies such as Fairfax Media and Rupert Murdoch's News Corporation (Thomson and White 2008). While variation remains in genres, styles and rhetorics of contemporary news reports around the world, the above-mentioned forces may be responsible for a push towards a seeming homogenization or globalization of styles and rhetorics. As Jan Blommaert notes, the homogenizing force of English as a global language can be encountered in dialects or local semiotic forms 'which are prepared to go global' and emerge in the context of technology-driven globalization processes (2012, 9). Such semiotic codes may be defined as supervernaculars, where the 'super' is an equivalent of 'trans-' and refers to semiotic complexes whose composition and circulation transcend those of local semiotic complexes. Following this line of thought, news discourse exists as the interplay between englobalization and deglobalization, in which language resources from complex local repertoires are being mobilized and deployed in meaning-making.

The analysis of online news discourse on climate-induced migration and its striking similarity with previous findings on British refugees and migrants provides a significant insight on how media discourse shapes translocal social knowledge, scripts and repertoires and creates translocal audiences. Moreover, the employment of discursive strategies to amplify negative affects such as fear and anxiety in news reports on climate-induced migrants may be regarded as an example of the role of news reporting in the modulation of transnational affect flows. The affective intensity and resonance of news reports is not particularly forceful as it travels within the subtlest and unnoticed surfaces of contact of everyday conversations. Yet, as Andrew Baldwin (2016) notes, 'Through affect we can better appreciate how racial sensibilities are mobilised for political purposes without the vocabulary of race ever being mentioned' (79). The images of migrants and refugees convey a disruptive, yet also comforting, passage of affective intensity, increasing but also setting a limit to the worry of 'ordinary' citizens for the future (Baldwin 2016). As Anderson notes, the political contract with the ordinary man 'of the twentieth century was arguably secured through the investment in affect: white power aimed at modulating the circulation and distribution of worry and fear, not in order to prevent and prescribe them but by – intensifying, multiplying, and saturating the material-affective processes through which bodies come in and out of formation' (Anderson 162). In this manner, the symbolic images of climate and environmental refugees may be read as an example of how the fantasy of border control is connected to the affective state of paranoia – a perception of white injury where worrying becomes the dominant affective mode of expressing one's attachment to the nation. In Ghassan Hage's words:

> They are constantly finding a source of concern: look at how many migrants there are, look at crime, look at ghettoes, look at tourists. Such pathological worry is that of people who use worrying to try to construct themselves as the most worthy Australians in the land. It should be remembered, however, that worrying can be the last resort of the weak. There are many people for whom worrying is the last available strategy for staying in control of social processes over which they have no longer much control. (1998, 10)

NOTE

1. A term may be defined as 'a lexico-semantic unit referring to a specific concept that is used in a specialised domain of knowledge and which is widely acknowledged by domain-expert language users' (Pecman 2014, 5).

REFERENCES

Anderson, Ben. 2010. "Modulating the Excess of Affect. Morale in a State of 'Total War'". In *The Affect Theory Reader*, edited by Melissa Gregg and Gregory J. Seigworth, 161–184. Durham and London: Duke University Press.

———. 2012. "Affect and Biopower: Towards a Politics of Life". *Transactions*, 37(1): 28–43.

Baker, Paul. 2006. *Using Corpora in Discourse Analysis*. London and New York: Bloomsbury.

Baker, Paul, Gabrielatos C., Khosravinik, M., Kryzanowski, M., McEnery Tony, Wodak Ruth. 2008. "A Useful Methodological Synergy? Combining Critical Discourse Analysis and Corpus Linguistics to Examine Discourses of Refugees and Asylum Seekers in the UK Press". *Discourse & Society*, 19(3): 273–306.

Baker, Paul, and Tony McEnery. 2005. "A Corpus-based Approach to Discourses of Refugees and Asylum Seekers in UN and Newspaper Texts". *Journal of Language and Politics*, 4(2): 197–226.

Baldwin, Andrew. 2013. "Racialisation and the Figure of the Climate-change Migrant". *Environment and Planning A*, 45: 1474–1490.

Baldwin, Andrew. 2016. "Premediation and White Affect: Climate Change and Migration in Critical Perspective". *Transactions of the Institute of British Geographers*, 41: 78–90.

Bates, Diane C. 2002. "Environmental Refugees? Classifying Human Migrations Caused by Environmental Change". *Population and Environment*, 23(5): 465–477.

Beeson, Mark and Matt Mc Donald. 2013. "The Politics of Climate Change in Australia". *Australian Journal of Politics and History*, 59(3): 331–348.

Bettini, Giovanni. 2013. "Climate Barbarians at the Gate? A Critique of Apocalyptic Narratives on Climate Refugees". *Geoforum*, 45: 63–72.

Biber, Douglas. 2003. "Compressed Noun-phrase Structures in Newspaper Discourse: The Competing Demands of Popularization vs Economy". In *New Media Language*, edited by J. Aitchison and D. M. Lewis, 169–180. London: Routledge.

Blommaert, Jan. 2010. *The Sociolinguistics of Globalization*. Cambridge: Cambridge University Press.

———. 2012. "Supervernaculars and their Dialects". *Dutch Journal of Applied Linguistics*, 1(1): 1–14.

Calsamiglia Helena and Teun A. van Dijk. 2004. "Popularization Discourse and Knowledge About the Genome". *Discourse & Society*, 15(4): 369–389.

Delanty, Gerard, Jones, Paul and Ruth Wodak (eds.). 2008. *Identity, Belonging and Migration*. Liverpool: Liverpool University Press.

Dreher, Tanja and Michelle Voyer. 2014. "Climate Refugees or Migrants? Contesting Media Frames on Climate Justice in the Pacific". *Environmental Communication*, 9(1): 58–76.

Farbotko, Carol. 2010. "Wishful Sinking: Disappearing Islands, Climate Refugees and Cosmopolitan Experimentation". *Asia Pacific Viewpoint*, 51(1): 47–60.

Fairclough, Norman. 1989. *Language and Power*. London: Longman.

———. 1995. *Media Discourse*. London: Hodder Education.

Goffman, Erving. 1974. *Frame Analysis: An essay on the Organization of Experience*. Cambridge, MA: Harvard University Press.

Hage, Ghassan. 1998. *White Nation: Fantasies of White Supremacy in a Multicultural Society*. Sydney: Pluto Press.

Jensen, Lars. 2011. "The Whiteness of Climate Change". *Journal of the European Association for Studies on Australia* 2(2): 84–97, edited by Katherine E. Russo, Anne Brewster and Lars Jensen.

Lewis, Bridget. 2015. "Neighbourliness and Australia's Contribution to Regional Migration Strategies for Climate Displacement in the Pacific". *QUT Law Review*, 15(2): 86–101.

Lipsitz, George. 1998. *The Possessive Investment in Whiteness: How White People Profit from Identity Politics*. Philadelphia: Temple University Press.

Louw, Bill. 1997. "The Role of Corpora in Critical Literary Appreciation". In *Teaching and Language Corpora,* edited by Anne Wichmann, Steven Fligelstone, Tony McEnery, and Gerry Knowles, 140–251. London: Longman.

Machin, David and Andrea Mayr. 2012. *How to Do Critical Discourse Analysis*. London: Sage.

Martin, John. R. and Peter R. R. White. 2005. *The Language of Evaluation: The Appraisal Framework*. Houndmills, Basingstoke: Palgrave Macmillan.

Massumi, Brian. 2009. "National Enterprise Emergency". *Theory, Culture & Society*, 26(6): 153–185.

McAdam, Jane. 2012. *Climate Change, Forced Migration, and International Law*. Oxford: Oxford University Press.

Pecman, Mojca. 2014. "Variation as a Cognitive Device: How Scientists Construct Knowledge through Term Formation". *Terminology*, 20(1): 1–24.

Reisigl, Martin and Ruth Wodak. 2001. *Discourse and Discrimination: Rhetorics of Racism and Antisemitism*. London and New York: Routledge.

Russo Katherine E., Brewster Anne, and Lars Jensen (eds.). 2011. "On Whiteness: Current Debates in Australian Studies". *Journal of the European Association for Studies on Australia*, 2(2): 2–5.

Stubbs, M. 2001. *Words and Phrases: Corpus Studies of Lexical Semantics*. Cambridge: Blackwell.

Thomson, Elizabeth and Peter R. R. White (eds.). 2008. *Communicating Conflict: Multilingual Case Studies of the News Media*. London: Continuum.

van Dijk, Teun. 1988. *News as Discourse*. Hillsdale, NJ: Lawrence Erlbaum.

———. 1991. *Racism and the Press*. London: Routledge.

———. 1993. *Elite Discourse and Racism*. London: Sage.

———. 1996. "Discourse, Power and Access". In *Texts and Practices: Readings in Critical Discourse Analysis*, edited by Cr.R. Caldas-Coulthard and M. Coulthard, 84–104. London: Routledge.

———. 1999. "Discourse and the Denial of Racism". In *The Discourse Reader*, edited by A. Jaworski and N. Coupland. London: Routledge.

———. 2008. *Discourse and Power*. Basingtoke: Palgrave Macmillan.

van Dijk, Teun A. 2009. *Society and Discourse: How Social Contexts Influence Text and Talk*. Cambridge: Cambridge University Press.

Wodak, Ruth, 2008. "Us and Them: Inclusion and Exclusion – Discrimination via Discourse". In *Identity, Belonging and Migration*, edited by Gerard Delanty, Ruth Wodak, Paul Jones, 54–77. Liverpool: Liverpool University Press.

Chapter 12

Rearranging Desire

On Whiteness and Heteronormativity

Andrew Baldwin

INTRODUCTION

Desire is an unlikely category for analysing 'climate change and migration'. As with many of the chapters in this volume, 'climate change and migration' is a relation that ordinarily appears within a juridico-political framework, constructed from an array of familiar political concepts. Sovereignty, containment, borders, militarism, neoliberalism, humanitarianism and law are only just a few of the concepts by and through which the relation between climate change and migration is called into being and scrutinized. But hardly ever do we consider 'climate change and migration' a relation of desire, constitutive of the way in which we inhabit the world, and by 'we' I mean inhabitants of the metropolitan 'West'. And yet when we turn to cinematic and literary portrayals of climate change, the popular genre of 'cli-fi', we find migration narratives densely interwoven with those of desire. This chapter considers two such cli-fi films: John Hillcoat's cinematic adaptation of Cormac McCarthy's *The Road* (2009) and Roland Emmerich's *The Day After Tomorrow (2004)*. The purpose is to locate desire as an affective force animating the relationship between 'climate change and migration'. Both films are suggestive of a cultural politics of 'climate change and migration' in which the heteronormative family form becomes the privileged economy of desire for surviving climate change. In contrast, Behn Zeitlin's science fiction fantasy *Beasts of the Southern Wild* offers a compelling counter-narrative in which surviving climate change entails the conscious refusal of desire domesticated into the heteronormative family. By celebrating mobility, creativity, even excess, *Beasts of the Southern Wild* presents a 'nomadic' model of survival, a model of life and of living, that serves as a useful metaphor for imagining new forms of kinship and belonging and, ultimately, new forms of political solidarity for climate change.

Desire is a central organising theme in both *The Day After Tomorrow* (*TDAT*) and *The Road*. Amidst scenes of societal breakdown, the protagonists in both films often yearn for their lost objects of desire: a restored state, the family home, a parent's embrace, the touch of a lover. This is the familiar expression of desire conceived in relation to subjective lack that one finds in psychoanalytic theory. Of course, desire can also be understood as an effect of power, as, for example, in the historicity of race and sexuality where a specific economy of desire is consolidated in the heteronormative family form as a prerogative of European colonialism (Stoler 1995, Carter 2008). But through these dystopic narratives we might also come to appreciate how desire shapes the wider affective schema of 'climate change and migration', although for this we need to think desire not only 'as a lack', as in the search for a lost object, but from the philosophy of Gilles Deleuze and Felix Guattari (1983) also as 'a process of production', or desiring-production (p. 26). Desire, in this second sense, is a world-shaping affective force that manifests materially in assemblages like, for example, 'climate change and migration'.

This chapter examines *TDAT* and *The Road* in order to consider how the affective force they exert relies upon elevating the white heteronormative family as the basic unit of human survival for climate change. Such elevation, I argue, gives rise to what might be called a 'white' desiring-production of climate change, an arrangement of desire that idealizes the heteronormative family, what Lauren Berlant (2011) might call 'the good life fantasy', even while we know the promise of 'the good life fantasy' – bourgeois suburban-ism, consumption, petro-modernity, and so forth – to be at the root of much of the current climate change crisis, not to mention the psychic traumas of het-eropatriarchy and racism (hooks 2004). 'Cruel optimism' is the term Berlant (2011) gives to describe this type of condition, a 'condition of maintaining an attachment to a significantly problematic object' (p. 24). As such, cruel opti-mism is precisely the condition in which we find ourselves bound to 'objects' or 'scenes of desires' whose 'continuity of form' allows for the 'continuity of the subject's sense of what it means to keep on living on' (Berlant 2011 p. 24). What *TDAT* and *The Road* convey then is not only a sense in which cruel optimism prevails as a sensory condition of climate change in much of the industrialized West (the protagonists remain attached to the suburban good life fantasy which we know to be a false promise), but that such a sensory condition is also one intimately bound to the histories of race and racism. Ultimately, what these two films communicate is a moral injunction: resolve the climate crisis, otherwise those psychically invested in the 'white' heteronormative good life might find themselves living out the humiliating fate of the 'climate refugee', that racially debased figure struggling to survive on landscapes bereft of life. They tell us that the white heteronormative family form might be torn asunder by climate change, or even more emphatically, that climate change might undo the very property relation that is the lifeblood of Western patriarchy.

But, to read 'climate change and migration' as a site of cruel optimism qua the heteronormative family form is neither to repudiate nor to celebrate the 'family' per se. For even while colonial and sexist exploitation continue to mark the heteronormative family in many subtle and not so subtle ways, the family can also be for many a site of creativity, nurturing and political and personal transformation without it being reducible to sexist oppression (hooks 2000). So, in the spirit of Eve Kosofsky Sedgwick (2003), the aim of this chapter is, instead, to cultivate a reparative dialogue, one that would prise open 'climate change and migration' as a site for unthinking sexist and racist exploitation, such that human life, and indeed human survival, in otherwise precarious times of climatic, economic and geopolitical upheaval might be *revalued* beyond the desiring-productions of bourgeois whiteness. In the final section, I consider how Angela Willey's (2016) concept of *biopossibility* might provide an imaginary capable of such revaluation.

ANTHROPORACIALITY AND THE POSTRACIAL ASSEMBLAGE OF 'CLIMATE CHANGE AND MIGRATION'

Climate change is bad enough. On its own, it can be understood as its own process of desiring-production. Air travel, automobility, central heating, meat consumption, and other fossil fuel-intensive forms of living, in one way or another, are all expressions of desire, a 'desire to live' (Butler 2015). In aggregate, such fossil fuel-intensive practices amount to an agglomeration of socio-technical and political economic forces which together give rise to a multiplicity of geophysical and socio-natural transformations (Hulme 2015, Randalls 2015), some actualized, some not. We have come to label these transformations 'climate change'. But 'climate change' is transmuted into a *racializing* assemblage when augmented by a second multiplicity, that of 'migration', where migration is conceived as exceptional to populations otherwise imagined as sedentary. When imagined as a singular relation, 'climate change and migration' comes to signify a coming heterogeneity in which the multiplicity of geophysical conditions (climatic upheaval) results in the ungovernable movement of bodies. For the purposes of this chapter, I take 'climate change and migration' to be an affective relation. Elsewhere I have argued that 'climate change and migration' is a virtual phenomenon characterized by its own excess (2013, 2016). What I mean by this is that 'climate change and migration' is objectively indeterminate, which means that it can never be known as such. This is not to say that it is not a real phenomenon, only that its realness is a *virtual* realness rather than an *actual* realness. It is not implausible to say that the geophysical manifestations of the desiring-production of climate change, that is, sea-level rise, extreme weather events and so forth, will affect human migration. The trouble arises, however, when we attempt to disaggregate climate change from all the other desiring-productions that shape human migration. The fact that we are unable to do this is the reason why it remains impossible to identify specific individuals as *actual* climate migrants or climate refugees (McAdam 2012). What concerns me in this chapter is the virtual realness, or virtual sensorium, of 'climate change and migration', and even more, the coming heterogeneity of bodies expressed by its virtual realness. Indeed, it is precisely this *sense* of a coming heterogeneity that makes 'climate change and migration' a virtual sensorium; one is able to *feel* a future of intermingling bodies hanging over the present but without that future ever being known as such. It can only be felt. This is also partly what I mean when I say that 'climate change and migration' is a racializing assemblage. It gives rise to a potentiality (a coming heterogeneity, the intermingling of bodies), such that this (always unactualized) potential becomes a performative force shaping the multiplicity that we know as 'the politics of climate change'.

However, by racializing assemblage, I also mean, following Alexander Welehiye (2015), 'a set of socio-political processes that discipline humanity into full humans, not-quite-humans, and nonhumans' (p. 4). In this sense, when the racializing assemblage of 'climate change and migration' expresses the potential ungovernability of heterogeneous, moving bodies, it induces an affect of anti-production; it diminishes our capacity to imagine the emancipatory or creative affordances of migration in the context of climate change (Baldwin 2016). Instead, we are forced to see in it only negative transformation (loss). It constrains the climate change imaginary to one in which human survival is said to depend on population control and in which only some forms of humanness are said to be desirable, hence the categorization of humanity into full humans (sedentary bodies), not-quite humans (adaptive migrants) and non-humans (maladaptive migrants). Conversely, this diminished capacity comes at the expense of more affirmative or creative imaginaries, such as those that might help us rethink the relationship between desire and human survival, or how power itself might be rearranged as a prerogative of life and living. There is a full-fledged humanism in this diminished capacity. To approach climate change as the imperative to control human mobility is to privilege a delimited vision in which 'the human' is conceived only as an agent of containment, or closure, as opposed to a vision in which the human is never fixed but always available to its creative reimagining. Some have described this diminished capacity as 'depoliticization' (Bettini 2013,

Methmann and Oels 2015). Elsewhere I have referred to it as a particular kind of affective orientation to climate change called 'white affect' (Baldwin 2016). The term 'white affect' is used because of the racial anxieties that attach to contemporary migration and the concomitant impulse to contain migrants. Jasbir Puar (2007) argues that 'identity is one effect of affect, a capture that proposes what one is by masking its retrospective ordering and thus its ontogenetic dimension – what one was – through the guide of an illusory futurity' (p. 215). The particular identity distilled from white affect is that of 'anthropoxacial man', a particular subjectivity David Theo Goldberg (2015, p. 139) has described as postracial.

The postracial is a contested concept. I use it in this chapter to name both a historical condition and a logic in which the structural racisms that persist as a result of slavery and colonial exploitation have been deemed irrelevant to contemporary political, social and environmental life, even while their effects continue to structure the life chances of 'racial' subjectivities as compared to those whose raciality masquerades as transparent, that is, 'white' subjectivities (Sharma and Sharma 2012, Goldberg 2015). Barack Obama symbolizes well the postracial inasmuch as the very fact of a black US president is oftentimes mobilized as evidence that America is no longer structured in racial domination even while the statistics of contemporary black incarceration in America tell a different story (Goldberg 2015, Shabazz 2015). The postracial is contemporaneous with and geographically inflected by the current racial situation that one finds in the United States, the United Kingdom and Europe as well as in racially structured settler societies, such as South Africa and Israel (Goldberg 2015). Its logics are multiple but function mainly through incessant race denial ('I am not a racist'), the fantasy of reverse racism (e.g. the charge that white people are disprivileged by virtue of their whiteness) and the pervasive insistence that racism is a thing of the past. As a unique form of racial power, postraciality functions by dehumanising people without any explicit reference to race or racism. It is, as such, a form of racial power that emerges when both race and the trace of race become imperceptible.

In his philosophy of the postracial, Goldberg (2015) also gives an account of what he calls the *anthropoxacial*, which, I argue later, is an apt descriptor of the racializing assemblage of climate change and migration. The anthropoxacial is a specific postracial expression that emerges when the figure of the human understood as the autonomous agent of historical modernity dissolves. As nature, technology and culture blur into *naturetechnocultures*, it has become commonplace to argue that discerning the human apart from its material embeddedness is impossible. This has given rise to a (re)new(ed) ontological awareness about the interspecies nature of human 'being' as, for example, in the new or vital materialisms (Bennett 2010, Coole and Frost 2010) and discussions about posthumanism (see also Brown, this volume).

But as Goldberg observes, 'In a counter-direction . . . with the erasing of distinctions between categories of the human, natural and technological, there is a heightening impetus to characterize the non-belonging, the rejected, and the alienated – the enemy, the dangerous, the threatening – as unrecognizably human' (p. 110). What he means is that in our present condition in which 'the human' is called radically into question, when, for example, climate change is said to threaten human survival, or the realization that our optimistic attachment to scenes of desire (i.e. the family) also threatens those very scenes, we find the concomitant hyper-*re*-inflation of the universal human through concepts like geoengineering and the Anthropocene and, I would argue, 'climate change and migration'. Anthroporaciality thus emerges as the form of the postracial in the space opened up by nature technocultures, a space in which the purportedly autonomous human agent is no longer fully discernible. Anthroporacial man is, thus, projected as the antidote to its own coming, self-made dissolution, to the threat of human (read: 'white') precarity. We can appreciate the full heft of the anthroporacial by quoting Goldberg at length:

> Anthroporaciality is not the older [racial] claim of inherent inferiority or superiority, nor one of historical immaturity. It is, rather, the assertion of 'the new man' (Anthropocene's literal meaning) claiming natural self-preservation in the face of supposedly racially hostile threats. Postraciality's 'new man' insists on self-defining and -refining his own destiny, making himself as he (re)makes his world. But he does so by necessarily denying the worlds of anyone antithetical to his world-making. He is, as a consequence, simultaneously paranoid and self-assertive, threatened and threatening, anxious and authoritarian, encircled and violently aggressive. In the deeply networked and interrelated globalities of movement and managed circulations, anthroporacial man has planetary designs and impacts. Anthroporaciality seeks inevitably for extended racist belittlement and exclusion, giving rise to while rationalizing them. Far from the end of racisms, anthroporaciality as postraciality's refining conception is their extended afterlife, renewed expression and heightened violent manifestation. (pp. 138–39)

Goldberg's notion of the anthroporacial is significant as it recalls how anthroporacial man invests in new forms of postracial expression as a prerogative of his own survival, or desiring-production. We might call this prerogative 'white ascendency'. In this sense, anthroporacial man enacts a form of biopower specific to the universal condition of the Anthropocene, creating 'caesuras within the biological continuum' (Foucault 2003 p. 255), a continuum of being that follows once the Anthropocene is announced as humanity's new universal condition. The idea advanced in this chapter is that 'climate change and migration' is one such postracial expression, the cut that anthroporacial man inflicts on the fabric of 'universal humanity' as a condition of its own self-remaking. It is in this sense, then, that 'climate change and migration' functions as a virtual sensorium of white affect, diminishing humanness in the face of climate change by disciplining 'humanity into full humans [*sedentary anthroporacial man*], not-quite-humans [*adaptive or labour migrants*], and non-humans [*maladaptive migrants; surplus populations*]' (Weheliye 2015 p. 4, my additions).

'Climate change and migration' functions as a postracial racializing assemblage when, for example, climate change is assumed to be either the cause or trigger of migration. Examples of this abound in popular media and political rhetoric. So, for example, when Prince Charles invokes the spectre of climate-induced mass migration to justify global climate governance, as he did during the opening plenary session of the Paris UNFCCC COP21, he engages in precisely this form of postracial expression. More nuanced accounts will mobilize the multicausal nature of migration, listing climate change as merely one of many variables that explain mobility (Cf. McLeman 2014). But in either case, the attribution of migration to climate change whether as cause or trigger enacts a degree of historical amnesia and thus racial dehumanization by decoupling migration from the oftentimes racial and colonial conditions that structure the migration decision-making calculus (see also Samaddar, this volume). But equally significant both cast 'climate change and migration' in a future-conditional grammar, an 'illusory future'. Notions like 'climate refugee' and 'climate migrant' are thus best conceived as postracial subjectivities inasmuch as the historical context of those deemed 'climate refugees' is violently disavowed when climate change is said to be the primary reason people migrate (Baldwin 2013).

FILMIC ANALYSIS

The remainder of this chapter zeros in on a somewhat oblique, even unlikely, moment in the anthroporacial assemblage of climate change and migration, namely its 'white' desiring-production, an arrangement of desire that elevates the white heteronormative family as the basic unit of human survival for climate change. My reason for zooming in on the heteronormative nuclear family is this: if 'climate change and migration' is a postracial racializing assemblage, resuscitating anthroporacial man (white ascendency) amidst his own self-made dissolution, then we should expect the resuscitation of anthroporacial man to entail at least in part resuscitating whiteness as a standard of value in the pursuit of anthroporacial man's survival. Roland Emmerich's *The Day After Tomorrow (2004)* and Cormac McCarthy's *The Road (2009)* are illustrative. In both, we find the elevation of the white heteronormative family as the basic and privileged unit of climate change survival. Stories of the flesh, these dystopic tales share much in common. Both are set within landscapes radically transformed by climate change or, in the case of *The Road*, some proximate environmental catastrophe. Both are set within political contexts in which state authority is either rapidly unravelling, weakened or, else, altogether absent. Both are predicated to varying degrees on the breakdown of heteronormative gender relations and both, in turn, feature protagonists, whose struggles for survival are partly migratory struggles to recuperate their lost object of desire: the 'white', heteronormative family. Additionally important, in neither of these portrayals do we find the usual racist expressions that animate popular rhetorics of migration and climate change: mass migration, 'swarms', 'tides' and 'hordes' of black migrants clamouring for entry to Europe or America. Instead, we find in both precisely the opposite: 'white', heterosexual, middle-class men, always a father and son and an absent mother, whose quest for survival and familial recuperation bears some relationship to racialized migration, either as an immediate survival tactic or as the promise of death. And so across both narratives we find the problem space of 'climate change and migration' defined as a futurized precarity, whether an emasculated or absent state authority, the heterogeneous mixing of migrating bodies, and/ or white precarity expressed as the optimistic attachment to the lost heteronormative family.

The Day After Tomorrow

The Day After Tomorrow (*TDAT*) is an obvious place to begin, given its popularity and genre-defining status. We find in it perhaps the most straightforward statement about white desiring-production inasmuch as we can read it as *both* the elevation of anthroporacial man *and* the recuperation of the white heteronormative family as the model of climate change survival.

Anthroporacial man is exactly the figure who inaugurates the Anthropocene by calling the Anthropocene into being and declaring it the new universal human condition. If the Anthropocene is said to be a new geological epoch in which humanity is now a distinctive geologic force, then it is one said to subsume *all* of humanity, even if not all humans are equally responsible for its making. The paradigmatic figure of the Anthropocene is the European or Western white male scientist (Yusoff 2015). This is the figure whose global imaginary allows for him to make universal declarations on behalf of all of humanity, his sophisticated knowledge of the earth system allowing him to warn humanity of its shared fate. Al Gore exemplifies anthroporacial man in climate change discourse. In *TDAT*, we find this figure in Jack Hall (Dennis Quaid), a climate scientist who travels seamlessly between his Antarctic field station, where he experiences the fracturing of the Larson B ice sheet first-hand, the United Nations, where he gives an impassioned plea to world diplomats indifferent to his science, and the corridors power in Washington.

But Jack is equally significant because he alone, or more accurately his science, insures the recuperation of the white heteronormative family during the acute climatic crisis that occurs during the film's short time span. Early in *TDAT*, we understand Jack's marriage to have broken down, the result of him prioritizing career over family. And so from the outset of *TDAT* the film's main storyline is set within the breakdown of heteronormative gender relations. The family, we also learn, is spatially fragmented. The mother, Lucy Hall (Sela Ward), is trapped in the hospital where she works as a physician. Lucy and Jack's son, Sam, is on a school trip in Manhattan, and Jack, now returned from his travels, lives alone in Washington. This is clearly an upper-middle-class family whose separation is further dramatized through a series of freak climatic events that take place in various parts of the world – massive hail in Japan, snow in India, multiple tornados that leave Los Angeles in ruins and a massive tidal wave that washes over all of Manhattan. And it's Jack's science which intervenes and, ultimately, saves the son from certain death and reunifies the family.

Following the Manhattan tidal wave, when Sam becomes trapped in the New York Public Library with hundreds of others, he is faced with a dilemma. He must either remain in the library or else submit to the only recognizable state authority amongst them, a black New York City police officer, who encourages the library refugees to seek refuge elsewhere. But through a telephone conversation with his father, Sam learns that a period of rapid freezing is about to take hold over the Northern Hemisphere. Jack convinces Sam to remain in the library and promises him rescue. So convinced, Sam attempts to convince the others to do the same, but they refuse his 'climate science' and instead blindly follow the state authority (the black officer) to their eventual death. On his approach to New York, Jack finds the frozen 'climate refugees' in the Upper Bay before reaching Sam, who survives the deep freeze by remaining sedentary and burning books in the library fireplace.

TDAT is not exactly a story about climate change and migration, and yet migration, or at least averted migration, remains central to it. Elsewhere in the film thousands of 'Americans' (assume 'white' Americans) are shown crossing the Rio Grande and entering Mexico, following an order from the US president. So, too, the US state authority seeks refuge in Mexico in an attempt to govern the heterogeneity and chaos from afar. In both cases, the climatic emergency is heightened through a trope of reversal, both when the exiled US state is forced to occupy the position of 'climate refugee' (in Mexico) and when its otherwise-sedentary citizens are themselves made into racialized refugees through an evacuation order by the soon-to-be-dead president. And so, it is precisely this reversal that makes Jack's plea to Sam all the more potent. The plea to remain is partly a plea to refuse state authority. But also significant is that it is a plea to the white son to refuse becoming a refugee, as seeking refuge from the chaos is a recipe for racial precarity and, in the case of those who followed the black police officer from the library, a recipe for racialized death (maladaptation). Survival thus depends not on seeking refuge elsewhere but on remaining put. But this is also a mode of survival that depends on a desire to reunite the heteronormative family unit and, in doing so, a mode of survival that reinvigorates anthroporacial man (Jack Hall) himself. And so amidst the scene of societal breakdown, a scene in which the state is left to govern the ungovernable while in exile and the earth system is swirling out of control, the white heteronormative family form remains the only stable point of reference, the only reliable form of sociality for surviving climate change.

The Road

The Road gives a radically different account of desire and family recuperation. Set in the US South, *The Road* unfolds as a dystopic future on a barren, desiccated landscape no longer capable of supporting agricultural life. Later in the film we learn that the landscape is the result of human inaction in relation to a looming environmental catastrophe, presumably climate change. This is a landscape without refuge where the only remaining humans – 'climate refugees' – wander the barren landscape without any real hope for survival and where the threat of cannibalism, the descent into race, is ever present. The film's central protagonists are a nomadic father and son who navigate this lifeless landscape, sustained only by their mutual love and trust and the false hope that their circumstance will improve if they move to the South by the sea. The father's false hope is sustained by the optimistic memory of family life prior to the catastrophe.

Memories of the absent mother recur throughout the film, mostly in the father's dreams, where he recalls her innocence: the homestead, the hearth, the wedding band, the family bed. In a world that seems completely devoid of meaning, her memory offers a point of reference that allows the father to continually reassure his son that they are the 'good guys'. Her memory offers as well the false hope, the mirage, that the family – the trinity of father, mother, son – might one day be reunited. This same false hope appears in various rituals of family life enacted throughout the film. When the father and son enter a burnt-out suburban gated community, they enter the father's childhood home. In his now burnt-out living room, he returns the cushion to the sofa and sits down, recounting the ritual of domestic comfort. And when father and son stumble upon a perfectly preserved bomb shelter, they re-enact the rituals of family life: mealtime, bedtime and memories of mom. Later in the film, again through the father's dreamscape, we learn that the mother left her husband

and child in the ultimate act of maternal sacrifice. He insists that survival is paramount, but she replies that she doesn't want to 'simply survive' and so she leaves, leaving father and son to fend for themselves. This is a survival story that can only really end with death. But in the final stages of the narrative, after the son holds vigil while watching over his father as he dies and prepares himself for his own survival and thus for his own death, the boy is visited by a lone man who turns out not to be a cannibal, but another one of the good guys, himself the father of two children. In the film's final scene, the children's mother holds out her hand to the boy and welcomes him into their family.

We can interpret *The Road* in all manner of ways, but for the purpose of this chapter it is the intersecting themes of survival, whiteness and the heteronormative family unit that demand our attention. As argued earlier, 'climate change and human migration' can be understood as a form of anthroporacial expression which rearticulates anthroporacial man's need for survival, or desiring-production, at the very moment (the Anthropocene, climate change) when its survival is being challenged. Specifically, 'climate change and migration' designates a coming heterogeneity and a condition of ungovernability, and *The Road* is emblematic of exactly this. It is a survivalist film in which white survival is called dramatically into question by a catastrophic future. It depicts a stateless world, an ungoverned world completely devoid of state sovereignty. This is an emasculated, lifeless world in which nature and culture are once and for all completely blurred and in which the migrating father and son cling to the false promise of familial sovereignty as way of overcoming their destitution. Throughout the film, as in *TDAT*, it's the loss and yearning to recuperate the white heteronormative family that holds the narrative together. In an otherwise bleak and meaningless landscape, the heteronormative family form not only comes to represent all that is 'good' in the world, but surfaces as the only refuge in a world that offers no refuge. And herein lies the moral injunction of the film: as we, the audience, bear witness to the slowly unfolding of climate change in the world around us, *The Road* reminds us that we are *all* threatened by the possibility of living a nomadic existence in a world without refuge. It warns us that we are all potential climate refugees, prone to resorting to cannibalism and other modes of racialized survival (e.g. theft, indigeneity), the only salvation from which is to be found by restoring the lost sovereignty of the white heteronormative family form.

BEYOND THE DESIRING-PRODUCTION OF WHITE HETERONORMATIVITY

This chapter has sought to emphasize the way that 'climate change and migration' designates a yet-to-come heterogeneity, the chaotic redistribution of bodies around the world as a result of climate change. The claim, in this sense, is not that 'climate change and migration' is an actually existing phenomenon, but a virtual one. And not just any virtual, but one that produces a sense of, or fealty for, a future in which all that one cherishes stands to be ripped apart. I have furthermore tried to suggest that 'climate change and migration' is a virtual sensorium, or affective schema, out of which the white heteronormative family form comes to be privileged as the main unit of survival for climate change, at least in these two popular 'cli fi' narratives. We find variations on this affective schema in both *TDAT* and *The Road*; the climate refugee or climate migrant is a racially configured body whose oppositional referent is the white heteronormative family. This is an arrangement of desire that consolidates the white heteronormative family. And finally I have suggested that the virtual sensorium of 'climate change and migration' functions as a kind of white desiring-production, a kind of machine that produces the world and in whose wake the world takes on a distinctive texture of closure.

We know, however, that the heteronormative family is not inevitable. As a norm of social (re)production and intergenerational survival, it is only ever an effect of power, and one whose imagined sovereignty is made possible through an exclusionary logic that displaces other forms of kinship and property relation as arrangements of social survival. Understanding this is important because it allows us to reimagine survival as a site of politics, contestation and possibility rather than as some sort of universal moral imperative in which the recuperation of a lost object, the reclamation of sovereignty, in this case, the white heteronormative family, is paramount. Instead, we might attempt to reimagine climate futures through an imaginary of *non*-sovereignty where our condition for being, even flourishing, in the world depends on our refusal of sovereignty and the embrace of and even desire for our relationality and openness to the world. We might even say that such a condition depends on the rearrangement of desire itself. The remainder of this chapter traces the lineaments of just such an imaginary, Angela Willey's (2016) concept of biopossibility. It then reads biopossibility as a concept of non-sovereignty in Benh Zeitlin's science fiction, climate change survivalist film, *Beasts of the Southern Wild*.

Willey builds her concept of biopossibility from an engagement with queer feminist science studies. Her concern is broadly to denaturalize and decentre sex and heterosexual reproduction and in their place to privilege 'affectivity and commitment' as the bases for human social bonding. Biopossibility emerges for Willey as a queer ethics or, more specifically, an erotics, albeit a 'non-sexual erotics', a term she borrows from Audre Lorde (1984), appropriate for reimagining social life in the space of the naturecultural. It is, as she puts it, 'a tool for naturecultural thinking' (p. 125). Central to Willey's ethics is what she calls the joy of possibility, a visceral joy aroused when one remains open to all possibilities. She calls this joy the 'crux of queer freedom', the practice of thinking 'against the logics of phallicized whiteness in which we find the comfort of the familiar, and to aspire to release assumptions about what we are and might become, in the service of imagination'. In this sense, biopossibility is an erotics of refusal. It is a refusal to accept the cruel optimism and presupposed sovereignty of the (naturalized) heteronormative good life, at the same time expanding 'our freedom to participate in the bringing into being of different futures' (p. 123). Biopossibility is thus an affect of openness the non-sovereignty of which derives from its always emergent relationality with its outside. I want to suggest that Willey's concept of biopossibility offers an erotics for reimagining social life in the space of climate change and its migratory futures. We can think of biopossibility as the inverse of anthroporaciality. If anthroporaciality is 'self-preservation in the face of supposedly racially hostile threats' (Goldberg 2015 p. 138), for example, a sedentary desire to avoid the descent into race or to recuperate a threatened white heteronormativity, then biopossibility is the pursuit of life and survival by maximizing one's creative engagement with the world. It 'opens a space for thinking natureculturally not only about friendship, community and/or our coevolution with nonhuman animals but also about human relationships to "things" – both abstract and material' (p. 138).

We can sketch out some of the lineaments of biopossibility in Benh Zeitlin's science fiction, climate change survivalist film, *Beasts of the Southern Wild*. The film tells the story of a five-year-old black girl called Hushpuppy, who, along with her father Wink and their rebellious, alcohol-fuelled comrades, both black and white, all of whom are poor, live illegally on a piece of land, called the Bathtub, on the wrong side of the levee that separates the bayou from the anodyne world of suburban Louisiana. Hushpuppy, Wink and their motley band live a kind of irreverent, anti-authoritarian wildness that actively resists capture from the health authorities that symbolize sanitized white America. They live on catfish, crab and stolen liquor, and when the storms come and the Bathtub floods, they seek refuge in artistic makeshift rafts, themselves manifestations of creative survival, until the floodwaters recede. Although one might take exception to Zeitlin's casual celebration of the triumph of resilience in the face of adversity, the Bathtub's unruly inhabitants are brilliant in their refusal of anodyne, white America in favour of a world of unbounded creativity, ungovernability and excess. This is a fugitive world defined as much by escape as by its potential to combine with itself to forge new ways of life that open out onto the world. Theirs is a world of self-organization lived deliberately as an act of political rebelliousness.

It is important to recall bell hooks (2012) and Agnes Woolley's (2012) respective critiques that *Beasts of Southern Wild* is remarkable for the way in which it uses myth to obscure the reproduction black stereotypes. The film can easily be accused of its uncritical embrace of various racial tropes which the audience is invited to overlook in favour of a narrative of black agency and survival in (presumably) the post-Hurricane Katrina context. Hushpuppy is the recurring figure of black female survival; Wink is abusive and absent; the black body as both animal and ecological savage. But if *Beasts of the Southern Wild* is read within the genre of climate cinema, then perhaps it can be read for more than simply its excessive racial logic. If *The Road* uses the figure of the climate refugee – the nomadic father and son – as a means for recuperating the white sovereign heteronormative family as the unit of survival for climate change, then *Beasts of the Southern Wild* uses the climate refugee – the nomadic father and daughter and their motley comrades – to offer an account of biopossibility that foregrounds non-sovereignty, collective well-being and rebelliousness as conditions of survival. This is not to suggest biopossibility as a fatalist response to climate change in which the struggle to abate climate change is abandoned in favour of biopossible life. Biopossibility is instead an erotics (a form of power) that might inform social life and political solidarity in the face of both the geophysicality of climate change *and* the social formations, such as institutionalized heteronormativity, that the cultural politics of climate change appear to privilege. In *Beasts of the Southern Wild*, biopossibility is a cross-race imaginary in which white and black co-conspire in their refusal of the anodyne world of white America situated on the other side of the levee. It is also a model of social reproduction in which commitment and trust are not coterminous with the family but are actively cultivated by those whose define themselves as a community of survivors. And alongside the struggle for survival are poetic moments – Hushpuppy and Wink adrift at sunset, Hushpuppy's imaginary beasts – that recall the simple joy of being.

If the levee symbolizes anthroporacial man's fantastical attempt to insulate himself and his anodyne community from the dangerous lives set adrift by climate change, then *Beasts of the Southern Wild* offers a metaphor for thinking creatively about social and political life in the context of climate change. In this sense, biopossibility offers a way of reimagining climate change and migration, not as a relation of loss, but instead as an occasion 'to release assumptions about what we are and might become', to rethink desire and to revalue life beyond the closures of heteronormative whiteness.

REFERENCES

Baldwin, A. 2013. "Racialisation and the figure of the climate change migrant". *Environment and Planning A*, 45(6): 1474–90.

————. 2016. "Premediation and white affect: Climate change and migration in critical perspective". *Transactions of the Institute of British Geographers*, 41(1): 78–90.

Bennett, J. 2010. *Vibrant Matter: A Political Ecology of Things*. Durham and London: Duke University Press.

Berlant, L. 2011. *Cruel Optimism*. Durham and London: Duke University Press.

Bettini, G. 2013. (In)Convenient convergences: 'climate refugees', apocalyptic discourses and the depoliticization of climate-induced migration. *Deconstructing the greenhouse: Interpretive approaches to global climate governance*. C. Methmann, D. Rothe and B. Stephan. Abingdon: Routledge: 122–36.

Butler, J. 2015. *Senses of the Subject*. New York: Fordham University Press.

Carter, S. 2008. *The Importance of Being Monogamous: Marriage and Nation Building in Western Canada to 1915*. Edmonton: University of Alberta Press.

Coole, D. and S. Frost, (eds.). 2010. *New Materalisms: Ontology, Agency, Politics*. Durham and London: Duke University Press.

Deleuze, G. and F. Guattari. 1983. *Anti-oedipus: Capitalism and Schizophrenia*. Minneapolis: University of Minnesota Press.

Foucault, M. 2003. *'Society Must be Defended' Lectures at the College de France*. New York: Picador.

Goldberg, D. T. 2015. *Are We All Postracial Yet?* Cambridge: Polity Press.

hooks, b. 2000. *Feminist Theory: From Margin to Centre*. London: Pluto Press.

hooks, b. 2004. *The Will to Change: Men, Masculinity, and Love*. New York: Washington Square Press.

————. 2012. "No love in the wild". NewBlackMan (in Exile) posted 6 September 2012.

Hulme, M. 2015. *Climate Change: One or Many?* Van Mildert College SCR Anniversary Lecture, 11 May 2015. Durham University.

Lorde, A. 1988. *Uses of the Erotic: The Erotic as Power*. In The Audrey Lorde Compendium: Essays, Speeches and Journals. New York: Harper Collins, pp. 106–18.

McAdam, J. 2012. *Climate Change, Forced Migration, and International Law*. Oxford: Oxford University Press.

McLeman, R. 2014. *Climate and Human Migration: Past Experiences, Future Challenges*. Cambridge: Cambridge University Press.

Methmann, C. and A. Oels. 2015. "From 'fearing' to 'empowering' climate refugees: Climate-induced migration in the name of resilience". *Security Dialogue*, 46(1): 51–68.

Puar, J. 2007. *Terrorist Assemblages: Homonationalism in Queer Times*. Durham and London: Duke University Press.

Randalls, S. 2015. Governing the Climate: New Approaches to Rationality, Power and Politics. In *Climate Change Multiple*, (eds.) H. Bulkeley and J. Stripple. Cambridge: Cambridge University Press.

Sedgwick, E. 2003. *Touching Feeling: Affect, Pedagogy, Performativity*. Durham and London: Duke University Press.

Shabazz, R. 2015. *Spatializing Blackness: Architectures of Confinement and Black Masculinity in Chicago*. Urbana, Chicago, Springfield: University of Illinois Press.

Sharma, A. and S. Sharma. 2012. "Post-racial imaginaries: Connecting the pieces". *dark matter* 9(1): no pagination.

Stoler, L. A. 1995. *Race and the Education of Desire: Foucault's History of Sexuality and the Colonial Order of Things.* Durham and London: Duke University Press.

Weheliye, A. 2015. *Habeas Viscus: Racializing Assemblages, Biopolitics, and Black Feminist Theories of the Human.* Durham and London: Duke University Press.

Willey, A. 2016. *Undoing Monogamy: The Politics of Science and the Possibilities of Biology.* Durham and London: Duke University Press.

Wooley, A. 2012. The politics of myth making: 'Beasts of the Southern Wild'. *Open Democracy.* 29 October 2012.

Yusoff, K. 2015. Towards a Black Anthropocene. Conference Paper. Living in the Anthropocene. Royal Geographical Society. London. 27 November 2015.

Afterword

Life Adrift in a Postcolonial World

Gaia Giuliani

Allow me to inaugurate the afterword of this important volume recalling the fantasies that lie behind the idea according to which a condition of 'permanent disaster' would offer 'opportunities of moral, cultural and political revitalisation' (Kevin Rosario 2007: 25). The idea of a post-catastrophe revitalization, which has surfaced repeatedly in visual mass culture since 9/11, invokes the utopian vision of a new foundation grounded on a particular understanding of our present societies, power relations and inequalities (Giuliani 2016). The fantasies entailed in the visual culture of catastrophe more often than not reproduce white hegemony, heteropatriarchy, class divisions and colonial subalternities within and across a militarized national and supranational 'body politic' in itself legitimized by the 'permanent emergency'. My contention is that these fantasies not only recentre the West, and postcolonial Europe in particular, in the global cartography of environmental and geopolitical changes. They are also neo-colonial in their commitment to a renewed global social order, one based on the rule of the survival of the civilized and the fittest, those subjects best able to survive the catastrophe and thereafter build and rule over a new global society at the expense of, and *against*, the uncivilized.

In what follows I challenge the fantasy of survival of an 'encamped' and isolated Europe by reflecting on constructions of 'monstrosity'. Monstrosity is useful in subverting the idea of Europe as a geographically and historically isolated entity. My claim is that monstrosity is a postcolonial trope in which the 'colonial archive' is reactivated when it is said that 'hordes' of incoming migrants and refugees are flocking to Europe. Particularly, monstrosity is evoked as representing the subversion of historical and contemporary borders between the encamped space of stability (of the nation, of Europe) and chaotic spaces structurally characterized by disaster, movement and dislocation, between civilization and barbarity, deservedness and killability, subjectivity and victimhood, and fitness and unfitness for the market (see Samaddar and Brown, in this volume). Here, migrants and refugees are looked upon as the 'returning colonised' (Sousa Santos 2011, Giuliani 2016b) whose very presence subverts, as Baldwin and Bettini highlight in the introduction to the present collection, not just the spatiality materialized by bordering processes, but also the normative historical separation between the (colonial) past, the (postcolonial/postracial/neoliberal) present and the future. A good example of this is found in popular cinematic representations of the cannibalizing zombie (Giuliani 2016a) and of apocalyptic disaster. In this afterword, I focus on the three films: *The Happening* (2008) and *Blindness* (2008), two examples of the dystopian genre, and *The Impossible* (2012), a disaster film about the 2004 tsunami in Indonesia and Thailand. Consistent with the use of visual texts by Colebrook, Baldwin and Goldberg (this volume), analysing these films allows me to explore Western and European fears of natural disaster in a way that subverts the normative spatial separation between civilization and barbarity.

I will close my afterword recounting Wendy Brown's reflection on the neoliberal construction of the individual as a market agent. My contention is that this construction reduces migrants and refugees to the 'figure of race' of the postcolonial monster (Giuliani 2016a) insofar as they cannot cope with the disaster, are unable to adapt (Bettini) and thus unfit market actors. These features make them into disposable subjects. This is examined in relation to an episode of *Black Mirror*, a UK/US series that thematizes 'unanticipated consequences of new technologies', including the moments of subjectivity they can inadvertently release.

PERMANENT CATASTROPHE, POSTCOLONIAL *WELTANSCHAUUNGS* AND THE RECENTRING OF EUROPE

American anthropologist Kevin Rozario (2007) has argued that moral, cultural and political renewal often invokes catastrophe as a tool of purification in which society is purified from sin, modernity's wrongdoings, the social barbarity of capitalistic individualism and racial mixing. Within such tropes of renewal, argues Rozario, the survival of those who come to be designated as 'the chosen' represents the hope of 'redemption' and 'endurance' of humankind. For my part, I consider this 'purification' intimately related to colonial *weltanschauungs* that in postcolonial times reread the world through dichotomies that oppose the fit for preservation to the unfit, the deserving to survive (and succeed) and the undeserving.

In line with my recent work on issues related to fears of disaster in the post–9/11 Western world, my analysis in this afterword draws on cultural studies and socio-anthropological interpretations of the discourse on disaster and catastrophe. It builds on the epistemological critique Bettini and Baldwin pose in their introduction, where they highlight how privileging climate change as migration's main 'agent', 'determinant' or 'trigger', in effect obscures the historical circumstances of migration. This afterword furthers this critique by contributing to its historical-theoretical import, offering an exploration of the postcolonial genealogy and the cultural effects of the 'figure of race'[1] of the climate change migrant/refugee within discourses that legitimize 'humanitarian interventions' (Giuliani 2016a) or depict migration as a measure of last resort (see Brad Evans, this volume).

I cannot stress enough the importance of 9/11 for understanding discourses on (climate change) migration and the production of refugees. In this, I follow Judith Butler (2009), who argues that the War on Terror, and its political, economic, military and securitarian cultural legacies represent a frame within which discourses on terrorism and its global power relations are forged. These discourses conflate ideas of security, secularism, war, social bounds and civilization, structured by a dichotomy between 'the good' and 'the bad' and on fears for the 'loss of (Western) civilisation' (Amoore and De Goede 2009 and Furedi 2007). In David T. Goldberg's (p. 113, this volume) own words, fear 'about the racially characterized migrant is at once the fear of a planet perceived to be climatologically out of control; and the fear of a planet climatologically run amok is the fear of racial invasion'. To be clear, my analysis does not imply that Europe is *the* stage where 'borders are performed' and become effective – as if there were no borders elsewhere and as if Europe's external confines were fixed once and for all (see Giuliani 2016c and 2017). Rather, I am suggesting that we view Europe as a 'discourse' more so than a 'place' (Bhambra 2016), one constructed and imagined as internally even, self-consistent, pacified and civilized, or, what Bettini and Baldwin (this volume) might say, is 'settled, sedentary and at some degree of remove from the transnational flows of labour, capital, and technology, imagined to lie beyond [European] borders' (p. 3). In this sense, Europe is constructed as a 'place-to-defend' *in opposition to* places that produce threats, both within the frame of the post-9/11 War on Terror and of climate change. Indeed, as much as the colonial European Self is imagined as even, its outside is uniformly constructed (for instance, by agencies engaging with climate change) as the 'place *for* disaster' (Giuliani 2016a), wherever this 'outside' might happen to be located. I view the distinction between a Self/inside as 'places of disaster' in contrast to an Other/outside as a 'place for disaster' as the re-elaboration of the colonial distinction between civilization and barbarity, or between those able to 'master nature' and those overwhelmed by natural elements. To better understand this distinction, I link these two constructions to the concepts of catastrophe and disaster, respectively. Catastrophe is a crisis, or a moment of transition, which occurs in the West, whereas disaster is an uncontrollable event located somewhere else in the world, outside the West.

CAUSALITY, AGENCY AND SUBJECTIVITY

In the frame of this postcolonial dichotomous understanding of the world, I move now to discuss the construction or reinforcement of the idea that the 'place of disaster', Europe, is also 'the place to be defended'. Rephrasing Hannah Arendt (1968) and following Judith Butler on 'precarity' (2006), Brad Evans (this volume) argues that 'the refugee will become one of the defining political problems of the 21st Century' (p. 70). My contention is that understanding the construction of the Self/inside untouched by disasters is key to appreciating what is at stake in the twenty-first-century cultural politics of the refugee. Or, in the reverse direction, it is through the symbolic and material construction of the figure of the refugee (as often opposed to that of the migrant) that we can understand how the hegemonic subject is constructed and which bodily features, behaviour, territory, class, gender, race and sexuality are ideally and materially assigned to him/her. To do this, I suggest we turn to postcolonial theory, critical race theory and critical whiteness studies in combination with the deconstructive approach of gender studies.

As mentioned by Wendy Brown in her opening chapter of this volume, the 'indispensable yet intensely colonial trope [ontogency recapitulates phylogeny] for framing civilizational infancy and maturity, difference and not only development, has for millennia organized our understanding of the human and its possibilities'. It is therefore *against* this colonial trope that we need to rethink the very concept of humanity in relation to disaster and humanitarian management. In fact, the humanitarian management of disaster and linked 'reconstruction' initiatives represent the primary site for the present-day production of a new Western and neocolonial discourse of *deservedness*, that is, the act of selecting who is 'deserving' and 'undeserving' of aid through the concept of humanitarian precedence. According to the discourse on deservedness (Ahmed 2008) and its (neo)liberal logic, the world population is of interest to humanitarian agencies according to a number of criteria that lie outside the conditions experienced by the affected populations. Such criteria include, for example, the impact on the interests of and opportunities for private capital; favouring both nation building processes, internal modernization and geographical connectivity; and political and military alliances (against communism in the past; against terror after 9/11) (Essex 2013: 38–39). For his part, Jamie Essex argues that such criteria are always 'ideological and geostrategic' (Essex 2013: 120). Here, the concept of deservedness is not unlike that of 'killability' found, for example, in work by Talal Asad (2007) and Achille Mbembe (2003). In fact I see a strict convergence between the fundamentally colonial attitude of classifying Western other(s) as 'expendable', which Achille Mbembe and Talal Asad trace in the War on Terror and its neocolonial forms of dominance, and the effect of an other-directed meaning of the disaster. Both entail a deprivation of subjectivity from the non-Western subjects or internal subaltern populations struck by disaster. As Ilan Kelman (2016) has noted in his reports associated with the 'Island Vulnerability' project, the 'vulnerability and resilience' of these subjects is adjudicated entirely by external humanitarian agencies, Western governments and local authorities that have internalized the imported logics of the 'international community' (Giuliani 2016a). In many cases, this interpretation reduces the multifactorial nature of the disaster to a single determining factor – such as global warming – thus giving rise to a dual outcome. On the one hand, it elides the multifaceted web of causes and forms of national and international complicity that underlie the disaster and its 'humanitarian' repercussions. And on the other, it erases any efforts by the non-Western populations struck by the disaster to protest or resist the power relations that structure their experience of disaster.

Specifically, negating the subjectivity of the people affected by disaster casts the non-West as a homogenous space that is 'naturally' defined as 'the place where disasters occur'. The definition of disaster itself therefore becomes instrumental in the way the West distinguishes itself from 'the rest', casting the latter as a space of barbarity, absent subjectivity and naturalized destruction. In this way, the space beyond the West, the 'out there', is once again positioned as a 'colonial object' in which the disaster functions as a framework of meaning in addition to being an actual event. As such, it must be subjected to strict military, political and governmental control through 'humanitarian intervention' or, when it comes to represent a 'security concern', through what Talal Asad (2007) has described as 'small colonial wars' (p. 35).

There is, however, the ever-present metropolitan fear that this 'spatially specific' and reassuring dichotomy between 'civilization' and 'barbarity' might be overturned, that 'disaster' might spill over Europe's borders in the form of the monstrified 'horde' of uncivilized migrants and refugees and that the social inequalities, climate change and political 'chaos' produced by global capitalism might come to reign over Europe itself. Or, in explicitly more racial terms, there is the fear that the border between encamped islands of whiteness and civilization, 'out there' in the middle of a domesticated 'place for disaster', could be overthrown by the racial chaos that is assumed to be 'inherent' to those places' and from which those islands of whiteness had been physically and symbolically separated.

MASS CULTURE, NATURAL DISASTER AND THE CAMP

Post-apocalyptic cinema is a useful site for illustrating the spatial politics of disaster. I begin my analysis of this genre with *The Impossible* by Juan Antonio Bayona (2012) because of the evocative way in which it depicts 'civilisation' being overturned by a tsunami. The movie is an account of a nature that sows death, involving an English family that falls victim to the Christmas Eve tsunami in 2004 while vacationing in Thailand. The film's title conveys exactly what I seek to address: the impossibility that white, Western, middle-class, 'respectable' people can fall victim to disaster, a fate ordinarily reserved for the colonized, in this case the 'homogenized' Thai population. In this sense, the events of the film are impossible by their very nature, representing as they do the dystopian manifestation of a permanent state of exception that, all of a sudden, involves even rich people.

As the movie shows through the image of the encamped resort, to prevent this dystopia from becoming reality, it is necessary to combat the natural incident with a precautionary mutation (of the body as well as of the space it inhabits) designed to strengthen non-killable subjects, or by carrying out a process of selection in their favour. These scenarios play into this dichotomous vision pitting 'citizens worth saving' against 'killable' victims that can be sacrificed. As many scholars have noted (Gilroy 1993; Chamayou 2014), the idea that we might control the risk of individual or societal degenerative metamorphosis by actively intervening to 'improve' the species through seclusion, bordering and biogenetic mutation has characterized modernity since the Enlightenment.

Consider the project of seclusion/bordering/mutation that is the 'encampment' – which is also at the very foundation of the nation state – in a broad perspective that necessarily includes and parallels the different strategies of encampment in colonial metropoles (i.e. European national states) and colonial and settler colonial locales (i.e. colonies 'for extraction' and colonies 'for settlement'). We see that 'camps' structured the colonial modern space in order to 'defend' the fit (the civilized and racially superior) and its civilization (capitalism) from 'the hordes' of barbarians peopling the 'out there'. The films I analyse in this afterword provide clear examples of this exact point: the dystopian device of natural disaster offers a renewed spatialization that preserves the 'to be defended' from the 'inferior'. This selection is aimed at drawing more rigid 'naturalized' boundaries separating along lines of class, gender and race, 'preserving' the sites of power as deeply codified bastions of white, upper-middle-class, patriarchal and (hetero)sexist control. The dichotomist racialized understanding of the global space as divided between 'inferiors' who deserve and who do not deserve to be included amongst the fittest is echoed by Kathrine Russo's analysis (this volume) of the use of the expression 'climate refugees' in Australian media.

The Postcolonial Camp and Natural Disasters

The Happening, *Blindness* and *The Impossible* together offer a vista on different functions the camp assumes. The bucolic, reassuring opening of *The Happening* by M. Night Shyamalan (2008) is the typical prelude suggesting something terrible is about to happen. The action is set in Central Park where, after a gust of wind rustles the leaves on the trees, time seems to freeze momentarily, along with all the people using the park. A moment later, everyone embarks either slowly or frantically on a mission to commit suicide.

The plot is set within a sequence of scenes depicting crowds of people escaping from those cities that appear to be the first to have been hit by a toxic storm. They flee towards areas they hope will be safe, but which turn out otherwise. Here, there is a sort of nostalgia of the 'camp' within which to find the reassuring structure that separates the healthy from the infected, a structure the state seems totally unable to provide. Nature has risen up against humans, who in turn have come to view nature as a pathogenic and destructive element. Nature is spreading spores that affect peoples' nervous systems, driving them to kill themselves and to 'punishing' anyone and everyone, including those who represent the most benevolent in American society. The film's central protagonist is a young white heterosexual middle-class couple from New York who adopt the orphan of a Latin American migrant couple who disappeared after the storm.

Blindness, by Fernando Meirelles (2008), based on the 1995 novel *Ensaio sobre a cegueira* by Portuguese novelist José Saramago, recounts the rebellion of nature, this time in the form of a virus that spreads through physical contact and blinds all its victims. In this case, the end (blindness causes accidents and death) is not the end of the world, but rather a dimension for experiencing the end of the world as we know it (driven by and organized according to the time and space of work, for instance) and rethinking the lives of individuals, both healthy and blind, in the industrialized space of global capitalism. Here, instead, the encampment functions to isolate the infected, to reduce their deadly charge as if they were the cause of the disease, as if the world outside could survive and reproduce itself 'eliminating' the diminished humans. The film lingers in this dimension of catastrophe-as-crisis for the world of 'survivors' created by the illness, highlighting the way this state of crisis exacerbates the most glaring examples of selfishness but also intensifies the most powerful forms of solidarity.

In both *The Happening* and *Blindness*, anxiety is generated by a subversion of the relation between privilege, camp, monstrosity and displacement. Those getting encamped as if they were dangerous monsters and thereby inoculating the disease are the middle-class bourgeois (*Blindness*), while the camp of the nation has collapsed (*The Happening*) forcibly displacing respectable citizens as if they were dangerous migrant/refugee in search of protection and survival.

Consider once again Bayona's *The Impossible*, only this time for the way in which it depicts natural disasters as phenomenon of natural selection and atonement. This remarkable work of art deals with a real tragedy, a disaster taking place 'out there' but which, by involving Westerners, turns into a 'catastrophe-as-turning point' with the power to re-establish the superiority of the 'First World'. Here the encampment corresponds to the luxury space of the five-star resort where the protagonists could live the experience of exotic tourism without getting enmeshed with the local society – a fantasy of isolation that gets destroyed by the tsunami. The tragedy is overcome by the protagonists all of whom survive the disaster and gather at the end – after a terrible trip in the devastated 'post-colony' where they do not enjoy the privileges of the condition of the colonizers – to fly back home. As such, *The Impossible* is a neocolonial tragedy, albeit one with a happy ending for the Western (white) protagonists (Hoad 2012). The happy ending, and here we agree with journalist Philip Hoad (2012), definitely marks the scope of the movie as 'conservative', as it 'settles for the nicely commercial afterglow of vague Spielbergian transcendence (the fact that the whole family escapes the ordeal intact is "the impossible" of the title) with which it ties up the tale'. The audience had imagined a world spatialized according to the logics of a global tourism market for whites when the catastrophe happened. They did not know if they would survive; they did survive. They did not know if they would be able to find the loved ones; they found them. They caught a nice plane and came back home where order was never upset and serves to locate 'here' and 'elsewhere', predictability and risk, life and death, peace and disaster in two highly distinct geographic and semantic terrains. The encamped space of reassuring 'civilisation' together with the dichotomy between 'here' and 'out there' have been restored, stopping the evolution – for the Western protagonists and audiences – of the catastrophe into disaster and relocating the second only in the reign of barbarity.

MONSTROSITY AND DISASTER

The trope of monstrosity is an important means by which discourses on climate change, migration, and particularly climate-induced migration, are framed in Europe today. Europe is seen as scarred by disasters in multiple ways. Disaster is presented both as the disorder brought about by 'the hordes' of migrants and refugees (as pictured by many films on zombies), and as disembodied forces that subvert the spatial division between 'here' and 'out there', and transform European citizens in to 'monsters' with no stability nor certainties (as pictured by *The Happening*). In both cases, such fantasies of disaster reactivate the colonial archive by representing the postcolonial other in the language of monstrosity. As Ranabir Samaddar (this volume) outlines, controlled and planned mobility within the space of the colonial object is inherent to the setting and reproduction of colonial capitalism. To nation states as engines of colonial capitalism and to the very few who benefit from it, stable notions of citizenship, sovereignty and territoriality – within the encamped space of the nation – have been *unsustainably* guaranteed in the Anthropocene. The subversion of the border resulting from the uncontrolled mobility of the colonial object necessarily produces fears of destruction of the colonial order. Those fears are sustained by constructions of monstrosity (the colonized as invading barbarian).

Climate refugees, much like other migrants and asylum seekers, are constructed as desubjectified and depoliticized subjects, whose inability to adapt to crises is exactly the reason they threaten to create crises in places such as Europe and the West, where 'disaster' is considered 'not structural'. As such, and recalling those figures of the colonial archive that depict colonial victims as potential threats to civilization, refugees and migrants are signified as 'immoral' monsters. That is, they are imagined as uncontrollable, unrestrainable deindividualized and dehumanized *forces* unable to adapt to their doomed condition (see Bettini, this volume) and thus undermine the presumed moral/economic superiority of the West by unleashing 'chaos' and giving visibility to the inequalities that belong to its uncivilized 'out there'.

As 'hordes' that subvert the borders between civilization and barbarity, deservedness and disposability, subjectivity and victimhood, order and disorder, fitness and unfitness, climate refugees are depicted as 'abusing' a dehistoricized order of things, a European order that is thought to be isolated in both space and time from its colonial past and from the contemporary postcolonial Global South. Boaventura de Sousa Santos (2011) refers to them as the returning colonised, a figure inscribed with fears of disaster and the violent demand for compensation for past colonial violence and contemporary postcolonial inequality (Giuliani 2016b). Such fears of disaster are not just connected to climate change, but, as Nigel Clark (this volume) argues, to a set of interrelated factors that highlights 'climate and its incitements to mobility *[as] even more deeply implicated* with politics, ethics and culture than we usually imagine'. As mentioned earlier, this desubjectified subject is often thematized in popular culture by the figure of the cannibalizing monster, the zombie, or the invading alien (Giuliani 2015). Their representations are the result of a complex intertwining of symbolic materials produced by security discourses, border management agencies, military departments, political debates and mass popular culture.

The mediated, filmic and discursive construction of the migrant/refugee as monster rearticulates, following Ann Laura Stoler (2002), what I referred to earlier as the *colonial archive*. It is from the colonial archive that the racialized figure of the colonized resurges and contributes in the tailoring of a discourse on climate change migrants and refugees that adopts dystopian metaphors to evoke the end of civilization. Similar representations recurred during the Brexit campaign as well as during the recent border closures in Hungary and Germany.

Depicted as animals that lack any sense of human 'sensitivity', 'justice' or, indeed, 'humanity', both zombies and aliens imaginatively represent the Other in its most extreme form. If zombies seek revenge, then aliens seek to appropriate and abusively destroy the essence of our European identity. Both are the outcome of a capitalist societal structuring that, as Samaddar (this volume) highlights, creates, manages and reproduces its internal/internal disasters and migrations. Faithful to Haraway's (1988) idea that positionality is the epistemological key for disrupting universalisms and for decolonizing the lens through which we interpret disasters and migrations, metaphors of zombies and aliens are for me tools that can help specify a politics of location, politics that in turn unveil the discursive apparatus built within both scientific and mass culture discourses. Rather than accepting the heuristic nature of these figures, what is required is a genealogical approach that reveals the power relations that structure the dichotomy and neocolonial ideology sustaining the global geopolitical and cultural functioning of neoliberal capitalism.

The figure of the monster is, definitely and undeniably, inherent to the global (dis)order of neoliberal capitalism. In fact, insofar as it contests capitalism's borders and dynamics, the construction of the migrant/refugee as monster should be understood as necessary *to* the construction of new borders and political dynamics (De Genova and Peutz 2010; Mezzadra and Neilson 2013). Revealing the symbolic matter out of which the racialized postcolonial figure of the monster is made is necessary for exploring the material construction of the hegemonic subject – the deserving that must be defended – as productive *for* the market.

5. UNPRODUCTIVE UNMARKETABLE MONSTERS AND THE RIGHT OF BUILDING AFFECTIVE COMMUNITIES

Let us recall once again Wendy Brown's reflection on the neoliberal construction of the individual as a market agent and reread it through my own reflections on the 'figure of race' that lies behind current constructions of migrants and refugees (Giuliani 2016a). The combination of these two angles reveals that the unfitness of their racialized figure is related to the incapacity of migrants and refugees to deal with the disaster (Goldberg, in this volume) and to adapt (Bettini this volume; 2014) and with their inability to become properly functioning market actors. To illustrate this I turn to an episode of the television series *Black Mirror* that thematizes rather well the above-mentioned construction.

'Nosedive' is the opening episode of the third season of *Black Mirror*, a television series created by Charlie Brooker and commissioned by Netflix. The series is often said to be 'speculative' because it grapples with issues that result from the 'unanticipated consequences of new technologies'. In 'Nosedive', the protagonist, Lacie Pound, lives in a world in which everybody can be rated five stars according to popularity, fitness, smartness, sympathy, coolness and success. Not surprisingly, Lacie is thus obsessed with being received well. She practises to smile properly and avoids facial expressions that might result in a bad rating. For Lacie, successes in life – access to a mortgage for an exclusive estate, a seat on the next flight after hers was cancelled, renting a fast car to arrive on time to the wedding of her highly rated friend, being her friend's maid of honour – all depends on her rating. This scenario represents the extreme consequence of a system – very similar to the one described by Wendy Brown – where the amount of 'likes' you give and collect functions as an exchange economy that transforms individuals into profit-seekers and market actors:

> Financialization changes the game for everything: from corporations that live and die by the stock market rather than quarterly earnings, to small businesses that live and die by Yelp ratings, to nation states that live and die by bond, credit and currency ratings, to educational institutions that compete for, manipulate and manage their rankings, to human beings whose value oscillates according to their Facebook "likes", and "favorited" tweets". (Brown, this volume)

Almost predictably, however, Lacie fails, trapped in a downward spiral by her falling rating. When she reaches the wedding venue, the highly rated bride has already repudiated Lacie as the maid of honour. After a problem with her outmoded, rented electric car, Lacie accepts a lift by an unrated female truck driver, steals a motorbike and is forced to break into the island wedding because her rating is now officially too low to gain legitimate entry. In her mud-stained outfit and smudged make-up, Lacie then pounces on the microphone and hastily performs her speech, exposing the bride's real face to the audience, revealing the bride's bossy and cheating behaviour when they were little girls and young women. She gets arrested and is subsequently jailed when she meets a man of colour wearing a well-fitting business suit. Lacie and the man begin to exchange insults, but slowly their mutual anger transforms into mutual delight as they both realize they are now free to speak without fear.

In this moment, Lacie becomes a less-worthy 'diminished-human' whose chances to live in her own society are reduced to those of the modern racialized and gendered *proletariat*, whose subjectivity is denied and whose possibility to participate in the *demos* is nullified. Her condition of internal abjection (Giuliani 2016b, c) pushes her to permanent mobility, not unlike the female truck driver. She's now a potential monster, whose construction resembles that of the postcolonial monster, but draws from a different archive, that of the miserable masses of early Western modernity. She is 'eugenically' ejected from a space whose borders are those produced and reproduced by the market and comes to personify the demise of democracy. As Brown puts it:

> When human beings are wholly reduced to market actors, the very idea of a self-ruling people vanishes . . . the *demos* is literally dis-integrated into bits of human capital, each preoccupied with enhancing its individual value and competitive positioning. So the idea of popular sovereignty becomes incoherent – there's no such thing in a market. (Brown, p. 36, this volume)

In conclusion, and building on Arun Saldanha's argument in this book, if like 'scarcity, waste, or environmental disaster, refugees are inevitable products of the violent territorialisations of capitalism itself' (p. 152), and if, as I argue, migrants and refugees are the ideologically charged outcome of territorialization, bordering and global exploitation, then we are compelled today to rethink the way we read migrations and specifically climate change migrations in order not to reduce them and their protagonists to parameters of stability that cannot represent migrations and migrants' conflictual, subversive and radical political charge.

Common to the present volume is the idea that displacement and migration are permanent (and not an emergency), for they are structural to an integrated system where climate change plays, together with subjectivity, the role of inherent forces. Nevertheless, if capitalism, through its own exploitative nature, has forcefully incremented displacement and movements, as outlined here by David T. Goldberg, Giovanni Bettini and Andrew Baldwin, neither capitalism nor climate change can alone explain why people decide to leave, move and get somewhere else. The 'right to escape', as epitomized by Sandro Mezzadra (2006), derives from migrants' and refugees' subjectivity and corresponds to a collective response to global capitalism. Subjectivity accounts for migrants' and refugees' 'desires and aspirations, as well as the deceptions that inform and drive migratory projects [and as such] avoids the voluntaristic and individualistic undertones that haunt the notion of agency' (De Genova et al. 2014: 29). As such, subjectivity renders an idea of migration and displacement as exceeding any reductive, atomizing and depoliticizing explanation as well as any bordering and constraining process that pretend to control and limit them.

In the face of the irreducible excess – the conflictual monstrosity – that is the subjectivity of people on the move, we are compelled to overcome the idea of the 'body politic' – and its ideological charge, be it the nation of the supranational Europe – and rethink Andersen's 'imagined community' (1982) in its global extension. This is the perspective through which the present volume can foreground a critique against the idea that nation states (necessarily hierarchical and exclusionary formations, as Claire Colebrook and Simon Dalby reminded us in this volume) and international law are the unique agents entitled to control the effects of climate change. Building on an understanding of human subjectivity as embedded in an inseparable natureculture integrated system, an epistemological as well as political project is envisioned here. In this project the capitalist reproduction of race, labour and border are caught in their multiple relations and at the core of an understanding of our times that engages with colonial past, postcolonial present and anti-capitalist futures.

NOTE

1. I define 'figures of race' as images that sediment transnationally over time and crystallize some of the meanings assigned to bodies, which are gendered and racialized in colonial and postcolonial contexts. 'They include that of the black man depicted as physically strong, with lower mental capacities and sexually dangerous; that of the Eastern European man as barbaric and violent; that of the Asian man as a naturalborn scam artist and involved in illegal and immoral business; that of the Arabic must-be-unveiled submissive woman; that of the Muslim man as fanatic and treacherous; and that of the black woman as a reassuring desexualised Mammy or a threatening hyper-sexualised Jezebel (Giuliani 2016b: 94). In the case of migrants and refugees, this symbolic material is reassembled according to who is migrating, how she/he is signified, and in which context. Within the frame of both the War on Terror and the paranoia about mass climate-induced displacement, migrants and refugees assume the connotation of the 'horde' of barbarians.

REFERENCES

Ahmed, Sara. 2008. "Multiculturalism and the Promise of Happiness". *New Formations*, 63: 121–137.
Amoore, Louise and Marieke De Goede (eds.). 2008. *Risk and the War on Terror*. New York: Routledge.
Anderson, Benedict. 1982. *Imagined Communities*. London: Verso Books.

Arendt, Hannah. [1951] 1968. *The Origins of Totalitarianism.* London: Harvest.

Asad, Talal. 2007. *On Suicide Bombing.* New York: Columbia University Press.

Baldwin, Andrew. 2013. "Racialisation and the Figure of the Climate-Change Migrant". *Environment and Planning*, 45: 1474–90.

Baldwin, Andrew. 2016. "Premediation and White Affect: Climate Change and Migration in Critical Perspective". *Transactions*, 41: 78–90.

Bettini, Giovanni. 2013. "(In)convenient Convergences: 'climate refugees', Apocalyptic Discourses and the Depoliticization of Climate-induced Migration". In *Deconstructing the Greenhouse: Interpretive Approaches to Global Climate Governance*, edited by Chris Methmann, Delf Rothe, Benjamin Stephan. Abingdon: Routledge, 122–36.

Bettini, Giovanni. 2014. "Climate Migration as an Adaption Strategy: Desecuritizing Climate-induced Migration or Making the Unruly Governable"? *Critical Studies on Security*, 2: 180–95.

Bhambra, Gurminder K. 2016. "Postcolonial Europe: Or, Understanding Europe in Times of the Post-Colonial". In *The SAGE Handbook of European Studies*, edited by Chris Rumford. London et al.: SAGE, 69–86.

Butler, Judith. 2009. *Frames of War: When Is Life Grievable?* New York: Verso Books.

Chamayou, Grégoire. 2014. *Les corps vils. Expérimenter sur les* êtres *humains aux XVIII et XIX siècle.* Paris: La Découverte.

De Genova, Nicholas and Nathalie Peutz, (eds.). 2010. *The Deportation Regime: Sovereignty, Space and the Freedom of Movement.* Durham: Duke University Press.

De Genova, Nicholas, Sandro Mezzadra and John Pickles, (eds.). 2014. "New Keywords: Migration and Border". *Cultural studies*, 29 (1): 55–87.

Essex, Jamie. 2013. *Development, Security, and Aid: Geopolitics and Geoeconomics at the U.S. Agency for International Development (Geographies of Justice and Social Transformation)* Athens, Georgia: University of Georgia Press.

Furedi, Frank. 2007. *Invitation to Terror: The Expanding Empire of the Unknown.* London: Continuum.

Gilroy, Paul. *Black Atlantic.* 1993. *Modernity and Double Consciousness.* London: Verso Books.

Giuliani, Gaia. 2015. "Fears of Disaster and (Post-)Human Raciologies in European Popular Culture (2001–2013)". *Culture Unbound*, 7 (3): 363–385.

———. 2016a. *Zombie, alieni e mutanti. Le paure dall'11 settembre a oggi.* Firenze-Milano: Le Monnier/Mondadori Education.

———. 2016b. "Monstrosity, Abjection and Europe in the War on Terror". *Capitalism Nature Socialism,* 27 (4): 96–114.

———. 2016c. "Afterword: The Mediterranean as a Stage: Borders, Memories, Bodies". In *Decolonising the Mediterranean: European Colonial Heritages in North Africa and the Middle East,* edited by Gabriele Proglio. Newcastle upon Tyne: Cambridge Scholars Publishing, 91–104.

Haraway, Donna. 1988. "Situated Knowledges: The Science Question in Feminism and the Privilege of Partial Perspective". *Feminist Studies*, 14 (3): 575–599.

Hoad, Philip. 2013. "Attempting the Impossible: Why does Western Cinema White-wash Asian Stories"? *The Guardian*, January 2.

Kelman, Ilan. 2016. *Catastrophe and Conflict: Disaster Diplomacy and its Foreign Policy Implications*. London: Brill.

Mbembe, Achille. 2003. "Necropolitics". *Public Culture*, 15 (1): 11–40.

Mezzadra, Sandro and Brett Neilson. 2013. *Border as Methods or the Multiplication of Labor*. Durham: Duke University Press.

Mezzadra, Sandro. 2006. *Diritto di Fuga. Migrazioni, Cittadinanza, Globalizzazione*. Verona: Ombre Corte.

Rozario, Kevin. 2007. *The Culture of Calamity. Disaster and the Making of Modern America*. Chicago: University of Chicago Press.

Santos, Boaventura de Sousa. 2011. "Para além do pensamento abissal: das linhas globais a uma ecologia de saberes". In *Epistemologia do Sul*, edited by Boaventura de Sousa Santos e Maria Paula Meneses. Coimbra: Almedinha.

Saramago, José. [1995] 1999. *Blindness*. London: Harvest.

Stoler, Ann Laura. 2002. "Colonial Archives and the Arts of Governance". *Archival Science*, 2: 87–109.

Films

Juan Antonio Bayona. *The Impossible* (USA e Spagna, 2012).

M. N. Shyamalan. *The Happening* (USA, 2008).

Chris Brooker. *Black Mirror* (GB and USA, 2016, season 3, episode 1).

Fernando de Meirelles. *Blindness* (USA, 2008).

Websites

http://www.islandvulnerability.org/;

Index

About the Contributors

Andrew Baldwin is Associate Professor in Human Geography in the Department of Geography, Durham University. From 2011 to 2015, he chaired COST Action IS1101 Climate Change and Migration: Knowledge, Law and Policy, and Theory, a pan-European research network of social scientists and humanists. His research examines the intersections of race, whiteness, migration and climate change.

Giovanni Bettini is Lecturer at Lancaster University. His research focuses on the genealogy and political effects of discourses on climate change, population and development, with a particular interest in the connections between climate change, adaptation and mobility.

Wendy Brown is Class of 1936 First Chair at the University of California, Berkeley, where she teaches political theory. Her most recent book is *Undoing the Demos: Neoliberalism's Stealth Revolution.*

Nigel Clark is Chair of Social Sustainability and Human Geography at the Lancaster Environment Centre, Lancaster University, UK. He is the author of *Inhuman Nature: Sociable Life on a Dynamic Planet* (2011) and co-editor of *Atlas: Geography, Architecture and Change in an Interdependent World* (2012), *Material Geographies* (2008) and *Extending Hospitality* (2009). He recently edited (with Kathryn Yusoff) a special issue of *Theory, Culture & Society* on Geosocial Formations and the Anthropocene. Current research interests include pyrotechnology, planetary capitalism, the politics of strata and speculative geophysical thought around the idea of the Anthropocene.

Claire Colebrook is Edwin Erle Sparks Professor of English at Penn State University. She has written books and articles on contemporary European Philosophy, gender theory, queer theory, poetry and literary theory. Her most recent book is *Twilight of the Anthropocene Idols,* co-authored with Tom Cohen and J. Hillis Miller (2016).

Simon Dalby is CIGI Chair in the Political Economy of Climate Change at the Balsillie School of International Affairs and Professor of Geography and Environmental Studies at Wilfrid Laurier University, Waterloo, Ontario. Simon Dalby was educated at Trinity College Dublin, the University of Victoria and holds a PhD from Simon Fraser University. He is the author of *Environmental Security* (2002) and *Security and Environmental Change* (2009) and recently co-edited (with Shannon O'Lear at the University of Kansas) *Reframing Climate Change: Constructing Ecological Geopolitics* (2016).

Brad Evans is Reader in Political Violence at the University of Bristol. The author of over ten books and edited volumes, he has recently been leading a series on violence for the *New York Times*. Brad is also the founder/director of the *Histories of Violence* project, along with being a Section Editor for the *Los Angeles Review of Books*.

Gaia Giuliani is FCT Postdoctoral Researcher at Centro de Estudos Sociais – University of Coimbra (PT). In 2009–2010 she was Endeavour research fellowship recipient (University of Technology Sydney). She then became an Assistant in Political Theory and Colonial and Postcolonial Studies at the Department of Social and Political Studies – University of Bologna, and undergraduate supervisor at the Department of Sociology – University of Cambridge (UK). Among her books are the authored *Zombie, alieni e mutanti: Le paure dall'11 settembre ad oggi* (2016), the co-authored *Bianco e nero: Storia dell'identità razziale degli italiani* with Prof. Cristina Lombardi-Diop (2013), winner of the AAIS best book prize for the category nineteenth–twentieth century, and the edited book *Il colore della nazione* (2015). In 2014 she cofounded the Interdisciplinary Research Group on Race and Racisms (InteRGRace) based at the FISPPA – University of Padova.

David Theo Goldberg is Director of the systemwide University of California Humanities Research Institute and Professor of Comparative Literature, Anthropology and Criminology, Law and Society at the University of California Irvine. He is the author and editor of some 20 books, the latest of which is *Are We All Postracial Yet?* (2015).

Katherine E. Russo, PhD, University of New South Wales (Sydney), is Tenure-Track Lecturer/Researcher at the Università degli studi di Napoli 'L'Orientale'. Her research focuses on media discourse, translation studies, gender, postcolonial and whiteness studies. She is the author of *Practices of Proximity: The Appropriation of English in Australian Indigenous Literature* (2010), winner of the ESSE Book Award (2012), and of *Global English, Transnational Flows: Australia and New Zealand in Translation* (2012). She is a member of the Board of the European Association for Studies of Australia and was a member of the Management Committee of the European COST Action IS1101 'Climate change and migration: knowledge, law and policy, and theory'.

Arun Saldanha is Associate Professor at the Department of Geography, Environment, and Society at the University of Minnesota in Minneapolis. He is author of *Psychedelic White: Goa Trance and the Viscosity of Race* (2007) and *Space After Deleuze* (2017), and co-editor of *Geographies of Race and Food: Fields Bodies Markets* (2013), *Sexual Difference Between Psychoanalysis and Vitalism* (2013) and *Deleuze and Race* (2013).

Ranabir Samaddar belongs to the critical school of thinking and is considered as one of the foremost theorists in the field of migration and forced migration studies. He has worked extensively on issues of migration and forced migration, the theory and practices of dialogue, nationalism and postcolonial statehood in South Asia, and new regimes of technological restructuring and labour control. The much-acclaimed *The Politics of Dialogue* was a culmination of his long work on justice, rights and peace. His co-authored work on new town and new forms of accumulation, *Beyond Kolkata: Rajarhat and the Dystopia of Urban Imagination* (2013) takes forward urban studies in the context of postcolonial capitalism. He is currently the Distinguished Chair in Migration and Forced Migration Studies, Calcutta Research Group.

Lightning Source UK Ltd.
Milton Keynes UK
UKHW01f1834040618
323710UK00001B/30/P